H. G. WELLS

LITERATURE AND LIFE: BRITISH WRITERS
Select list of titles in this series:

Complete list of titles in the series available from the publisher on request.

H. G. WELLS

Brian Murray

A Frederick Ungar Book
CONTINUUM • NEW YORK

1990

The Continuum Publishing Company
370 Lexington Avenue
New York, NY 10017

Printed in the United States of America

Library of Congress Cataloging-in-Publication Data

Murray, Brian.
    H. G. Wells / Brian Murray.
       p.   cm. — (Literature and life. British writers)
    "A Frederick Ungar book."
    Includes bibliographical references
    ISBN 0–8264–0468–5
    1. Wells, H. G. (Herbert George), 1866–1946—Criticism and
interpretation.   I. Title.   II. Series.
PR5777.M87   1990
823'.912—dc20   89–71199
                                          CIP

For my parents,
and for Patricia and Jim

"Truthfully, my child, have you ever read a book of Wells'?"

"Yes, I have."

"Tell me—but the truth, just between you and me."

"I read one book, Father."

"One? One book by Wells is like trying to bathe in a single wave. What was the book?"

"It was about God."

"*God the Invisible King?*"

"That's the one."

"Did you finish it?"

"No."

"Neither did I."

"Oh, Father—you?"

"I just couldn't read it. Human evolution with God as Intelligence. I soon saw the point, then the rest was tedious, garrulous."

"But it was *so* intelligent. I read a few pages and was so thrilled. I knew he was a great man, even if I couldn't read the whole book. You know I can't read an entire book. I'm too restless. But you've read all his other books."

"No one could read them all. I've read many. Probably too many."

—Saul Bellow, *Mr. Sammler's Planet*

Contents

Acknowledgments

I am grateful to A. P. Watt Ltd. on behalf of The Literary Executors of the Estate of H. G. Wells for permission to quote from *Exasperations,* his unpublished memoir housed at the University of Illinois, Urbana-Champaign. For their assistance and expertise, I would also like to thank Gene Rinkel of the Rare Book Room at the University of Illinois, and Alex Freeman, Local Studies Librarian at the Bromley Central Library, Bromley, Kent. For their continuing interest and support, I am particularly grateful to Evander Lomke, Ursula Appelt, and—as always—Corinna del Greco Lobner.

Chronology

1866 Herbert George Wells is born September 21, in Bromley, Kent. His father, Joseph, is a cricket player and shop-keeper. His mother, Sarah, works variously as a house-keeper and lady's maid.

1874 Enters Thomas Morley's Commercial Academy in Bromley.

1880 Begins serving the first of his draper's apprenticeships with the firm of Rodgers and Denyer, Windsor.

1881 Works briefly with Samuel Cowap, a pharmacist in Midhurst.

1883 Enters Midhurst Grammar School as a teaching scholar.

1884 Enrolls in The Normal School of Science in South Kensington, where he studies biology with Thomas Huxley and comes to edit the *Science Schools Journal.*

1887 Teaches at the Holt Academy in Wrexham, North Wales.

1889 Teaches at the Henley House School, London.

1890 Earns B.Sc. from London University. Begins teaching at the University Correspondence College in London, where he remains for the next three years.

1891 Marries cousin, Isabel Mary Wells. Begins publishing articles and reviews on subjects relating to science and education.

1893 *Textbook of Biology* published.

1895 Marriage to Isabel ends in divorce. Four books, including *The Time Machine* and *The Wonderful Visit,* are published. Marries Amy Catherine Robbins.

1896   *The Island of Dr. Moreau* and *The Wheels of Chance* are published.

1897   *The Invisible Man* published.

1898   *The War of the Worlds* published. Begins friendships with Henry James, Joseph Conrad, and Ford Madox Hueffer.

1899   *When The Sleeper Wakes* published.

1900   Builds "Spade House" in Sandgate, his residence for the next nine years. *Love and Mr Lewisham* published.

1901   First child, George Philip, born. *Anticipations* and *The First Men in the Moon* are published.

1903   Second son, Frank, born. Joins the Fabian Society.

1904   *The Food of the Gods* published.

1905   *Kipps* and *A Modern Utopia* are published.

1906   Visits the United States and meets President Theodore Roosevelt. *In the Days of the Comet* and *The Future in America* are published.

1908   *The War in the Air* and *First and Last Things* published. Leaves the Fabian Society.

1909   Moves to London. *Tono-Bungay* and *Ann Veronica* published. A daughter born to Wells and Amber Reeves.

1910   *The History of Mr. Polly* published.

1911   *The New Machiavelli* published.

1912   Moves to Easton Glebe, Essex. *Marriage* published.

1913   *The Passionate Friends* published.

1914   Visits Russia. A son, Anthony West, born to Wells and Rebecca West. *The Wife of Sir Isaac Harman* and *The World Set Free* published.

1915   *Boon* published.

1916   *Mr. Britling Sees it Through* published.

1917   *God the Invisible King* published.

1918   Works for the establishment of the League of Nations. *Joan and Peter* published.

1920 Visits Russia for a second time and meets with Lenin and Maxim Gorki. *The Outline of History* published.

1922 Runs unsuccessfully for Parliament as a member of the Labour Party.

1923 Again contends for seat in Parliament without success. *Men like Gods* published.

1924 Establishes winter residence, "Lou Bastidon," later "Lou Pidou," on the French Riviera. *The Dream* and *The Story of a Great Schoolmaster* are published. Begins relationship with Odette Keun.

1925 *Christina Alberta's Father* is published.

1926 *The World of William Clissold* is published.

1927 Catherine Wells dies following brief struggle with cancer.

1928 *The Book of Catherine Wells* and *Mr Blettsworthy on Rampole Island* are published. Assumes active role in PEN.

1930 *The Autocracy of Mr. Parham* and *The Science of Life* are published.

1931 *The Work, Wealth and Happiness of Mankind* is published.

1932 *The Bulpington of Blup* published.

1933 *The Shape of Things to Come* is published. Begins relationship with Moura Budberg.

1934 Travels again to Moscow; interviews Stalin. *Experiment in Autobiography* is published, a lengthy work of unusual candor and extensive self-analysis.

1935 Moves to 13 Hanover Terrace, London. Completes film script, *Things to Come*.

1936 *The Croquet Player* published.

1938 *Apropos of Dolores* published.

1940 Undertakes final speaking tour of the United States. Returns to Hanover Terrace, where he remains throughout the war years. *The Rights of Man* published.

1941 Last novel, *You Can't Be Too Careful*, published.

1944   Earns D.Sc. from London University after submitting *Thesis on the Quality of Illusion in the Continuity of the Individual Life in the Higher Metazoa, with Particular Reference to the Species Homo Sapiens.*

1945   *Mind at the End of Its Tether* is published.

1946   Death of H. G. Wells, August 13, at Hanover Terrace.

1

The Life

Over the course of a career that spanned nearly fifty years, H. G. Wells produced well over one hundred books, many of them novels, the rest devoted to a remarkably wide range of subjects and themes. Wells wrote about politics, science, economics, religion; in his lifetime he was probably better known for *The Outline of History* than *The Time Machine*. At the height of his fame—in the early 1920s—Wells was widely assumed to be one of Britain's most important authors, his name linked with John Galsworthy, Arnold Bennett, Rudyard Kipling, and George Bernard Shaw. Of these perhaps only Shaw equaled Wells in literary genius and intellectual voltage. But it is doubtful that even Shaw matched Wells in notoriety and influence—in sparking discussion and debate that shaped modern attitudes toward, among other things, the role of women and the function of the state. It is impossible, of course, to gauge precisely the lingering influence of any writer; certainly, Wells was not the only prominent voice of his generation calling for the vast reorganization of society, arguing that values and attitudes that prevailed in the Victorian era were now obsolete; he was not alone in insisting that, through science and education, men and women could come to acquire a clearer understanding of themselves and their place in the universe. But Wells was rather more than a writer; he was, in his prime, a widely recognized public figure, a man who met with Soviet leaders and American presidents. Moreover, many of his books were not only aggressively promoted and prominently displayed: they sold. Writing in 1941—five years before Wells's death—George Orwell suggested that "thinking people who were born about the beginning of this century are in some sense Wells's own creation." "I doubt," wrote Orwell, "whether anyone writing books between 1900 and 1920, at any rate in the English language, influenced the young so much. The minds of all of us, and therefore the physical world, would be perceptively different if Wells had never existed."[1]

Wells's life began, inauspiciously, on September 15, 1866, in Bromley, Kent—a rapidly growing London suburb. His father, Joseph—a skilled cricket player—kept a small shop that stocked china, glassware, and sporting gear. The Wells family lived in adjacent quarters, in what Wells graphically depicts as "grim and dismal" surroundings. There were battered chairs and bureaus and frayed rugs; there was the lingering reek of paraffin that Joe deployed in his unending struggle with legions of bugs. There was, below ground, a cramped kitchen reached by a "murderously narrow" staircase and dimly illumined by a grate in the street. An open gutter cut through the family's small yard of brick and dirt; from a nearby butcher's shed penned cattle primed for slaughter mournfully bellowed. "Home Sweet Home," Wells writes, "meant nothing to me."

In a memoir published shortly after Wells's death, Bernard Shaw insisted that Wells tended to play up the hardships of his childhood, and had in fact "never missed a meal, never wandered through the streets without a penny in his pocket, never had to wear seedy clothes, never was unemployed, and was always indulged as more or less an infant prodigy."[2] True, Wells had been spared the utter despair and squalor—the crime, illiteracy, and cholera—that marked the lives of many in Victorian England, and that Henry Mayhew, for one, rendered so vividly in *London Labour, and the London Poor* (1861–62). Wells's parents had been taught to read and managed to maintain steady, if modest, earnings throughout most of their lives. Joe, moreover, was a kind of celebrity, known throughout much of Kent as the man who—as Wells liked to recall—"clean bowled four Sussex batsmen in four successive balls, a feat not hitherto recorded in county cricket."

Still, even as a child, Wells sensed that his family's claim to respectability was tenuous; that a very thin margin divided the lower middle class from the desperately poor. His mother's father, an innkeeper, ended up destitute. His Uncle William—Joe's brother—was a draper who died bankrupt in a workhouse infirmary. Joe's own business was forever struggling, facing increasingly stiff competition from the Army and Navy Cooperatives and other forerunners of the modern department store. Wells would recall long periods when his family's funds were so low that, in fact, "there was not much to eat," and he and his older brothers, Frank and Fred, wore ill-made, patched-up clothes. Sarah had no household help and was often left in charge of the family shop; "she became," Wells writes, "the unpaid servant of everybody." In his sixties Wells could still picture his mother "struggling up or down stairs with a dust-pan, a slop pail, a scrubbing brush or a greasy dishclout." Her hands, he wrote, "had become enlarged and distorted by scrubbing and damp, and I never knew them otherwise."

Wells records that his father was an inept businessman, an "economic innocent" far less interested in selling tea sets and pickling jars than in picking up small sums as a part-time cricket player and coach. Joseph also lacked "sympathy for the woman's side of life," and, Wells admits, ought to have been more sympathetic to Sarah's ordeal. But Wells does not condemn his father for his financial failings, for hatching grand schemes for the family's emigration that never came to pass. Instead, Wells portrays his father as a bright and energetic man who liked to read and could "do clever things with his brain and hands and body," but who, like other members of his class, had been wretchedly educated and barely encouraged, made to understand that his options in life were meager and few. More genial than aggressive, Joe Wells was additionally disadvantaged in what his son calls "a social order where all the good things go to those who constitutionally and necessarily, watch, grab and clutch all the time"; where men like Joe Wells are "shoved out of play and wasted altogether"—simply "hustled out of existence by the smarties and pushers." Wells writes that a constant factor in his "developing socialism" was his "increasingly conscious impulse" to "anticipate and disarm the smarty and pusher and make the world safe for the responsive and candid mind and the authentic, artistic and creative worker."

Sarah was forty-three when "Bertie" was born, little more than a year after her favorite child, Frances or "Possy," the family's only daughter, died of acute appendicitis at the age of nine. Certainly, Sarah doted on her youngest and most headstrong son, generally putting up with his outbursts and pouts. She taught him his letters and numbers, helping him write his first word, "butter," which, Wells recalls, "I traced over her handwriting against a pane of the window." But she also tended to smother Bertie with cautions and prohibitions, telling him to keep tidy and steer clear of the sort of children who might teach him to swear. Thus "my universe of discourse was limited," Wells writes. "She preferred to have me indoors rather than out."

Sarah Wells had been reared in a strict, Low Church Protestant household; the Bible and the English catechism were, she believed, wholly, irrefutably true. Sundays she led Bertie to a local church where he learned of God's impatience and wrath; sometimes she sent him to a special children's service where—as he recalls in *Exasperations,* a late, unpublished memoir—"a great parson, named very appropriately, Woolley, baa'd at us about how God loved us." Wells was, by his own account, "a prodigy of Early Impiety," confused by such conflicting messages and convinced of "the unsoundness" of Christianity well before he could articulate why. His fear of Hell was harder to shake, and "was indeed good enough to scare me and prevent me calling either of my brothers fools, until I was eleven or twelve." But then, in a nightmare, Wells saw "Our Father in a particularly malignant phase, busy basting a poor broken sinner rotating slowly over a fire built under the wheel. I saw no Devil in the vision; my mind in its simplicity went straight to the responsible fountain head." In *Exasperations,* Wells calls the dream "a perfect resolution of my distresses. I knew He, that awful He, was impossible. I was left to struggle with a vast number of minor philosophical issues, but I believed in God Almighty no more. There might be friends and powers to help me against evil, but this religious stuff they were putting over me was palpably absurd."

In the 1930s, Wells called much of Christianity an "unintelligible mix-up of bad metaphysics and grossly materialistic superstition." He described himself as either "an outright atheist or an extreme heretic on the furthest verge of Christendom—beyond the Arians, beyond the Manichaeans." Still, throughout his life, Wells remained deeply attracted to the figure of Jesus, calling him "the dominant figure in history," praising his "tremendous challenge to the established institutions of mankind." Moreover, as both his novels and nonfictional writings show, Wells draws repeatedly upon the language and imagery of Christianity. He warns of the apocalyptic horror and suffering that will surely come if men and women continue to give in to their baser impulses; he calls for the construction of a kind of earthly heaven, its resources "economized and used with scientific skill for the maximum result," its cities "finely built," its citizens "finely bred and taught and trained." Wells calls repeatedly for the formation of a secular priesthood, men and women of exceptional will and self-

self-discipline who stand prepared to guide the wayward masses to this "World City of Mankind." Indeed Wells was, in his way, an evangelist, obsessed with helping direct the fate of humanity and discerning for himself the true nature of God. He was even prepared—in the prime of his career—to proclaim allegiance to "the Invisible King," to describe himself as being "under a divine imperative," the "humble and willing servant of the righteousness of God." "There is no author," wrote Rebecca West of Wells in 1912, "who has a more religious faith; nor one who speaks his gospel with such a tongue of flame."[3]

Wells was seven when he first found his imagination fired by literature, and began to realize that, beyond Bromley, there existed a more diverse and enthralling world. He broke his leg, and wound up "enthroned on the sofa," the happy recipient of books and periodicals his father fetched from the local library. "I mingled with Indians," Wells recalls in *Experiment in Autobiography*, "I learnt about whaling and crossed the drift ice with Esquimaux." Reading John George Wood's *Illustrated Natural History*, "I conceived a profound fear of the gorilla, of which there was a fearsome picture, which came out of the book at timesafter dark and followed me noiselessly about the house." Reading *Punch*, he discovered drawings of "lovely feminine figures," Britannia, Columbia, La France, all of them "bare armed, bare necked, showing beautiful bare bosoms, revealing shining thighs"—a "revelation" to a boy brought up "in an age of flounces and crinolines," and by a mother who had often stressed "the impropriety of not wearing clothes." "My first consciousness of women," Wells writes, "my first stirrings of desire were roused by these heroic divinities."

Wells continued to read incessantly throughout his childhood and adolescence, despite the fact that his parents—uncertain of the healthiness of such omnivorousness—sought to scotch the habit soon after his leg had healed. Sarah was certain, however, that Bertie did need at least a bit of schooling to make his way in the world, and so sent him to a nearby "academy" that aimed modestly to prepare boys for success as bookkeepers and clerks. Thomas Morley, the school's sole instructor was, at least in Wells's recollection, like one of Charles Dickens's inventions—a "portly spectacled man with a strawberry nose and ginger-grey whiskers" who relied on the cane for discipline and, when not snoring at his desk, demanded the rote memorization of names and dates. In his autobiography, Wells concedes that Morley helped him acquire a good "mathematical apparatus" and "the ability to use English with some precision and delicacy, even if the accent was a Cockney one." But elsewhere Wells makes it clear that Morley's school came to represent for him all that was haphazard and absurd about the English system of education, noting that "my brothers, my school friends, and I realized we were abominably educated for the world we had to face: not even taught to speak our own language, undertrained physically and mentally, and thrust into employment without hope or pride. I saw their lives being crippled and their hopes mocked, and only by the most desperate efforts did I escape the same frustrations."

In the autumn of 1877, Wells's father fell from a ladder and fractured his thigh. Left lame, he was finished, finally, as a semi-professional cricketer. Money became particularly tight in the Wells household; the tension that had long marked the marriage of Joseph and Sarah grew particularly severe. In 1880 Sarah left Bromley—and her husband—to take on the post of housekeeper at Uppark, a large country house in Sussex where, before her marriage, she had worked as a maid. Sarah also decided that, like his brothers, Bertie should become a draper, basically a trained clerk in a fabrics store. Helped by a relative, she found him an apprenticeship with Rodgers and Denyer, a prestigious firm of "silk-mercers, linen drapers, lacemen, court milliners and dressmakers" located quite close to Windsor Castle.[4] Sarah could not have imagined a more fortunate start. She was a staunch Royalist, and "her belief in drapers" was, as Wells explains, "almost as unquestioning as her belief in Our Father and Our Saviour." "To wear a black coat and tie behind a counter was," she believed, "the best of all possible lots attainable by man—at any rate by man at our social level."

In his autobiography, Wells slams the system of trade apprenticeships that, throughout his lifetime, continued to lock lower-class boys into dead-end jobs not of their choice. He recalls the sight of his brother Freddy savoring one last game of marbles before giving in to a routine of "stock-keeping, putting things away, tidying things up, bending over the counter, being attentive and measuring off" that would presumably persist for the next "forty-odd years of his life." The more defiant Bertie was even less eager to forfeit the pleasures of youth: he knew he was bright, and had already begun to hope vaguely for a more varied career. He was not then one of Rodgers and Denyer's more fervent employees. He regularly wandered off from his post at the cash desk, often sneaking into the warehouse, where—in a quiet corner—he could furtively read. He returned change sloppily; his cash sheets rarely jibed. In a business that demanded a neat appearance, Wells was, by his own admission, "shabby and untidy," sporting "a black velvet cap with a peak and that was all wrong." He was soon known as a "tiresome boring little misfit" who was "either missing when he was wanted or in the way when he wasn't." He was, not surprisingly, sacked.

Bertie went next to Wookey, where a distant relative, an "Uncle" Alfred Williams, had recently taken charge of a local school. Wells worked as a pupil-tutor with Williams—an odd, long-winded man who liked to talk of his wide travels and his disdain for organized religion, his comments flavored by an acute sense of the many varieties of human folly. Williams was fired, however, when local officials learned that he had lied in his application, greatly embellishing his educational qualifications. Wells was also sent packing, having stayed in Wookey for less than a month. Later, he came to appreciate the fact that Williams had supplied him with "a new angle from which to regard the universe"—allowing him to see it as "an essentially absurd affair, good only to laugh at." "That," Wells writes, "seemed in many ways a releasing method of approach. It was a fresh, bright way of counterattacking the dull imperatives of life about me, and taking the implacable quality out of them."

After leaving Wookey, Wells lived briefly and happily at Uppark. With its large rooms and lovely grounds and well-stocked library, Uppark was a world away from crowded, chaotic Bromley, and left a lasting imprint on his adolescent mind. The Utopian worlds that Wells would later construct derive in large part from his sense of what life would be like if, ultimately, the entire world were to become one vast Uppark, a serene and civil place where men and women of brilliance and grace could talk freely of science and art, their single goal the steady improvement of the human race. "Modern civilization," Wells suggests, "was begotten and nursed" in such households, where—in the seventeenth and eighteenth centuries—members of "the minor nobility" set up the first museums, picture galleries, and laboratories. The country house stands, Wells writes, as "the experimental cellule of the coming Modern State."

Bertie then went to Midhurst, where Sarah had apprenticed him to Samuel Cowap, a pharmacist who manufactured his own "heartening Cough Linctus"—and would later serve as a principal model for Edward Ponderevo, the colorful tonic-blender whose entrepreneurial escapades Wells chronicles in *Tono-Bungay*. Wells enjoyed rolling pills and mixing medicines and exploring Cowap's shop, with its drawers full of senna pods, flowers of sulphur, and squills; he even considered pursuing his own career in pharmacy. Encouraged by Cowap, Wells thus went to the local grammar school for a course in basic Latin—at that time the official language of the druggist's trade.

Horace Byatt, the headmaster of the Midhurst Grammar School, proved to be one of the most important people in Wells's life. Byatt not only tutored Wells in Latin, but helped him prepare for a series of government-sponsored examinations designed to locate students capable of college-level study. Wells was delighted. He liked the amiable Byatt. He liked preparing for the tests, discovering that he could learn rapidly "by reading alone without any nursing in class." This method of quickly absorbing and then reassembling, under pressure, large numbers of theories and facts "has at any rate the great merit of imposing method and order in learning," Wells writes. It was essentially the same method he would later use to compile several of his best-known nonfictional books, including *The Outline of History* (1920).

But again Sarah intervened, certain that her son had spent quite enough time poking about in books. Wells had barely settled in with Byatt when Sarah ordered him to report to yet another draper's shop—this time in Southsea. Edwin Hyde, its proprietor, was "a fairly civilized employer," Wells recalls, providing his trainees with uncommon amenities, including private "cubicles" and their own chests of drawers. He had also installed a small library where, most evenings, Wells worked his way through a large encyclopedia—"one of those compilations for the mentally hungry that have played so important a part in supplementing the deficiencies of formal educations in the British communities in the nineteenth century." But, again, Wells could muster no zest for endless hours of "blocking, rolling and folding." "The hour I unpacked my bag in the 'prentices' dormitory of Mr. Edwin Hyde's Drapery in Kings' Road, Southsea," he writes in *Exasperations,* "was the most frightful in my life. I thought I was caught and damned to a life of suffocating servitude beyond any hope of escape. I could see no way out." The frustration and rage that Wells now experienced cannot be overemphasized; it stayed with him for the rest of his life. As a novelist, he repeatedly portrays characters who find themselves stuck in circumstances that fail to match their talents and expectations; whose sense of suffocation is matched by an equally intense yearning for flight.

After two years in Southsea, Wells found a route of escape. He wrote to Byatt and again secured a place at Midhurst—as well as a second chance to study for his Board of Education exams. Initially, Sarah refused to sanction the move, reminding Bert that she would forfeit a large deposit by breaking a four-year commitment to Hyde. "I felt extraordinarily desperate," Wells recalls. "I behaved very much like a hunted rabbit that turns at last and bites." Certain that he was facing his final chance for a more fulfilling existence, Wells regaled Sarah with pleas and threats and, finally, hints of suicide. She relented, leaving him with what he would term "the two guiding principles of my life. 'If you want something sufficiently, take it and damn the consequences,' was the first and the second was: 'If life is not good enough for you, change it; never endure a way of life that is dull and dreary, because after all the worst thing that can happen to you, if you fight and go on fighting to get out, is defeat, and that is never certain to the end which is death and the end of everything.' "

Wells excelled in his exams, winning a scholarship to the Normal School of Science in South Kensington, its aim the production of teachers capable of staffing the growing number of science courses being offered in Britain's schools. "When I first took my fragile, unkempt self and my small black bag through its portals," Wells writes, "I had a feeling of having come at last under definite guidance and protection. I felt as I think a civilized young citizen ought to feel towards his state education. If I worked hard, did what I was told and followed the regulations, then I thought I should be given the fullest opportunity to develop whatever fine possibilities were in me and also that I should be used to the best advantage for the world and myself."

Though his formal education had been patchy, Wells was already remarkably well read. At Uppark he had grazed freely in the library, which reflected the tastes of the estate's first owner— Sir Matthew Fetherstonhaugh, a "Free Thinker" whose interests in science and philosophy earned him a membership in the Royal Society. Here, Wells discovered works by Voltaire, Jonathan Swift, and Thomas Paine, many of which strengthened his religious skepticism and his growing sense that the history of human society is, in the main, a saga of stupidity and waste. He read or reread the works of Percy Bysshe Shelley—a particularly notorious advocate of political and sexual liberation. At Uppark Wells also read, and long remembered, Plato's *Republic*, calling it "a very releasing book indeed for my mind." For while his "Uncle" Williams had already taught Wells "the trick of mocking at law and custom," the *Republic* offered "the amazing and heartening suggestion that the whole fabric of law, custom and worship, which seemed so invincibly established, might be cast into the melting pot and made anew."

In his youth Wells also discovered Winwood Reade's *The Martyrdom of Man* (1872), perhaps the single work that most shaped his values and ideas. Reade was a novelist, explorer, and social historian whose earlier *Savage Africa* (1863), based upon his travels through Gabon, is a vivid and often witty work unfortunately marred by the kind of racist assumptions that were commonplace in colonialist nations of the nineteenth century. *The Martyrdom of Man*, which Reade calls a "plain, unvarnished story of the human race," is also representative of its era, the product of an intellectual eager for meaning and mooring, but no longer able to embrace the doctrines of official Christianity, which—throughout the nineteenth century—had been challenged by various scientific findings and historical inquiries.[5] Charles Lyell's *Principles of Geology* (1830–33) appeared to refute the notion—widely held by fundamentalist Christians—that the earth had been assembled, rather abruptly, around 4000 BC. Ernest Renan's *The Life of Jesus* (1863) raised provocative questions about the identity of Jesus as it examined him within the cultural and historical context of his times.[6] Even more explosive, of course, was Charles Darwin's *Origin of Species* (1859), with its strong implication that human beings do not represent a privileged species, but are linked with all other beings in a biological chain that reaches back to the very beginnings of life. The world is not then operated according to the meticulous designs of a benign Creator, but rather by accident; species adapt and change in response to shifting environmental facts. As Darwin portrays it, the world of Nature is an indifferent and often cruel realm where most of the energy of living is consumed in the daily struggle to survive. He writes of "the severe struggle for life," of "the Survival of the Fittest"; of the "incessant struggle of all species to increase in numbers," for "the more diversified the descendants become, the better will be their chance of success in the battle for life."[7]

Reade accepts Darwin's central contentions, noting that "since the 'Origin of Species' appeared, philosophical naturalists no

longer deny that the ancestors of man must be sought for in the
lower kingdom"; that "we are all of us naked under our clothes,
and we are all of us tailed under our skins." Reade devotes a fair
part of *The Martyrdom of Man* to denouncing the doctrines of
orthodox Christianity, including its insistence that thinking men
and women must revere "the Jehovah of the Pentateuch" who
"rejoiced in offerings of human flesh" and the "God of Job," a
"sultan of the skies, who, for a kind of wager, allowed a faithful
servant to be tortured, like that man who performed vivisection
on a favorite dog, which licked his hand throughout the operation." In its institutionalized form, Christianity has, according
to Reade, "plundered mankind of thousands of valuable minds,
exiling earnest and ardent beings from the main-stream of humanity, entombing them in hermitage or cell, teaching them to
despise the gifts of the intellect which Nature has bestowed,
teaching them to waste the precious years in barren contempla-
tion and in selfish prayers." It has remained insular and hide-
bound, and grown ever more irrelevant, its "worship is a conven-
tionality," Reade writes, its "churches are bonnet shows, places of
assignation, shabby-genteel *salons* where the parochial At Home
is given, and respectable tradesmen exhibit their daughters in the
wooden stalls."

Reade is not, however, an atheist. There is a God, he insists,
"but not a God who is gratified by compliments in prose and
verse." It is an "Unknown God," the "supreme and mysterious
Power by whom the universe has been created, and by whom it
has been appointed to run its course under fixed and invariable
law." Reade believes that God's true nature will be more clearly
understood as ancient superstitions fade and humanity's collective
knowledge grows; that God "is an image of the mind, and that
image is ennobled and purified from generation to generation
as the mind becomes more noble and more pure." "We do not
wish to extirpate religion from the life of man," Reade asserts,
"we wish him to have a religion which will harmonize with his
intellect, and which inquiry will strengthen, not destroy. We
wish, in fact, to give him a religion, for now there are many who
have none."

That religion, Reade explains, is based on a hatred for unexamined assumptions—a loathing for selfishness and greed. It respects free inquiry as well as compassion and civility; it seeks "to
develop to our utmost our genius and our love"; indeed, writes
Reade, "our Faith is the Perfectibility of Man." "Changes so pro-

digious," he adds, "can only be effected in prodigious periods of
time. Human nature cannot be transformed by a *coup d'état,* as
the Communists imagine." It may require decades of education
and collective effort; it will require—above all else—the triumph
of science, which will finally enable human beings to "conquer
Nature" by discerning the "laws which regulate the complex phe-
nomena of life." Having done so, we can, in effect, take the place
of Nature, even learning "to predict the future, as we are already
able to predict comets and eclipses and planetary movements." As
a result, the earth, "which is now a purgatory, will be made a
paradise."

The "heavenly commune" that Reade envisions is very like the
more perfect world—the Eden-to-come—which Wells repeatedly
portrays. Reade similarly foresees the rise of "aerial locomotion"
and, with it, the elimination of distance, the blurring of national
boundaries. Like Wells, he looks forward to a time when people
will "look at this star as their Fatherland"; when "Love, not
Fear, will unite the human race"; when "the whole world will be
united by the same sentiment which united the primeval clan."
Hunger, starvation, and poverty will vanish; "luxuries will be
cheapened and made common to all." Man will "subdue the
forces of evil that are without"—as well as "those that are
within." He will learn to "repress the base instincts and proper-
ties which he has inherited from the animals from below"; he will
"worship the divinity within him." Writes Reade:

These bodies which now we wear belong to the lower animals; our
minds have already outgrown them; already we look upon them with
contempt. A time will come when Science will transform them by means
which we cannot conjecture, and which, even if explained to us, we
could not now understand, just as the savage cannot understand electricity, magnetism, steam. Disease will be extirpated; the causes of decay
will be removed; immortality will be invented. And then, the earth being
small, mankind will migrate into space, and will cross the airless Sa-
haras which separate planet from planet, and sun from sun. The earth
will become a Holy Land which will be visited by pilgrims from all the
quarters of the universe. Finally, men will master the forces of nature;
they will become themselves architects of systems, manufacturers of
worlds. Man then will be perfect; he will then be a creator; he will be
therefore what the vulgar worship as a god.

The basic assumptions that inform *The Martyrdom of Man* are
apparent in the writings of many of Reade's better-known con-

temporaries who similarly argued that, with Christianity's decline, Western men and women must take care not to lose their ethical bearings, their commitment to building juster, saner, more humane societies. In *Culture and Anarchy* (1869) and elsewhere, Matthew Arnold, for example, calls repeatedly for the pursuit of "human perfection," a process of "growing" and "becoming" that aims to subdue "the great obvious faults of our animality." Arnold would "do away with classes" and "make the best that has been thought and known in the world current everywhere." He recognizes, moreover, that traditional Christianity, though invaluable as a humanizing force, has been unfortunately marked by a "Puritan's ideal of perfection" that remains "narrow and inadequate."[8] In her poem "Oh May I Join the Choir Invisible" (1867), George Eliot reveals a religious fervor as she signals her longing not for the Christian conception of heaven, but for a radically transformed earth where "discords" are "quenched by meeting harmonies," and "Die in the large and charitable air." She condemns "miserable aims that end with self"; she hopes not for immortality, but for the chance to partake fully in the hard but ennobling process of human progress, to "Enkindle generous ardor, feed pure love, / Beget the smiles that have no cruelty—/ Be the sweet presence of a good diffused, / And in diffusion ever more intense."[9]

Such beliefs can also be found in many of the writings of Thomas Huxley, by far the best-known instructor at the Normal School of Science in South Kensington. Huxley was known internationally for his research in biology, and for a series of elegant, accessible essays on various social and scientific topics. Wells respected Huxley enormously, calling him "the acutest observer, the ablest generalizer, the great teacher, the most lucid and valiant of conversationalists." Wells considered the year he spent in Huxley's class to be "the most educational" of his life.

In "The Struggle for *Existence in Human Society*" (1888)—a piece that foreshadows many of Wells's central views—Huxley stresses that evolution does not ensure progress, only a continuing adaptation or "remodeling of the organism" in response to changing environmental circumstances.[10] In fact, "Retrogressive is as practical as progressive metamorphosis," Huxley writes. And "if what the physical philosophers tell us" is accurate, that the earth is "in a state of fusion" and "gradually cooling down," then the time will inevitably arrive "when evolution will mean adaptation to an universal winter, and all forms of life will die out, except such low and simple organisms as the Diatom of the arctic and antarctic ice and the Protococcus of the red snow." Thus, if the earth is

proceeding from a condition in which it was too hot to support any but the lowest living thing to a condition in which it will be too cold to permit of the existence of any others, the course of life upon its surface must describe a trajectory like that of a ball fired from a mortar; and the sinking half of that course is as much a part of the general process of evolution as the rising.

"This may not be," Huxley observes, "the best of all possible worlds, but to say that it is the worst is mere petulant nonsense." There is, after all, much "natural beauty" in the world; there are "a vast multitude of pleasures" available to human beings, "bits of good which are to all appearances unnecessary as inducements to live, and are, so to speak, thrown into the bargain of life." Huxley notes too that human beings are a resourceful, resilient lot; "there can be no doubt in the mind of any reasonable person," he writes, "that mankind could, would, and in fact do, get on fairly well with vastly less happiness and far more misery than find their way into the lives of nine people out of ten. If each and all of us had been visited by an attack of neuralgia, or of extreme mental depression, for one hour in every twenty-four—a supposition which many tolerably vigorous people know, to their cost, is not extravagant—the burden of life would have been immensely increased without much practical hindrance to its general course." "Men with any manhood in them," Huxley asserts, "find life quite worth living under worse conditions than these."

Indeed, Huxley writes, there is ample evidence that—in the face of pain, fear, and uncertainty—human beings have done much to advance. He points to the rise of "ethical man" who—unlike "the primitive savage"—sought to escape "from his place in the animal kingdom" where life is a continual bloody conflict; to establish instead a "kingdom of Man" where cooperation and a shared concern for the future is the rule, and "the struggle for existence" is mitigated by the cultivation of the intellect and the intelligent control of population. Even now, Huxley notes, "the finer spirits look to an ideal *civitas Dei*—a state when, every man having reached the point of absolute self-negation, and having nothing but moral perfection to strive after, peace will truly reign, not merely among nations, but among men, and the struggle for existence will be at an end."

Selflessness, cooperation, stoic endurance; the end of war and the triumph of reason: these are the ideals that Wells's work consistently celebrates. It is precisely this Huxleyan "kingdom of Man" that he spent his life seeking to build, supplying its blueprints in such work as *Anticipations* (1902), and *A Modern Utopia* (1904), and *The Open Conspiracy* (1928).

In his writings, Wells often describes London's dirt and disorder—symptoms of a city built in a continuing climate of chaos and brutal self-seeking. But as a student Wells found himself fascinated by the city's many distractions, frequently leaving his studies to explore its streets. ("London took hold of me," is how he puts it in *Tono-Bungay*, "and Science, which had been the universe, shrank back to the dimensions of tiresome little formulae compacted in a book.") He attended political meetings where young reformers, socialists, condemned the inequities of a class-ridden society, calling for the nationalization of industry, old-age pensions, and a minimum wage—policies that Wells too would come to support. In Hammersmith, Wells watched William Morris hold court. Wells could never embrace Morris's vision of Utopia—where, as Hugh Kenner puts it, "human satisfactions are those of leisurely handicraft."[11] But Wells welcomed what he would describe as Morris's indictment of "the contemporary theory that the search for gain, the desire to possess and to possess still more and the consequent competition to possess, constituted the main driving force of human association."

Meanwhile, Wells's own search for the company of a woman intensified; he now found himself full of "suppressed and accumulating cravings." He was, however, poor and insecure, acutely aware that he was simply a small, skinny, guinea-a-week scholarship boy wearing worn clothes and a rubber shirt collar that cost nothing to launder, but that, over time, yellowed with "something rather like the tartar that discolours teeth." ("I wanted a beautiful body and I wanted it because I wanted to make love with it," he writes, "and all the derision and humour with which I treated my personal appearance in my talking and writing to my friends, my caricatures of my leanness and my unkempt shabbiness, did not affect the profundity of that unconfessed mortification.") Wells's cravings were assuaged when, during his first year at South Kensington, he took a room with his Aunt Mary (the widow of his bankrupt Uncle William), who now lived with her daughter Isabel and several boarders in a large, rather ramshackle house near Bloomsbury. Wells was drawn immediately to Isabel, who

worked as a retoucher in a photographer's shop and showed little
interest in books or radical ideas; who, rather like Sarah Wells,
had no trouble standing up for Church and Queen. But Isabel
was pretty and, Wells recalls, generally patient as he regaled her
with talk "of atheism and agnosticism, of republicanism, of the
social revolution, of the releasing power of art, of Malthusianism,
of free-love and such-like liberating topics."

Inspired by Huxley, Wells did well during his first year at
South Kensington, and began to think seriously of working toward a doctorate in zoology. But Huxley, in poor health, offered
no courses during Wells's second and third years at the school.
Wells quickly decided that his next series of instructors were
plodders and perfunctory performers; one of them "maundered
amidst-ill-marshalled facts," another sought to "over-control" his
students—to "mess about with their minds." Wells, in turn, devoted more time to Isabel and a wide range of extracurricular
activities, including a student publication, the *Science Schools
Journal*. Through these pursuits he found several lifelong friends,
among them Richard Gregory, later editor of *Nature*—one of
Britain's most respected scientific publications. "We loitered in
the corridors," Wells writes, "made groups in the tea-shop
at lunch-time, lent each other books and papers and developed
each other's conversational powers." "These faithful associates,"
he writes, "bolstered up my self-respect and kept me from becoming a failure absolutely. They stimulated me to make good in
some compensatory way that would atone for my apathy in the
school work."

Wells crammed furiously for his third-year examinations—but
not in time. His poor showings in Astronomical Physics and Advanced Geology meant that, despite his strong start, Wells left
South Kensington without a degree and little more than a strong
reputation among his peers as a promising writer and wit. Having
blown his chance for either a scientific career or a reputable
teaching post, Wells wound up at an obscure academy in rural
Wales, its head an eccentric and ill-trained man who liked to
drink and declined to bathe. Soon after arriving, Wells sustained
a crushed kidney when, during a football match, he was deliberately fouled by one of "the bigger louts." Although he was weak
and passing blood, Wells kept teaching, finally developing what
local doctors diagnosed as tuberculosis. He was promptly returned to Uppark, and duly installed by Sarah in a "chintz-
furnished, fire-warmed sunlit room."

Wells was now certain that he wanted to be a writer, and used his convalescence to study works by Nathaniel Hawthorne and Robert Louis Stevenson, among others, "with an attention to language and style that I had never given these aspects of literature before." He was also certain that he wanted desperately to live— a decision he reached one "sun-drenched" afternoon "turgid with vitality" when he lay amid "a great outbreak of wild hyacinths." "I have been dying for nearly two-thirds of a year," he told himself, "and I have died enough." "I stopped dying then and there," Wells would recall in his autobiography, "and in spite of moments of some provocation, I have never died since."

Upon recovering, Wells returned to London and looked for work, finally landing a teaching job at a small school run by John Vine Milne—whose son, Alan Alexander, would later become famous as the author of the children's classic *Winnie-the-Pooh*. Wells respected Milne, a man of intelligence, warmth— and limited financial means. Thus Wells, poorly paid, supplemented his income by marking papers for the Briggs Correspondence College, and reviewing, for the *Educational Times,* "practically every work upon education that was being published at that time." In years to come, Wells would write frequently about education, often recalling when he was an instructor and asked himself: "What on earth am I really up to here? Why am I giving these particular lessons in this particular way? If human society is anything more than a fit of collective insanity in the animal kingdom, what is teaching for?"

In what remained of his free time, Wells managed to study successfully for a series of examinations that, in 1890, enabled him to earn, externally, a bachelor of science degree from London University. He now moved from Milne's school to Briggs's new, London-based "tutorial" college in Red Lion Square, helping students prepare for the biology sections of college entrance exams. Wells focused, therefore, not only on matters of science, but on "the peculiar mental habits of the university examiners," simulating the likely thrust of their questions in a long series of drills. He was uneasy participating in a process that stressed strategy as much as substance. But he was well paid, and soon gathered enough lecture material to compile a book, his first, a *Textbook of Biology* (1893).

In October 1891, Wells and Isabel were married, taking a house in a sober London suburb. It was, from the start, an unfortunate match, leaving Wells aware that—even in presumably enlightened times—men and women were entering into marriage utterly unprepared for its demands and complications. Smouldering for years, Wells was set "for flame meeting flame." But he was also, he admitted, "a very ignorant as well as an impatient lover." And Isabel proved skittish—suspecting, apparently, that consummation involved a procedure one endured more than enjoyed. There were other difficulties. Isabel, badly schooled and—as Wells puts it—"book shy," could not understand why her husband, burdened with paperwork and class preparations, should want so badly to do "quite other writing besides." She was puzzled too, Wells writes, by his widely shifting moods, his tendency to "fly off from something in the newspaper to scorn, bitterness, and denunciation." There was, Wells now realized, "an unalterable difference not only in our mental equipment and habits, but in our nervous reactions"; there was "no contact nor comparison between our imaginative worlds."

Wells was drawn more and more to other women, including Amy Catherine Robbins, one of his students. Her father, recently deceased, left little. Thus Catherine—despite her own uncertain health—decided to become a schoolteacher to support both her mother and herself; she was, Wells writes, a "valiant little figure" with her "schoolgirl satchel of books and a very unwieldy microscope someone had lent her." The two talked "over our frogs and rabbits." They exchanged books and notes and occasionally met for tea. "Our friendship," Wells writes, "grew swiftly beyond the bounds of friendship and I was amazed to find that she could care for me as much as I did for her. When I told her I had smashed a kidney at football and lost a large part of one lung, that seemed to her merely a reason for immediate action. I do not think either of us expected to live ten years. But we meant to live every minute there was for us to live."

This friendship developed during a period that was particularly taxing for Wells. His father's shop had finally folded. Sarah, grown quirky and deaf, had been relieved of her duties at Uppark. With his brothers unemployed or barely working, Wells suddenly found himself the main source of his family's support. He was teaching heavily and supplementing his income with a steady flow of articles and reviews. Under the strain, Wells's health once again broke; he began coughing violently, bloodily, "and this time the blood came and came and seemed resolved to choke me for good and all." He was, in fact, close to death—and bedridden for weeks.

To recuperate, Wells went to the coastal town of Eastbourne, where he read a novel that, for better or worse, greatly shaped his sense of what constituted literary success. The novel, *When a Man's Single* by J. M. Barrie (better known as the author of *Peter Pan*), features a group of journalists, one of whom reminds a younger colleague that "you beginners seem able to produce nothing but your views on politics, and your reflections on art, and your theories of life, which you sometimes even think original." Editors, he asserts, want neither art nor philosophy. They want not yet another meditation on evolutionary theory, but (for instance) a few brisk paragraphs "saying you saw Herbert Spencer the day before yesterday gazing solemnly for ten minutes in at a milliner's window."[12] For Wells, the point was plain. One made money by selling articles, and one sold articles by pleasing editors who liked things timely, lively, direct. At Eastbourne, Wells promptly tossed off "On the Art of Staying at the Seaside," assuming the voice of a seasoned tourist complaining breezily of the frequently overlooked drawbacks of a holiday by the sea. "Proper bathing," he concludes, is best done "up the river" and never in the sea. A river, after all, is "strewn with flowers"; its water falls fresh from the sky. But the sea harshens the skin and leaves the hair sticky; for its water, "geologists tell us, has not been changed for fifty-million years!"

Wells sent "The Art of Staying at the Seaside" to the *Pall Mall Gazette,* one of many newspapers and magazines competing fiercely for readers at a time when broadening educational reforms had increased literacy throughout Britain. Harry Cust, editor of the *Pall Mall Gazette,* so liked "The Art of Staying at the Seaside" that he asked Wells for more material in a similar vein. Wells delivered. Over the next several years, he wrote regularly for Cust and other editors affiliated with the popular press, turning in pieces that resemble—but never surpass—those collected by Dickens in his *Sketches by Boz*. Light, funny, often facetious in tone, they feature characters and situations meant to be easily recognized by those familiar with the variety of London life. Wells portrays an exasperating visit to a haberdashery in "The Shopman"; in "Of Blades and Bladery" he is the urban sophisticate reminding the would-be man-about-town to keep his hat jauntily tilted and his tie slightly askew; to carry a walking stick and practice carefully until he can swing it just so. Approaching a bar, the young blade must never appear "too tame," avoiding such simple declarations as "I will take a gulp of ale if you please, miss."

Instead, "at present, we may assure the Blade neophyte, it is all
the rage to ask for 'two of swipes, ducky.' " So, Wells urges, "Go
in boldly, bang down your money as loudly as possible, and shout
that out at the top of your voice. If it is a barman, though, you
had better not say 'ducky.' "

H. G. Wells was a complex man, too aware of weightier realities to want to devote the whole of his career to writing glib essays and corny jokes. Thus in "The Extinction of Man," another
of his early pieces, one finds Wells reminding his mostly middle-
class readers of their uncertain place in a savage world—something he would persist in doing for the next forty years. The
future, he notes, might not provide "perfect comfort and security"; we should not expect to "go to work at ten and leave off at
four and have dinner at seven for ever and ever." Like "the sabre-
toothed lion" and countless other prehistoric beasts, human beings could soon enter a time when they can no longer regard
themselves the reigning species. Consider, Wells suggests, the
menace posed by other animals. Huge crabs or octopi of "intense
pugnacity" could, for example, acquire the ability to maneuver
on land—as well as a liking for human nutriment, "just as the
Colorado beetle acquired a new taste for the common potato and
gave up its old food-plants some years ago." "Then perhaps,"
Wells drolly adds, "a school or pack or flock of *Octopus Gigas*
would be found busy picking the sailors off a stranded ship, and
then in the course of a few score years it might begin to stroll up
to the beaches and batten on excursionists. Soon it would be a
common feature of the watering-places. Possibly at last com-
moner than the excursionists."

There are more dangers. In "The Extinction of Man" Wells
describes Central Africa's migratory ants, already capable of
clearing out villages and sending "men and animals before them
in a headlong rout." "At present," he writes, "they have their
natural checks"—including "ant-eating birds." But, Wells warns,
"it may be that the European immigrant, as he sets the balance of
life swinging in his vigorous manner, may kill off these ant-eating
animals, or otherwise remove the checks that now keep these ter-
rible little pests within limits." Of course, bacilli can also multiply rapidly and, Wells suggests, "have no more settled into their
final quiescence than have men." A new disease could very probably wipe out humanity; for, after all, "science has scarcely
touched more than a fringe of the possibilities associated with the
minute fungi that constitute our zymotic diseases." "No," Wells

asserts, as he would repeatedly, "man's complacent assumption of the future is too confident." "Even now," he concludes, "the coming terror may be crouching for its spring and the fall of humanity be at hand."

Wells began publishing fiction when, in 1894, Lewis Hind, the editor of the *Pall Mall Budget,* asked him for a series of "single sitting" stories built upon scientific issues or themes. "The Stolen Bacillus," the first of these, involves a political terrorist—"the Anarchist" Wells calls him—who steals, from "the Bacteriologist," a tube that brims with what he believes to be "bottled cholera." The Anarchist ingests the tube's contents, hoping to make himself a political martyr—and a walking source of mass contamination. But he is foiled. The vial contains not a virus, but a substance that simply turns his skin a very vivid blue. "The Stolen Bacillus" is certainly slight—but of interest for several reasons. It features, in "the Bacteriologist," one of Wells's first scientist-heroes. It also combines humor with suspense—a tendency Wells would more brilliantly display in *The Invisible Man* and *The First Men in the Moon.* That Wells should focus so readily on an anarchistic threat is also revealing. Much of his later fiction shows a similar fear of social and intellectual disorder, a sense that without the intervention of vigilant, well-meaning scientific minds humankind can simply count on a future replete with chaos and brutality.

Other stories produced by Wells during the 1890s bluntly illustrate his preoccupation with nature's capriciousness and savagery. In "The Flowering of the Strange Orchid" (1894), a mild-mannered flower breeder buys an exotic plant that one day sprouts "leech-like suckers" capable of seizing a man by the throat. In "The Star," one of the best of Wells's early pieces, a "pallid great white star" nearly smacks the earth in a swift and fiery descent, producing storms and floods and an earth full of "ruined cities, buried granaries, and sodden fields." In "The Sea Raiders" (1896) Wells describes the invasion of a small coastal town by herds of flesh-eating sea monsters who—with their "flexible tentacles" and leathery skins—anticipate the Martians that Wells would come to portray in *The War of the Worlds* (1898). "The Empire of the Ants" similarly expands upon one of the grim scenarios offered in "The Extinction of Man." Here, an Englishman accustomed to seeing Nature "hedged, ditched, and drained into the perfection of submission" travels to Brazil, where he is struck by "the inhuman immensity" of the land: by forests where "man at most held a footing upon resentful clearings, fought weeds, fought beasts and insects for the barest foothold, fell a prey to snake and beast, insect and fever, and was presently carried away." He discovers too that huge, highly intelligent ants now reign in this hostile terrain, devouring whole populations on their way to world domination. "By 1911," the story's narrator notes, "they ought to strike the Capuarana Extension Railway, and force themselves upon the attention of the European capitalist. By 1920 they will be half-way down the Amazon. I fix 1950 or '60 at the latest for the discovery of Europe."

In "The Red Room" Wells focuses on fear—a key factor, he believed, in the hampering of human possibility. Its narrator and central figure is a young man who agrees to pass the night in Lorraine Castle, in a large room filled with shadows and alcoves and, reputedly, restless ghosts. Initially, he vows to remain brave and cheerful, lighting numerous candles and reminding himself that "nothing supernatural could happen." But the candles fail, and in the "ponderous blackness" of the closed room the narrator feels his self-possession fade. He winds up howling, banging headlong into the furniture in a frantic effort to escape. In the morning, he is far wiser for his ordeal, aware that he was victimized by his own imagination; that his own frenzied gyrations snuffed the flames. "There is neither ghost of earl nor ghost of countess in that room," he tells his host, "but worse, far worse," the "worst of all things that haunt poor mortal man"—namely, "Fear! Fear that will not have light nor sound, that will not bear with reason, that deafens and darkens and overwhelms."

Another early story, "The Argonauts of the Air" (1895), signals Wells's lifelong interest in technology and shows something of his growing ability to combine a dramatic story with characters who are rather more than mere sticks. Its principal figures—one Monson and his assistant, Woodhouse—construct a "flying machine" several years before the Wright Brothers take off at Kitty Hawk. Wells describes the device thoroughly, noting its "two small petroleum engines" and its "canoe-like recess" where Monson and Woodhouse sit, shielded by "two plate-glass windows" from "the blinding rush of air." The men die on their debut flight, smashing straight into the Royal College of Science (formerly the Normal School of Science at South Kensington) and setting off great explosions and flames. It was not the last time Wells would use fiction to destroy something that failed to meet his expectations: he would ravage the earth itself on numerous occasions. "The Argonauts of the Air" also stresses the theme, one of his favorites, that the advance of humanity requires courage and risk. Monson's work, the story's narrator notes, will now inspire and guide "the next of that band of gallant experimentalists who will sooner or later master this great problem of flying."

By 1896, Wells was widely recognized as the author of a continuing flow of stories and sketches, and of four books—*The Stolen Bacillus, Select Conversations With An Uncle, The Time Machine,* and *The Wonderful Visit*—all published in 1895. *The Stolen Bacillus* collects more than a dozen of his earliest stories, most of them stressing weird or unsettling incidents above the careful development of character or plot. The similarly brief, brisk pieces in *Select Conversations* center on the acerbic figure Wells based loosely on his "Uncle" Alfred Williams. *The Time Machine* is by far the most significant of these early titles—and, surely, one of the best known works of fiction in the English language. Its central character is an English scientist who constructs an ingenious device that speeds him far forward through the centuries, enabling him to witness, among other things, the barbarism of a regressing humanity and, finally, the slow death of the earth itself, the "universal winter" to which Huxley alludes in "The Struggle for Existence in Human Society." The book impressed several reviewers with the power of its descriptions and the vitality of its prose; but one, Israel Zangwill, himself a novelist, pointed out that the tale does present lapses in logic that some readers have always found hard to ignore. As Zangwill observes, it never occurs to Wells's "Time Traveller" that he will have to repeat "these painful experiences of his, else his vision of the future will have falsified itself—though how the long dispersed dust is to be vivified again does not appear." Moreover, writes Zangwill, had the Time Traveller "travelled backwards, he would have reproduced a Past which, insofar as his own appearance in it with his newly invented machine was concerned, would have been *ex hypothesi* unveracious." For of course had he "recurred to his own earlier life, he would have had to exist in two forms simultaneously, of varying ages." These "absurdities," writes Zangwill, "illustrate the absurdity of any attempt to grapple with the notion of Time"; they prove too that "there is no getting into the Future, except by waiting."[13]

The social and cosmic pessimism evident in *The Time Machine* is displayed too in *The Wonderful Visit,* a largely overlooked work that, as Ingvald Raknem points out, appears to owe more than a little to Grant Allen's 1895 novel, *The British Barbarians*. Wells describes the strained visit to an English village by an angel—an "angel of Italian art, polychromatic and gay"—who is befriended by a local vicar with a fondness for metaphysical speculation and shooting birds. Though many of its incidents and characters, including the vicar, are rather comically drawn, *The Wonderful Visit* examines the pathos of life and indicts the human propensity to suspicion, jealousy, and social prejudice—none of which the angel knew while he remained secure and serene in his "Angelic Land." At one point, for example, he is pelted with beechnut husks by local schoolboys who object to his shoulder-length hair. "The strange thing," the amazed angel tells the curate, "is the readiness of you Human Beings—the zest, with which you inflict pain." "Yes," agrees the Vicar, "It's fighting everywhere. The whole living world is a battle-field—the whole world." "Pain," he tells the angel, "is the warp and the woof of this life."

By the end of 1895, Wells was writing full-time, his income healthy, his confidence high. In January of that year, Wells and Isabel were divorced; in October he married Catherine Robbins, or "Jane" as he came to call her. But Wells remained fond of Isabel, even attempting, after their divorce, an impulsive, rather pathetic attempt at reconciliation that ended with his weeping "like a disappointed child" in Isabel's arms. For years Wells continued to provide financial support to his first wife and, eventually, to her second husband; years later, "in a world far removed from the primitive jealousies, comparisons, and recriminations of our early years," they began a cordial, "cousiny" relationship they maintained until Isabel's death, in 1931, from complications resulting from diabetes—a condition that Wells late in life discovered he shared.

Between 1895 and 1900, Wells added greatly to his reputation, producing three of the novels for which he remains best known. In *The Island of Dr. Moreau* (1896), one of his most thoroughly bleak works, Wells abandons his protagonist on a small Pacific island where a notorious vivisectionist—Moreau—attempts to fashion humanlike beings from a variety of animals, including dogs, apes, and pigs. Wells would later note that he wrote the novel in order to remind his readers "that humanity is but animal rough-hewn to a reasonable shape and in perpetual internal conflict between instinct and injunction"—something he would continue to do throughout his career. *The Invisible Man* (1897) looks

similarly at a grotesquely self-centered physicist who takes to
crime after discovering a formula that leaves his flesh and bone
"as transparent as glass." In *The War of the Worlds* Wells describes the destruction of much of England by invading forces
from Mars; this novel—like *The Invisible Man*—was widely perceived to be a highly original exercise; Joseph Conrad, in a letter
to Wells, called it "uncommonly fine." "I suppose," Conrad
wrote,

you'll have the common decency to believe me when I tell you I am always powerfully impressed by your work. Impressed is *the* word, O Re-
alist of the Fantastic! whether you like it or not. And if you want to
know what impresses me it is to see how you contrive to give over
humanity to the clutches of the Impossible and yet manage to keep it
down (or up) to its humanity, to its flesh, blood, sorrow, folly. *That*
is the achievement. In this little book you do it with an appalling
completeness.[14]

Wells's "A Story of the Days to Come" (1899) is also significant as one of his first attempts to provide a detailed portrayal of
a future society—one where technology has thoroughly transformed the human landscape. Its opening pages present one
Mwres, "a prosperous person," whose home boasts the latest in
domestic gadgetry. Mwres does not read a newspaper (there are
none); he gets the news from a "phonographic machine" complete with built-in calendar and clock. If he gets bored, Mwres
"had only to touch a stud" and the machine "would choke a little
and talk about something else." Mwres eats processed foods,
"pastes and cakes of agreeable and variegated design, without any
suggestion in colour or form of the unfortunate animals from
which their substance and juices were derived"; more fancifully,
he wears "pleasant pink and amber garments of an air-tight material, which with the help of an ingenious little pump he dis-
tended so as to suggest enormous muscles."

As Kingsley Amis points out, "A Story of the Days to Come,"
is among the very first in a long line of modern literary and cinematic dystopias, with its depiction of a society where "advertising matter is everywhere bawled out of loudspeakers" and
"phonographs have replaced books"; where "huge trusts reign supreme, an army of unemployables is maintained by a kind of
international poorhouse called the Labour Company"; where
"deviates get their antisocial traits removed by hypnosis, dreams

can be obtained to order, and as a last detail, a prophecy so universal nowadays as to justify panic in razor-blade circles, men don't shave anymore, they use depilatories."[15]

In *When the Sleeper Wakes* (1899) Wells again assembles a futuristic set from which novelists and filmmakers would frequently borrow. Here, in the London of 2100, are "huge metallic structures" and "gossamer" suspension bridges; the "telephone, kinematograph and photograph" have replaced "newspaper, book, schoolmaster, and letter"; there is, everywhere, the effect of "a gigantic hive." Both "A Story of the Days to Come" and *When the Sleeper Wakes* reveal something of Wells's fondness for technological ingenuity—for cities that are efficient, uncluttered, clean. But by no means are the societies Wells presents here meant to look ideal; indeed, both works illustrate his belief that technology without ethics can be dangerous; that clever gadgets and sparkling cities do not represent "progress" if the social order is still rotten at the core. Those with power in *When the Sleeper Wakes* enjoy plenty of amenities, including a "Pleasure City" replete with "splendours and delights." But for "common men" there is nothing but unrelenting labor in subterranean work zones thick with dust and gloom; here, beneath the soaring city, are "pale features, lean limbs, disfigurement and degradation." In his autobiography, Wells describes *When the Sleeper Wakes* as "an exaggeration of contemporary tendencies: higher buildings, bigger towns, wickeder capitalists and labour more downtrodden than ever and more desperate." It is "our contemporary world in a state of highly inflamed distension."

As the twentieth century began, Wells set out to widen his range. He was tired of being known, in some quarters, as "The English Jules Verne"—with its implication that he was less a serious author than a maker of startling stories meant to divert adolescent boys. In 1899, Wells published *Love and Mr. Lewisham,* the first of his more "realistic"—and overtly autobiographical— novels. Like the young Wells, Lewisham is at eighteen bookish and driven, so determined to know something about virtually everything that he divides his day into numerous well-defined blocks of time—rising at five, for example, to memorize French verbs, and then rushing through breakfast so that, before heading for work, he can devote twenty-five minutes to memorizing extracts from Shakespeare's plays. Like Wells, Lewisham wins a scholarship to the Normal School of Science in South Kensington, where he studies biology with Thomas Huxley, and, after an impressive start, winds up falling behind in his studies, his attention split between science, "the Social Revolution," and Ethel Henderson, the young woman he hastily weds. They are a diverse, struggling pair soon ensnared in a cycle of fights and long silences. But when Ethel becomes pregnant, Lewisham vows to stick it out, painfully aware that his great plans, including "his red-hot ambition of world mending," would remain unrealized. "It is almost as if Life had played me a trick," Lewisham thinks. "Promised so much—given so little!"

Mr. Lewisham is still quite young at the novel's close; he has gained self-knowledge and could, perhaps, find a way to the great career he has always craved. But neither the book's tone nor its structure suggest that such a result is likely. Lewisham is the trapped, strapped lower-class figure that Wells knew he too would have become if he had not been so obsessively driven, willing to risk all in order to insure the full use of his talents. *Love and Mr. Lewisham* is then Wells's dramatization of his own struggle to avoid the fate of his father and his brothers; it also reveals—through the figure of Lewisham's father-in-law—many of Wells's darkest assumptions regarding the true nature of human society. Chaffery, a quack spiritualist, reminds Lewisham that the average man is hopelessly simple, full of "lust and greed tempered by fear and an irrational vanity"; that life is, in the end, simply "a struggle for existence, a fight for food."

Wells worked hard on *Love and Mr. Lewisham,* cutting, he claimed, "twice as much stuff as still stands in the story." Reviews were not particularly enthusiastic: one critic complained of "that air of weary disillusionment which has spoiled the artistic effect of so much of Mr. Wells's later works"; another suggested that the novel's readers must "wallow in gloom from cover to cover amid a succession of dreary episodes," so that "we come away with a choking sensation as from the worst stations of the underground railway."[16] When Wells's friend Arnold Bennett urged Wells to return to the sort of speculative romances that had brought him fame, Wells fumed. "Why the hell," he wrote Bennett, "have you joined the conspiracy to restrict me to one particular type of story?" "I want to write novels," he insisted, "and before God I *will* write novels."

In *Anticipations,* a work of nonfiction, Wells again seeks to portray the impact of technology as he offers an extended and remarkably accurate forecast of life in the twentieth century. Examining recent scientific discoveries and the continuing implications of social trends, Wells describes, among other things, the total triumph of the automobile—at a time when many still considered the "horseless carriage" a passing craze. In the decades to come, Wells writes, new highways will more effectively link city and country; the truck will rival the train as a hauler of consumer goods; suburbs will sprawl. New "solvents" will simplify household cleaning; electricity, replacing coal, will make cooking a "pleasant amusement" instead of a sooty, time-wasting trial. He notes too, more cautiously, that "probably before 1950, a successful aeroplane will have soared and come home safe and sound."

In his *Autobiography*, Wells describes *Anticipations* as "the keystone to the main arch of my work." Its later sections offer the first extended presentation of Wells's version of the ideal society—a "New Republic" administered by men and women unbound by outmoded religious and social attitudes. These "artists in reality" will deny "the self-contradictory absurdities of an obstinately anthropomorphic theology." They will assume that God is a mystery, "His purpose" discernible, albeit dimly, only to those who strive "to understand the order and progress of things." Wells's leaders believe that "the essential being of man in this life is his will"; that he exists "only to do"—to work unceasingly to make life more thoroughly fulfilling for more and more human beings. To that end, Wells's future leaders will construct an educational system designed to replace the likes of Mr. Morley (those "heavy-handed barber-surgeons of the mind") with carefully trained instructors comprising "the most important profession in the world." And because they will be acutely aware of the need to limit population, these "New Republicans" will promote the wide use of ever more effective methods of contraception; they will assume, however, that codes restricting the sexual practices of consenting adults will inevitably loosen. In fact, Wells's New Republicans are not interested in thwarting responsible sexual play; they seek instead to assure what Wells depicts as a more beneficial pattern of procreation, one that will end the continuance of "base and servile types, of fear-driven and cowardly souls, of all that is mean and ugly and bestial in the souls, bodies, or habits of men"; that will favor instead "the procreation of what is fine and efficient and beautiful in humanity—beautiful and strong bodies, clear and powerful minds, and a growing body of knowledge."

Rebecca West would note that Wells was "by temperament and conviction a democrat," and full of "proletarian resentments" that stemmed from his drive for success in a country where, commonly, luck of birth meant more than talent and zeal.[17] But Wells was never a democrat in the sense that, say, William Jennings Bryan was a democrat. Wells consistently attacks the concentration of wealth in the hands of obtuse and irresponsible plutocrats; he repeatedly insists that educational and social opportunities must greatly expand; in "Democracy under Revision" (1927) he observes appreciatively that "the whole world of modern science became possible, and could only become possible, through the immense mental releases of ascendent Democracy." But Wells offers no rhapsodies to "the common man"; he suggests, moreover, in "Doubts of Democracy" (1927), that "the primitive theory of electional democracy" has largely failed; that those who have come to govern are not in fact chosen "for their known gifts and virtues." For "the business of getting elected proved to be susceptible to considerable complication, and demanded almost from the outset something more than conspicuous public services and utility to ensure a candidate's return." "The would-be ruler," Wells writes, "found it incumbent to divert so much of his time from being good and great to the task of getting elected, and he had to bind himself in such close relationship with others engaged in the same task, that his individual goodness and greatness speedily became a minor consideration. His interest in what was good for his country and mankind has been, and is, entirely subordinate to what will gain and lose votes. Independence of mind, magnanimity and greatness of desire are positive disadvantages for him." Thus, "we find in all the great democratic countries that the direction of affairs has passed into the hands of men who are great merely as politicians, and who are otherwise neither remarkably intelligent, creative, nor noble beings."

Certainly, as *Anticipations* shows, Wells's own ideal societies do not function like modern-day democracies: they are deliberately planned, hierarchical systems run by well-disciplined elites for whom the notion of liberty is meaningless without, first, an uncompromising commitment to the pursuit of perfection and the abolition of waste. The "New Republicans" he portrays in *Anticipations* are particularly powerful, willing to guarantee a cycle of "fine and efficient" procreation through a variety of often stringent means. "They will rout out and illuminate urban rookeries and all places where the base can drift to multiply"; they will presumably count, among the "base," the "mean-spirited, under-

sized, diseased little man" who is "quite incapable of earning a
decent living for himself," and very probably "married to some
under-fed, ignorant, ill-shaped, plain, and diseased little woman,
and guilty," then, "of the lives of ten or twelve ugly, ailing children." Wells's ruling class will sterilize—even eliminate—those
who, defying the state's guidelines, attempt to reproduce; they
will regard "the modest suicide of incurably melancholy or diseased or helpless persons as a high and courageous act of duty
rather than a crime." ("Most of the human types, that by civilized
standards are undesirable, are quite willing to die out," Wells
muses, "if the world will only encourage them a little.") The
New Republicans will keep an especially close watch on "inferior
races," in whose ranks Wells appears to include—in addition to
Asians and Negroes—Jews. Though he insists that he cannot
grasp "the exceptional attitude people take up against the Jews,"
Wells gratuitously lists their supposed faults, and notes hopefully
that, through social pressure and intermarriage, Jews will "cease
to be a physically distinct element in human affairs in a century
or so." And what, he asks, "for the rest, those swarms of black,
and brown, and dirty white, and yellow people, who do not come
into the new needs of efficiency?"

Well, the world is a world, and not a charitable institution, and I take it
they will have to go. . . . So far as they fail to develop sane, vigorous, and
distinctive personalities for the great world of the Future, it is their portion to die out and disappear.

As William Lyon Phelps observed in 1916, Wells was—by
1910—"a world figure"; "his books were in the window of every
important book-shop in Germany," for example, "where he was
studied rather than read."[18] It seems reasonable to suggest, then,
that much of Wells's early work, with its continuing emphasis on
order and efficiency, its admiration of will, social unity and careful breeding—revealed again in *A Modern Utopia* (1904)—con-
tributed to the formation of a mental atmosphere in which fascist
attitudes could achieve respectability, enabling Hitler and other
advocates of genetic and racial "purity" to come to the fore. Certainly, Wells himself was not obsessively anti-Semitic; he formed
friendships with men and women of varying races and creeds,
and can be found ridiculing racial prejudice of any kind in several
of his later writings. But anti-Semitic undertones continue to persist in Wells's work; as Anthony Burgess puts it, Wells was not

above perpetuating "a *Stürmer* stereotype of 'the Jew.' " And despite his growing demands for a global community, Wells seems
to forget at times that the world's population is not exclusively
European and white. "Presumably," observes Burgess, "both
blacks and Jews have opted out" of Wells's "great biological experiment; the laboratory is an Anglo-Saxon preserve."[19] Indeed,
particularly in the 1920s, Wells reveals a qualified sympathy for
the kind of collective energy and will that both fascism and communism can ignite in populations heretofore indifferent to political issues and grand schemes of social engineering. In 1927, for
example, one finds Wells surveying contemporary Italy and suggesting that "there is good in these Fascists. There is something
brave and well-meaning about them."

It should be stressed, however, that Wells's later works are not
preoccupied with questions of human breeding.[20] His loathing for
militarism and nationalism is quite consistent, and sufficient to
disqualify him as a proto-Nazi. Wells regularly ridicules Hitler
and Mussolini in his later writings; he would add—in 1927—
that "mixed up" with "this goodness" in Italian Fascism is "much
sheer evil, a puerile malignity and the blood-lust of excited
beasts." Such novels as *Kipps* and *The History of Mr. Polly* certainly reveal Wells's ability to empathize with social underdogs;
The Island of Dr. Moreau and *The Invisible Man* suggest that he
was quite capable of understanding that all sorts of horrors are
possible when arrogant, self-seeking men break their bond with
the rest of humanity.

It is also worth noting that at the turn of the twentieth century
talk of eugenic solutions to social problems was much in the air;
writers and politicians of varying views backed policies that, in
the wake of Hitler, Himmler, and Mengele sound chilling indeed.
Winston Churchill, for example, was intrigued by the idea of using X rays to sterilize the mentally impaired; George Bernard
Shaw would suggest that the socially unfit be rounded up and,
quite simply, gassed.[21] In 1925, in the United States, Wells's
friend Margaret Sanger, a leading advocate of birth control and
women's rights, argued that a nation that believed so strongly in
"efficiency, accuracy, and sound economic policy," ought to consider more closely the "haphazard, traditional, happy-go-lucky
methods" that were producing "the Americans of tomorrow."
Writing for *Collier's*, Sanger complained of the high sums "ex-
pended upon the upkeep of asylums for the feeble-minded and
insane, the mentally defective, the criminal, the congenitally de-

fective, the delinquent and the dependent"—the "billions, literally billions keeping alive thousands who never, in all human compassion, should have been brought into this world." "We are spending more on maintaining morons," writes Sanger, "than in developing the inherent talents of gifted children." She quotes with approval the observation, offered by noted botanist Luther Burbank, that " 'America . . . is like a garden in which the gardener pays no attention to the weeds.' " " 'All over the country today,' " Burbank complains, " 'we have enormous insane asylums and similar institutions where we nourish the unfit and criminal instead of exterminating them. Nature eliminates the weeds, but we turn them into parasites and allow them to reproduce.' "[22]

Not surprisingly, the scheme of relentless planning that Wells proposes in *Anticipations* left him vulnerable to satire; Max Beerbohm, for example, deftly mocks the Wells of *Anticipations* in "Perkins and Mankind," one of several parodies he collected in *A Christmas Garland* (1912). As he mimics the clipped prose and the offhand scientific allusions that mark the style of much of Wells's early short fiction, Beerbohm quotes lengthily from "Sitting Up For The Dawn," which he attributes to "H. G. W*lls," and which advocates, among other things, a "General Cessation Day," when those who have reached the state-prescribed age-limit for existence will stroll to "the Municipal Lethal Chamber," contentedly accepting their fate, happy "to 'make way' for the beautiful young breed of men and women who, in simple, artistic, antiseptic garments, are disporting themselves so gladly on this day of days." For of course here "there will be no deaths by disease. Nor, on the other hand, will people die of old age." Children start life knowing they have "a certain fixed period" before them; citizens will revere "the Future," their chief concern "the welfare of the great-great grand-children of people they have never met and are never likely to meet."[23]

It is likely, however, that, for most of Wells's contemporaries, the appeal of *Anticipations* was not found in its fanciful presentation of a "New Republic," but its rather daring attempt to describe the forthcoming century at a time when "futurology" had yet to be invented; when projections of things-to-come were still left largely to astrologers and the readers of tea leaves. *Anticipations* was something like the *Future Shock* (1970) of its day, selling well and prompting wide debate. Its breadth, depth and celebration of human possibility impressed many of Britain's most influential intellectuals, including Beatrice and Sidney Webb, leading figures in the socialist Fabian Society. With the support of the Webbs, Wells now took an active part in Fabian activities and brought spark to meetings and debates, despite the fact that he was awkward at the podium and spoke in a voice that his contemporaries have variously described as high-pitched, squeaky, and shrill. (Tapes of Wells's BBC radio broadcasts of the 1930s suggest John Houseman as imitated by Truman Capote.) But Wells soon irritated many Fabians, including the Webbs, by insisting that the society had become sluggish and ineffective and was itself in need of massive reform. He called for an aggressive campaign to increase membership, particularly among the working class; he wanted colorfully packaged Fabian tracts prominently displayed on newsstands throughout the British Isles. Many in the society objected to Wells's manner as much as his message: he was a cocky, vaguely Cockney presence suddenly asserting himself among members of the upper-middle-class, university-trained men and women more comfortable with dinner table discussions and parliamentary maneuverings than with engineering massive propaganda crusades.

From 1900 until 1910, Wells lived near the coastal town of Sandgate, in a home—Spade House—that had been designed for him by Charles Voysey, an architect well known for similarly stark and elegant white-stucco structures. At Spade House (so named for the spade-shaped letter plate near its front door), Wells entertained a growing number of literary friends, including Bennett, George Gissing, Joseph Conrad, and Henry James. Here, two sons were born—George Philip in 1901 and Frank Richard in 1903. At Spade House Wells produced several of his best-known books, including *A Modern Utopia,* a more thorough presentation of the Wellsian utopia first sketched in *Anticipations.*[24]

The narrator of *A Modern Utopia* is not named: he is simply "the owner of the voice," like Wells an admittedly "fleshly" man in his early forties. During a walking tour of the Alps, he suddenly realizes that he has been projected utterly elsewhere, to a place that resembles the earth in climate and topography, but has gradually developed a system of social organization quite unlike any in this planet's history. Immediately, the narrator is impressed by what he finds. The streets are clean, well paved; vehicles and buildings delight the eye. Everywhere he sees people free of the "puffy faces" and "nervous movements" that "haunt one" in a typically grim London crowd. They are graceful, unaffected, colorfully clad. "Compared with our world," the narrator realizes, this "is like a well-oiled engine beside a scrap heap."

In this "whole and happy place" Wells's parents would not have been sentenced to lives of servitude; young Bert would have been spared his hard and treacherous climb. For the citizens of Utopia are encouraged to view life as "an adventure," to develop the full range of their "possibilities." They are assured shelter, food, and basic income, for the state aims "not to rob life of incentives but to change their nature, to make life not less energetic, but less panic-stricken and violent and base, to shift the incidence of the struggle for existence from our lower to our higher emotions." This "World-State" does permit some private enterprise; it regards the "private morals" of its inhabitants to be beyond its concern: there are, indeed, "few or no commands." Still, it closely supervises the reproductive practices of its citizens, requiring that no man can form a family unless he is employed and free of debt and disease. The state provides direct subsidies to women who bear children, granting more to those whose offspring is particularly healthy and bright. Utopia holds "that sound childbearing and rearing is a service done, not to a particular man, but the whole community."

All the citizens of Utopia—males and females—are thoroughly, equally educated until "differentiation" becomes clear and they are tracked into occupations that match their interests and abilities. The "Poietic" possess imaginations "that range beyond the known and accepted"; they become artists, inventors. Those in the "Kinetic" class, "clever and capable" people "distinguished by a more restricted range of imagination," become judges, managers, engineers. The irredeemably sluggish, muddled, or slow—the "Dull" Wells calls them—are assigned less taxing chores. Above them all are the "voluntary" caste of "Samurai." Resembling the "Guardians" of Plato's *Republic* and the Roman leaders whom Plutarch portrays in his *Parallel Lives* (a work of enormous popularity in the eighteenth century, and one Wells very probably encountered in the Uppark library), the "Samurai" are a serious, highly disciplined group, willing to devote themselves entirely to the welfare of the state. They bathe in cold water and "sleep alone four nights in five"; they keep their "nerves and muscles in perfect tone" and, once a year, go alone, "bookless and weaponless, without pen or paper or money" into "some wild and solitary place"—an exercise designed to test the "sturdiness" of body and mind. Such rigors ensure that "timorous, merely abstemious" people are excluded from the Order—which Wells, in *First and Last Things*, calls "an ideal of clean, resolute and balanced living."

Wells was neither an original nor a systematic thinker; the tenacious reader who works chronologically through all of his fictions and what he called his "social speculations" will encounter a host of qualifications and contradictions. But in *A Modern Utopia* Wells does present a thorough version of what would remain, in essence, his ideal state. It does not exist to promote and protect private wealth and the transient pleasures of a limited few, but to ensure security, stimulation, and opportunity for all of its citizens. It refuses to consign intellectuals to marginal roles. It is perfectly logical, and in many respects intrusive—and thus not likely to appeal to those who believe that governments work best when they govern least, confining themselves to providing police protection and working sewers. Its leaders recognize that "order and justice do not come by Nature," or through a vague belief in "the sweetish, faintly nasty slops of Rousseauism that so gratified our great-great-grandparents." "These things," notes the narrator of *A Modern Utopia*, "mean intention, will, carried to a scale that our poor vacillating, hot and cold earth has never known." Indeed, "what I am really seeing more and more clearly is the will beneath this visible Utopia." He continues:

Convenient houses, admirable engineering that is no offence amidst natural beauties, beautiful bodies, and a universally gracious carriage, these are only the outward and visible signs of an inward and spiritual grace. Such an order means discipline. It means triumph over the petty egotisms and vanities that keep men on our earth apart; it means devotion and a nobler hope; it cannot exist without a gigantic process of inquiry, trial, forethought and patience in an atmosphere of mutual trust and concession. Such a world as this Utopia is not made by the chance occasional co-operations of self-indulgent men, by autocratic rulers or by the bawling wisdom of the democratic leader. And an unrestricted competition for gain, an enlightened selfishness, that too fails us.

The novel *Kipps* (1905), which followed *A Modern Utopia*, is the account of a draper who learns about himself and English society after unexpectedly inheriting a sizable sum. It was commercially successful, and helped bolster Wells's reputation as a "serious" novelist with the Dickensian knack of combining social criticism with a strong plot and memorable, often comical, characterizations. In 1906, Wells sailed for the first time to the United States, hoping to promote his work among a potentially vast readership that—before *Kipps*—he had barely tapped. He visited New York, Boston, Washington DC, and Chicago, recording his impressions in a series of newspaper articles that in 1906 were gathered into a book, *The Future in America*.

At its outset, Wells asserts that "the essential factor in the destiny of a nation, as of a man and of mankind, lies in the form of its Will, and in the quality and quantity of its Will"; he arrived "full of curiosity about America," anxious to discern and analyze the exact character of "a great nation's Will." In Washington, Wells met with President Theodore Roosevelt, and was pleased to find not "the Teddy of the slouch hat, the glasses, the teeth, and the sword," but an inquisitive, open-minded man whose "range of reading is amazing"—who in fact represents "the seeking mind of America displayed." Chicago, however, left Wells especially dismayed. What Carl Sandburg would praise as the "City of the Big Shoulders" was, for Wells, "a Victorian nightmare," the "most perfect presentation of nineteenth century individualistic industrialism I have ever seen in its vast, its magnificent squalor." Wells points to "the monstrous fungoid shapes, the endless smoking chimneys, the squat retorts, the black smoke pall of the Standard Oil Company." He describes "Packingtown," the place that "feeds the world with meat," as "a centre of distribution for disease and decay, an arena of shabby evasions and extra profits, a scene of brutal economic conflict and squalid filthiness, offensive to every sense." "Want of discipline!" Wells shouts: "Chicago is one hoarse cry for discipline!" For here, as in "Lancashire, in South and East London, in the Pas de Calais, in Western Prussia," one sees the results of "the shoving unintelligent proceedings of underbred and morally obtuse men." One realizes that "each man is for himself, each enterprise; there is no order, no pre-vision, no common and universal plan." "Modern economic organization," Wells asserts, "is still as yet only thinking of emerging from its first chaotic stage, the stage of lawless enterprise and insanitary aggregation, the stage of the prospector's camp."[25]

In the Days of the Comet offers yet another portrait of a more satisfying world, situated not in a realm of pure fantasy but in a twentieth-century England that has been thoroughly transformed by "a rush of green vapors" that a passing comet has left in its wake. Willie Leadford, the novel's narrator, recalls that—before the comet—much of London, like much of Chicago, was a place of "smoke and drifting darkness," of "groping imbecility," where "humanity choked amidst its products, and all its energy went in increasing its disorder, like a blind stricken thing that struggles and sinks in a morass." But the magical gas creates what Wells believed science and education and collective will could one day achieve. Finally, nations agree to cooperate; truces are declared. The London of old disappears; it becomes a clean, glimmering place, its citizens "learning, living, doing, happy and rejoicing, brave and free." Like everyone else, Leadford now finds himself feeling tranquil and whole; he becomes aware that, heretofore, his own life "has been foolishness and pettiness, gross pleasures and mean discretions." No longer does Leadford consider killing the man—Edward Verrall—who bested him in competition for the affections of a young woman, Nettie Stuart. Instead, at the novel's close, Leadford and his lover Anna appear ready to join Nettie and Verrall in an intimate foursome, becoming "friends, helpers, personal lovers in a world of lovers." For jealousy too has vanished; couples must no longer, "like old-time men and women," go "apart in couples, into defensive little houses, like beasts into little pits," where—intending to love—they become instead the jealous guarding of "an extravagant mutual proprietorship." After reading the novel, George Bernard Shaw wrote to Wells demanding: "What is all this in the *Comet* about a ménage à quatre? What does it mean? Why does the book break off so abruptly? Why not take some green gas and be frank?"[26]

For many readers, the book's closing scenes were frank enough. Wells was already well known as an advocate of relaxed sexual standards; in *Anticipations,* for example, he suggests hopefully that—with the development of better methods of birth control—"the question of sexual relationships will be entirely on all fours with, and probably very analogous to, the question of golf. In each case," Wells writes, "it would be for the medical man and the psychologist to decide how far the thing was wholesome and permissible, and how far it was an aggressive bad habit and an absorbing waste of time and energy." By 1909, many in London's literary and political circles were aware that much of Wells's own energy was being absorbed in a continuing series of affairs; that he had fathered the child that Amber Reeves was about to bear. Reeves, nineteen, was independent and unrepentant. But her parents, both of them prominent Fabians, were far from pleased: Mr. Reeves, Wells recalls, "declared his intention of shooting me."

The Webbs were also vexed, fearing that spreading gossip about Wells's activities could well push the entire socialist movement into the glare of bad publicity. The *Times Literary Supplement* had already found in *In the Days of the Comet* the suggestion that "Socialistic men's wives" are, "no less than their goods, to be held in common," noting that "free love, according to Mr. Wells, is to be of the essence of the new social contract."[27]

The appearance of *Ann Veronica* (1909) added much to Wells's reputation as a daring and controversial figure. Its title character, a young woman of twenty-one, defies her father by leaving his home in search of self-reliance and unhindered intellectual inquiry; she becomes the lover of her science instructor, an unhappily married man. Ann is certainly more frankly sexual than most of the women portrayed in the fiction of the period—although in this respect she closely resembles Herminia Barton, the heroine of Grant Allen's notorious and somewhat more melodramatic novel, *The Woman Who Did* (1895). As Wells would record, *Ann Veronica* was "among the first studies ever made of the young woman of the English intelligentsia," and proved popular with "advanced young people" throughout Europe and the United States. The book was banned in some places, and roundly denounced in the British press—perhaps most famously by John St. Loe Strachey, writing anonymously in the *Spectator*. Strachey, a perceptive man, respected Wells's imagination and narrative skills, insisting that "as a writer of scientific romances he has never been surpassed." But Strachey loathed *Ann Veronica*, calling it "depraved" and "capable of poisoning the minds of those who read it" by "undermining that sense of continence and self-control in the individual which is essential to a sound and healthy State." According to Strachey, *Ann Veronica* proposed that "if an animal yearning or lust is only sufficiently absorbing, it is to be obeyed"; it depicts, then, "a community of scuffling stoats and ferrets."[28] Wilfred Whitten, writing as "John O'London" agreed, calling the novel an open invitation "to run amuck through life in the name of self-fulfillment." *Ann Veronica* "will be read and talked about this winter by the British daughter," Whitten warned. "All I can say is that I hope the British daughter will keep her head."[29]

Tono-Bungay, appearing the same year, did not provoke the same animosity. Wells had spent several years working on this novel, hoping to provide what he later described as an unusually "spacious" view of "the contemporary social and political system in Great Britain, an old and degenerating system, tired and strained by new inventions and new ideas and invaded by a growing number of mere adventurers." With power and gusto, *Tono-Bungay* follows the career of one of those "adventurers," a provincial chemist who achieves wealth and influence through the skillful marketing of a worthless patent medicine. Wells called *Tono-Bungay* his "finest and most finished novel." Contemporary critics tend to agree: *Tono-Bungay* is, on the whole, Wells's most accomplished work of fiction.

In *The History of Mr. Polly* (1910) Wells created, in Alfred Polly, one of his best characters, a memorable study in frustration and resolve. But with *The New Machiavelli* (1911) Wells begins to reveal a growing impatience with fashioning well-defined characters and carefully paced plots; Richard Remington, its central character and narrator, functions principally as a vehicle for Wells's wide-ranging social and political views. *The New Machiavelli* is, broadly speaking, the account of Remington's scandal-making relationship with a young journalist, Isabel Rivers; it features thinly masked and unflattering portraits of several of Wells's well-known contemporaries, including the Webbs, who appear as Oscar and Altiora Bailey, a pair of manipulative governmental insiders who—after boosting Remington's political career—abet his fall. Clearly, with *The New Machiavelli,* Wells was out to settle a score with the Webbs, who had generally objected to his Fabian reforms and apparently helped orchestrate the criticism that swelled in the wake of his involvement with Amber Reeves. After its publication, Wells complained that too many readers were preoccupied with tracing the novel's autobiographical strains; in fact, in the years to come, he often felt compelled to point out that his protagonists are not simply portraits of himself lightly disguised. But in fact—much of the time—they are. Wells was one of the most overtly autobiographical novelists of his generation, writing repeatedly of his domineering mother and his loss of faith—of the intellectual rapture he felt during his time of study with Thomas Huxley. Wells's central characters tend to grow restless in their marriages; they look in vain for perfect love and take up the all-consuming task of remolding the world. Remington, for example, grows up in "Bromstead," a sprawling, ill-planned suburb that obviously owes much to Bromley; he remembers the peculiar harshness of his mother's low-church theology, with its "dark allusions" and "sinister warnings." Remington's relationship with Rivers recalls the case of Wells and

Reeves. Like Wells, Remington wants to "invigorate and reinvigorate education"; to "make the best and finest thought accessible to everyone"; to emancipate women and ensure world peace. This, Remington believes, cannot be achieved under the guidance of the Baileys and the rest of their bureaucratically minded ilk; instead there must arise a true "aristocracy" of public-spirited men and women who can combine both brilliance and diligence, who detest the very idea of a "rule-of-thumb world."

Marriage (1912), Wells's next novel, has always had its admirers—including, curiously, C. S. Lewis, who would later attack what he would come to dub "Wellsianity," particularly in *That Hideous Strength* (1945). As he explained in a letter to Arthur Greeves, Lewis appreciated the willingness of *Marriage* to address "all the big, outside questions"—something it does while striking, at its close, a frankly religious tone.[30] The novel's principal characters, Marjorie and Richard Trafford, are uneasily wed. She is bright but unfocused and so busies herself by buying things; he is a research scientist who becomes a businessman and, in the process, gets rich. Trafford eventually realizes, however, that he needs more than wealth and prestige. Like Remington, like Wells—like so many of Wells's heroes—Trafford sees inefficiency and squandered energy everywhere: he decides that—given direction and will—human beings can transform the world. And like several of the key characters in the novels Wells produced between 1910 and 1920, Trafford feels a strong metaphysical pull. "Since we don't know God," he tells Marjorie, "since we don't know His will with us, isn't it plain that all our lives should be a search for Him and it?" That "search," he asserts, will require the "perpetual extension and refinement of science," the "research that every artist makes for beauty and significance in his art," and the "perpetual extension of this intensifying wisdom . . . till all men share in it, and share in the making of it."

Structurally, however, *Marriage* is something of a mess, a bloated narrative largely devoid of characters of complexity and depth. It is verbose. At one point its narrator notes that Trafford's father, "a brilliant pathologist," had died "before he was thirty through a momentary slip of the scalpel." He observes again, some thirty pages later, that Trafford's father "had been killed by a scratch of the scalpel in an investigation upon ulcerative processes, at the age of twenty-nine." The *Freewoman*, a feminist publication, simply shredded the novel, its anonymous reviewer complaining that Wells's "mannerisms"—including his habit of "spluttering at his enemies"—had become more "infuriating than ever."[31]

As Wells soon learned, the anonymous author of this review was a young woman who called herself "Rebecca West," hoping to signal a kinship with the strong-willed character of that name in Ibsen's *Rosmersholm*. (She was also convinced, as she later explained, that her own name, Cicely Fairfield, implied "something blond and pretty like Mary Pickford.")[32] Wells could be prickly; he was known to explode at even slight criticism of his work. But he was impressed by West's obvious brilliance and verve—traits that would continue to characterize her diverse and extensive collection of fiction, criticism, and social history. Wells and West met and began to correspond; they became lovers. And although Wells had announced—in *Anticipations*—that "procreation is an avoidable thing for sane persons of even the most furious passions," they produced, in August of 1914, an unplanned child, Anthony. In his 1984 biography of Wells, Anthony West—a fine writer in his own right—recalls that he was ten before he was given the true identity of his father; before then, "I was allowed to call him *Wellsie*, but expressly forbidden to speak to him or of him as *father, papa*, or *daddy*." Still, West writes that Wells often showed him interest and affection, "so much so that the warming memory of his presences buoyed me up through his absences."[33]

Wells remained married to Jane. In 1911 they moved into a country house at Easton Glebe, in Essex, which Wells fondly depicts in yet another highly autobiographical novel, *Mr. Britling Sees It Through* (1916). Nevertheless, Wells and West remained intimate until the early 1920s, often generating much gossip and scorn, and thus moving their "ménage"—as Wells calls it—"from house to house and from place to place and Anthony was shifted from school to school." This sense of furtiveness—combined with Wells's disinclination to divorce—brought growing strain to what was, from the start, a volatile relationship, one that has been frequently chronicled and analyzed. Wells himself portrays his relationship with West in *The Research Magnificent* (1915); in *The Secret Places of the Heart* (1922), she appears, less attractively, as an "emotionally adhesive" young woman named Martin Leeds.[34] And yet, in later years, West was able to speak of Wells with liking and respect, recalling, for example, that to be in his company was "on a level with seeing Nureyev dance or hearing Tito Gobbi sing."[35] Wells would come to regard his years with West with similar affection, remembering that "we did at times love

each other very much. We love each other still. We both had
streaks of broad humour, strong desires and keen interests, and
when these streaks got together we could be very happy." Some
sense of this shared exhilaration can be seen in their earlier correspondence, wherein Wells appears as "Jaguar" and West as
"Panther," a pair of highly intelligent cats frolicking wittily in
what West's biographer Victoria Glendinning calls "a private my-
thology," a "secret erotic world."[36]

Late in the summer of 1914, as German troops drove toward
Paris, Wells completed one of his least readable works of fiction,
Boon (1915). Packaged as the "literary remains" of George Boon,
a recently deceased British author, this odd collection of conver-
sations and sketches—purportedly collected by one "Reginald
Bliss"—stands as proof that, alas, Wells was willing to publish
almost anything, even his scraps; it is today best known for its
lambasting of Henry James, who was twenty-three years Wells's
senior. Although he still respected Wells's intelligence and energy,
James was disappointed with the structural slackness evident in
Wells's more recent novels, and had been particularly critical of
Marriage in "The Younger Generation," an extensive evaluation
of several practicing novelists that appeared in the *Times Literary
Supplement* in early 1914.[37] In this essay, James—as Hugh Kenner puts it—"held Wells aloft in public by the tail, a naughty
mouse."[38] James does duly praise Wells's intelligence and creative
energy, his "extraordinarily various, extraordinarily reflective"
mind. But James also reveals, again, that he preferred novelists
who thoroughly examine the intricacies of human psychology to
those who, at the expense of precise characterization, bluntly es-
pouse political themes. He prized subtlety, precision, and authorial distance—qualities he found missing in Wells's fictions,
including *Marriage,* which reveals "a certain quite peculiarly
gratuitous sacrifice to the casual." Wells, James implies, does
not scrupulously, artistically select: he saturates, pours forth,
dumps—creating vivid and effective scenes, but, regrettably, a
rather sloppy whole more suffused with the personality of the
author than with the presence of effectively realized characterizations.

Wells, in response, wheeled out his heaviest guns. Through the
voice of *Boon,* Wells suggests that James's work is, in its own
way, superficial and incomplete. It focuses too frequently on "de-
natured people," the equivalents in fiction of "those egg-faced,
black-haired ladies, who sit and sit, in the Japanese colour-

prints." James's characters "never make lusty love, never go to angry war, never shout at an election or perspire at poker": his novels include "no people with defined political opinions, no people with religious opinions, none with clear partisanships or with lusts or whims, none definitely up to any specific impersonal thing. There are no poor people dominated by the imperatives of Saturday night and Monday morning, no dreaming types—and don't we all more or less live dreaming?" James, asserts Boon, is too selective, effeminate, discrete: he "sets himself to pick the straws out of the hair of Life before he paints her." Boon also mocks James's elaborate—often baroque—prose style, his "palatial metaphors" covering what Boon suggests is a hollow core. Having "first made sure that he has scarcely anything left to express," James, according to Boon, "then sets to work to express it, with an industry, a wealth of intellectual stuff that dwarfs Newton." As Boon puts it, the author of *The Ambassadors, The Golden Bowl,* and *The Portrait of a Lady,*

spares no resource in the telling of his dead inventions. He brings up every device of language to state and define. Bare verbs he rarely tolerates. He splits his infinitives and fills them up with adverbial stuffing. . . . His vast paragraphs sweat and struggle; they could not sweat and elbow and struggle more if God Himself was the processional meaning to which they sought to come. And all for tales of nothingness. . . . It is a leviathan retrieving pebbles. It is a magnificent but painful hippopotamus resolved at any cost, even at the cost of its dignity, upon picking up a pea which has got into a corner of its den. Most things, it insists, are beyond it, but it can, at any rate, modestly, and with an artistic singleness of mind, pick up that pea.

Such remarks do reveal a certain insight into the style and tone of James's fiction.[39] But of course it is the limited insight of the caricaturist who can quickly discern a subject's most distinguishing or eccentric traits and—with a few quick strokes of the pen—complete a portrait that is recognizable but, inevitably, crude. Never one for subtlety, Wells sent James a copy of *Boon;* James, who took himself—and his art—quite seriously, was less than amused. He found *Boon* wounding, an unfortunate end to the affectionate relationship—a kind of father-son bond—that began when James praised the genius apparent in Wells's earliest novels and stories. "It is difficult of course," James wrote Wells,

for a writer to put himself *fully* in the place of another writer who finds him extraordinarily futile and void, and who is moved to publish that to the world—and I think the case isn't easier when he happens to have enjoyed the other writer enormously, from far back; because there has then grown up the habit of taking some common meeting-ground between them for granted, and the falling away of this is like the collapse of a bridge which made communication possible.

When Wells, writing back, claimed lamely that *Boon* "is just a waste-paper basket," something he found while "turning over some old papers," James, with customary incisiveness, replied: "Your comparison of the book to a waste-basket strikes me as the reverse of felicitous, for what one throws into that receptacle is exactly what one *doesn't* commit to publicity and make the affirmation of one's estimate of one's contemporaries by."

Wells published *Mr. Britling Sees It Through* as the war in Europe intensified. Its title character is yet another of Wells's self-projections, a loquacious and "unusually short" writer (Wells stood around five foot five) who, in his middle forties, lives with his wife and son in a home that, like Easton Glebe, sits prettily in the Essex countryside. Like Wells, Britling enjoys driving speedily about in a motorcar; he is a superb host to a steady flow of bright and lively guests. Like Wells, Britling chafes in a marriage "in neutral tint"—one that is friendly but long without physical passion. Britling has affairs, but these tend to leave him dissatisfied, fearing that he has simply made "a mess" of "the whole scheme of his emotional life"; that "loving a woman is a thing one does thoroughly once for all—or so—and afterwards recalls regrettably in a series of vain repetitions, and that the career of the Pilgrim of Love, so soon as you strip off its credulous glamour, is either the most pitiful or the most vulgar and vile of perversions from the proper conduct of life." Britling is sometimes anxious, depressed; there are "black nights" when, sleepless, he thinks himself "a soul naked in space and time wrestling with giant questions," wondering: "Was Huxley right, and was all humanity, even as Mr. Britling, a careless, fitful thing, playing a tragically hopeless game, thinking too slightly, moving too quickly, against a relentless antagonist?"

Mr. Britling Sees It Through was among the decade's most successful serious novels—and not, one supposes, because it provided yet another glimpse into Wells's private dramas. Its appeal undoubtedly stemmed from its often deeply moving portrait of Britain's homefront during a time of war. For Britling, the war regularly brings news that people close to him have been slaughtered, among them his elderly aunt, who dies when a German zeppelin bombs her little town, killing fifty-seven, some of them children. Another victim is Heinrich, the young Geman who tutored Britling's sons; who was playful and passionate about learning and life and who dies fighting for his country, at the Russian front. Another victim is Britling's own son, Hugh, an aspiring artist. He too dies in combat, shot through the eye, "blown to bits by some man who had never known what he did." Though Wells's own sons were too young for military duty, Wells renders, in Mr. Britling, a convincing portrayal of parental grief. Britling had delighted in Hugh's letters, and "their youthful freshness," reading them repeatedly, "until their edges got grimy." Now, he recalls Hugh's infant hair, like "silk, spun silk," like "the down on the breast of a bird." He pictures him again "playing, climbing the cedars, twisting miraculously about the lawn on a bicycle, discoursing gravely upon his future, lying on the grass, breathing very hard and drawing preposterous caricatures." Hugh "came into life as bright and quick as this robin looking for food," Britling tells another character. Now, "he's broken up and thrown away. . . . Like a cartridge case by the side of a covert."

In his maturity, Wells often expressed his admiration for the writings of the American philosopher William James, Henry's brother; there are echoes in *Mr. Britling Sees It Through*—and in much of Wells's later writings—of James's well-known essay, "The Moral Equivalent of War" (1906). Here, James observes that much of human history amounts to little more than "a bath of blood": he points to the *Iliad,* "one long recital of how Diomedes and Ajax, Sarpedon and Hector *killed.*" James calls for the eventual abolition of war, believing that "common sense and reason ought to find a way to reach agreement in every conflict of honest interests"; he "devoutly" believes "in the reign of peace and in the gradual advent of some sort of a socialistic equilibrium." This he hopes can be achieved without the loss of "intrepidity, contempt of softness, surrender of private interest, obedience to command"—virtues long associated with military activity. This will require, then, the establishment of "moral equivalents" to war—the channeling of humankind's "competitive passion" into "healthier sympathies and soberer ideas," into the taming of Nature and the betterment of human society.[40] Britling expresses a similar view, calling for the establishment of "the great republic of the United States of the World"; "Why," he wonders, "do we bother ourselves with loyalties to any other government but that?"

At its close, *Mr. Britling Sees It Through* strikes an openly religious note that surprised many familiar with Wells's pro-science stance, but undoubtedly added to the book's enormous appeal. Britling now wants to tell the world about God, the "Captain of the World Republic," the "Presence" providing inspiration and strength to men and women who are receptive to the good, who seek "the establishment of a new order of living upon the earth." "Religion," Britling asserts, "is the first and last thing, and until a man has found God and been found by God, he begins at no beginning, he works to no end." "I must tell all my world of Him," he decides, " . . . the inevitable King, the King who is present whenever just men forgather," who "fights through men against Blind Force and Night and Non-Existence; who is the end, who is the meaning."

Wells promptly amplified his religious views in *God, the Invisible King* (1917). The book created a great stir, perhaps largely among agnostics and atheists who—on the basis of such works as *The Island of Dr. Moreau*—had come to assume that H. G. Wells shared their views.[41] In fact, *God, the Invisible King* contains little that Wells had not already expressed, less directly, in earlier writings. In *First and Last Things,* for example, published a decade before, Wells objects to orthodox Christianity, but—like Winwood Reade—appears quite willing to accept belief in a more remote and mysterious God who somehow drives human beings toward beauty, love, and the fulfillment of perfection. "I am greatly attracted by such fine phrases as the Will of God," Wells writes, "the Hand of God, the Great Commander."

The extent of the attraction is made very clear in *God, the Invisible King,* which Wells calls "a religious book written by a believer," one "seeking religious consolation at this present time of exceptional religious need." Indeed, Wells proclaims himself "sympathetic with all sincere religious feeling," while distancing himself considerably from the tenets of orthodox Christianity, from "dogmas very widely revered." Wells rejects the concept of the Trinity. He insists that God is not an "Avenger"—nor a "sedulous governess retraining and correcting the wayward steps of men." He believes that "religion cannot be organised, because God is everywhere and immediately accesible to every human being." He believes in "the God of the Heart," who is neither "be-

nevolent or malignant toward men," but who nonetheless "calls
men and women to his service and who gives salvation from self
and mortality only through self-abandonment to his service."
God, according to Wells, is

a finite intelligence of boundless courage and limitless possibilities of
growth and victory, who has pitted himself against death, who stands
close to our inmost beings ready to receive us and use us, to rescue us
from the chagrins of egotism and take us into his immortal adventure,
that we who have realised him and given ourselves joyfully to him, must
needs be equally ready and willing to give our energies to the task we
share with him, to do our utmost to increase knowledge, to increase order and clearness, to fight against indolence, waste, disorder, cruelty,
vice, and every form of his our enemy, death, first and chiefest in ourselves but also in all mankind, and to bring about the establishment of
his real and visible kingdom throughout the world.

God is potentially present, then, "in every government, great
and small, from the council of the world-state that is presently
coming, down to the village assembly." God, Wells insists, seeks
to work

through a continually better body of humanity and through better and
better equipped minds, that he and our race may increase for ever, working unendingly upon the development of the powers of life and the mastery of the blind forces of matter throughout the deeps of space. He sets
out with us, we are persuaded, to conquer ourselves and our world and
the stars. And beyond the stars our eyes can as yet see nothing, our imaginations reach and fail. Beyond the limits of our understanding is the
veiled Being of Fate, whose face is hidden from us.

Like Britling, Wells had backed Britain during the first stages
of World War I; as late as 1918 he was working for the government, heading a "Policy Committee for Propaganda in Enemy
Countries." Many of the pieces that Wells produced during the
war's first years were prompted by spreading allegations of
German atrocities and are, by his own account, "intensely indig-
nant," revealing a "pro-war zeal" he came to regard as "incon-
sistent with my pre-war utterances and against my profounder
convictions." For like Britling, Wells eventually realized that what
came to be called "the Great War" was—if nothing else—stark
proof that the human race could no longer depend on its armies
for solutions to its diplomatic and economic controversies; that,

in light of poisonous gas and massive aerial bombing, war itself must be made obsolete. To that end, Wells devoted considerable effort, in 1918, to the campaign that soon produced the League of Nations, an organization that—before collapsing at the outset of World War II—established a model for the more comprehensive United Nations, chartered in 1945. Indeed, Wells now began to evoke the ideal of a harmonious World State in nearly all of his writings, projecting himself as a citizen of the globe, traveling widely and spreading the message that nothing was more essential than international cooperation born of the wide realization that the human race, linked by common roots and desires, is far more similar than diverse.

Soon after the war, in the autumn of 1920, Wells made his second trip to the Soviet Union (his first was in 1914). The Russian Revolution, begun in 1917, was now complete; Wells—accompanied by his son George, called "Gip"—was eager to renew his friendship with the writer Maxim Gorki, and to observe Europe's first communist government in its incipient stage. Wells's findings, collected in *Russia in the Shadows* (1920), do not underplay the country's difficulties. "Our dominant impression of things Russian is an impression of a vast irreparable breakdown," Wells writes, detailing scenes of shabbiness, poverty, and hunger. In Moscow, Wells met briefly with Lenin, finding him "creative" and frank; in Lenin's Bolshevik regime, despite its suppressions, he discerned the best long-term hope for a more just and efficient Russia—a view that incensed Winston Churchill and the playwright Henry Arthur Jones, both of whom attacked Wells in print, and thus helped set off a long series of public debates on the issue of Western support for the new Soviet state.[42] Though he would remain on friendly terms with officials in the Soviet government for many years to come, Wells was never an orthodox Marxist; in fact, in *Russia in the Shadows* he calls Marx a "Bore of the extremest sort" and his *Das Kapital* "a cadence of wearisome volumes," a "monument of pretentious pedantry." "Temperamentally I dislike Communism," Wells adds in *A Year of Prophesying* (1924). "I am a collectivist but not a communist. I have always clung and still cling to the belief that the sprawling social and economic life in which I have grown up might be progressively organised into a secure, generous, and scientific system without any abrupt and violent destructive change."

For Wells, the key to that change was education. In 1918, with Jane's help, he began the exhausting work that would produce, in

1920, the first—and most crucial—volume of his own continuing educational crusade. This was *The Outline of History*, one of the most widely discussed literary projects of the decade—and, in its various editions, one of the best-selling books of all time. Its aim, as Wells would explain, was to produce "present universal history as a manageable 'subject' capable of direct application to college and school use." But it was history that would avoid parochialism and stress humanity's shared achievements. Wells's *Outline* would not celebrate war or the triumphs of militaristic dictators—one of whom, Napoleon, Wells calls a figure "of almost incredible self-conceit," an aper of Caesar and Charlemagne who simply lacked the imagination required to build "a world republic and an enduring world peace" and who, victorious, "could do no more than strut upon this great mountain of opportunity like a cockerel on a dunghill." Wells wanted *The Outline of History* to be a more thorough version of Reade's *The Martyrdom of Man*, similarly emphasizing humanity's growing awareness that it could determine the shape of its collective destiny. Wells aimed for a work far "more objective and comprehensive and coherent" than those traditional sources upon which people had, "consciously or unconsciously," based their understanding of the human enterprise—namely "the historical portion of the Bible, supplemented by some scraps of classical literature, and their own national record."

But suspicions quickly arose regarding Wells's qualifications as a historian and thus of the worth of his *Outline*, which first appeared serially in a magazine format that bore dramatic illustrations of dinosaurs and carried ads for such products as Frye's Breakfast Cocoa and Waterman's Pens. At first, Wells drew heavily upon the *Encyclopaedia Britannica* as well as such vivid but less than definitive sources as Edward Gibbon's *The Rise and Fall of the Roman Empire* and Thomas Carlyle's *The French Revolution*; indeed, as he would concede in *Exasperations*, he and Jane worked without "the meticulous squeamishness of responsible 'scholars' who live in a paralysing atmosphere of small mistakes." He was, then, wide open to attacks from academics, one of whom, A. W. Gomme, a classicist, argued that the author of the *Outline*, though exuding confidence, should have done his homework more carefully before passing judgment on ancient Greece and Rome. Like any "non-expert" seeking to negotiate difficult intellectual terrain, Wells—Gomme wrote—did not always know "what expert to follow, nor how far" and occasionally made "the most absurd blunders by using the wrong book or misunderstanding the methods of the right one."[43] Later, Wells himself would admit as much. The first editions of *The Outline of History* were frequently, he admitted, "ambiguous" and "sometimes confused." Subsequent editions drew far more extensively upon scholarly and editorial advice Wells gathered from such respected authorities as Gilbert Murray, Ray Lankester, and Ernest Barker. Moreover, to his credit, Wells never claimed that *The Outline of History* was a definitive study meant to survive close scrutiny for several generations. He understood, rightly, that it would soon be superseded "by far better work along the same lines."

In its revised editions, the *Outline* continued to have its critics, including those who objected to the book's Darwinistic suppositions and anti-Catholic slant.[44] But from the outset, Wells's history was regarded by many more critics as a kind of masterpiece, a lively and informative chronicle that undeniably filled a need. E. M. Forster, for example, called *The Outline of History* "a great book; a possession forever."[45] H. L. Mencken complained that Wells was "quite idiotic" for indicating in the *Outline* that "military genius is a thing of a very low intellectual order, and scarcely to be distinguished from a talent for ordinary crime"; for believing too in the efficacy of popular education. As Mencken perceptively noted, "popular education, no matter what efforts are made to improve it, must inevitably remain but little more than a device for perpetuating the ideas that happen to be official—in other words, the nonsense regarded as revelation by the powers currently in control of the state." Still, Mencken recognized that *The Outline of History* "comes near being a genuinely great book," and proof that Wells "is an enormously clever, well-taught, reflective, courageous and original fellow."[46] It also left him an enormously wealthy fellow. From the start, sales of the book were huge, and remained steady for the next two decades. Late in life, Wells estimated that the book added "well over a quarter of a million pounds to my brassy self-assurance."[47]

As always, Wells stood ready to capitalize on a fresh success. During the 1920s, he aired his political and social views in a series of columns that appeared in newspapers and magazines throughout Britain and the United States. Wells relished his access to such a vast audience, and—despite much initial complaining about hasty, space-saving cuts—decided he found it "amusing to try saying what one has to say in as editor-proof a form as possible." In 1922, on the Labour ticket, he ran unsuccessfully for Parliament; in 1923, he offered a fairly complete account of his educational views in *The Story of a Great Schoolmaster*, a tribute to F. W. Sanderson, the well-respected head of the Oundle School and, Wells writes, "beyond question the greatest man I have ever known with any degree of intimacy."

According to Wells, Sanderson had managed to maintain "that adolescent power of mental growth throughout life," understanding that "the fundamental instinct of life is to create, to make, to discover, to grow, to progress." Wells supplies long extracts from Sanderson's speeches and writings; in them, the influential headmaster reveals that, like Wells, he was convinced that education was the key to the cause of human evolution; that Britain's preparatory schools, badly outdated, were in quick need of deep reform. Sanderson criticized curricula that continued to stress the study of ancient writers at the expense of courses in science and technology. A modern school, Sanderson believed, should include machinery halls, wood-working shops, and laboratories set up for extensive study in biology and chemistry. Sanderson believed contemporary students should read works on contemporary problems—works by such writers as Shaw, Galsworthy, John Ruskin, and not surprisingly, Wells. He believed that "the great purpose" of modern education "is to enlist the boys or girls in the service of man to-day and man to-morrow."[48] Wells agreed. It was "our conviction," he writes,

that the present common life of men, at once dull and disorderly, competitive, uncreative, cruelly stupid and stupidly cruel, unless it is to be regarded merely as a necessary phase in the development of a nobler existence, is a thing not worth having, that it does not matter who drops dead or how soon we drop dead out of such a world. Unless there is a more abundant life before mankind, this scheme of space and time is a bad joke beyond our understanding, a flare of vulgarity, an empty laugh, braying across the mysteries. But we two shared the belief that latent in men and perceptible in men is a greater mankind, great enough to make every effort to realise it fully worth while, and to make the whole business of living worth while.

Such extreme proclamations—the proclamations of Wells the prophet, not Wells the comic novelist—continue to inform the later writings, including two novels, *Men Like Gods* (1923) and *The Dream* (1924). In *Men Like Gods,* a political journalist, Alfred Barnstaple, drives down a country road that takes him three thousand years into the future, into a world where peace and beauty prevail. Its citizens, the products of centuries of careful planning and selective breeding, are "gentle-mannered and gracious"; they have a "firm clear beauty of the face and limbs," displaying then the kind of physical grace and beauty that Wells—by his own admission—had long desired. They are telepathic—and nude. "That nudity," Wells would later clarify, "had a symbolical value too great to be mitigated. It emphasized that uncompromising frankness, that stark reality, which is the very soul of the new world of the author's hope and desire"—a place where men and women, having refined away "the beast in our inheritance," need no longer submit to restraining taboos.

As Urthred, one of the Utopians, explains, these healthy and serene citizens have long since gotten past the belief that "the universe is being managed for them better than they can control it for themselves"; they have, in fact, finally beaten "Mother Nature," who is—in Urthred's words—an "old Hag" both "purposeless and blind," capable of "savage moods" and quite incapable of caring for her offspring, whom she created "by accident" and tortures or rewards "without rhyme or reason." Exercising "the Word and the Will," Urthred and his fellows have "suppressed" Nature's "nastier fancies, and washed her and combed her and taught her to respect and heed the last child of her wantonings—Man." Like the enlightened citizens of the future envisioned by Winwood Reade, they have "taken over the Old Lady's Estate," constantly learning how to "master this little planet."

According to Urthred, the Utopians regard Barnstaple's own era, the early twentieth century, as the "Age of Confusion." They recall that its literature preached "selfish violence as though it was a virtue"; that its citizens struggled in a class-ridden world, their minds trained "to conflict, trained to insecurity and secret self-seeking." Barnstaple sees the truth of such insights, and defends the Utopians and their ways in debates with a group of earthlings who, like him, have accidentally entered this exotic realm. One of them, Rupert Catskill—on earth a politician, the Secretary of State of War—decides that the Utopians are "altogether too gentle" and have "drunken the debilitating draught of Socialism." Catskill wants to defeat the Utopians in combat, for he fears they will use strange powers to lure the earthlings into practicing similarly "degenerate" ways: "they may," he warns, "trifle with our ductless glands." Catskill clearly bears some re-

semblance to Winston Churchill, with whom Wells had frequently—but not irreparably—argued. (Wells's 1937 novel, the
eminently forgettable *Star-Begotten,* is dedicated to Churchill.)
Catskill functions here as one of Wells's stock bad guys, a flat
and predictable figure who, with other flat and predictable characters, is moved rompishly through what amounts to a kind of
extended comic strip, a political cartoon.

The Dream (1924) is in fact the dream of Sarnac, a man living
two thousand years hence. In deep sleep, he becomes Harry Mortimer Smith, born a shopkeeper's son in Kent. Sarnac, the resident
of another one of Wells's more orderly worlds-to-come is greatly
distressed by what he experiences and sees. As Smith, he spends
much of his boyhood below his father's shop, in a "cold, cavernous, dark place" filled with the stench of paraffin and rotting
vegetation. He learns little in a school that is ill-equipped, ill-run;
he suffers through Sunday school, learning of the "ambiguous
lives and doings of King David of Israel and Abraham, Isaac, and
Jacob and the misbehaviour of Queen Jezebel and the like topics."
As Smith, Sarnac never learned that "there was so much as a human community with a common soul and an ultimate common
destiny." As *The Dream* comes to a close, one of Sarnac's
friends—amazed by this account of endemic ignorance, frustration and greed—cries out: "Oh, poor, little, pitiful pitiless creatures! . . . Why were they all so hard upon each other and so deaf
to the sorrow in each other?" "We knew no better" Sarnac explains. "This world now has a tempered air. In this world we
breathe mercy with our first fluttering gasp. We are taught and
trained to think of others that their pain is ours. But two thousand years ago men and women were half-way back to crude Nature. Our motives took us unawares. We breathed infections. Our
food was poisoned. Our passions were fevers. We were only beginning to learn the art of being human." "A lifetime," another
of Sarnac's friends proclaims, "a whole young man's lifetime, a
quarter of a century, and this poor Harry Smith never once met a
happy soul and came only once within sight of happiness! And he
was just one of scores and hundreds of millions! They went
heavily and clumsily and painfully, oppressing and obstructing
each other, from the cradle to the grave."

The "Age of Confusion," Sarnac muses, was "a life, and it was
a dream, a dream within this life; and this life too is a dream.
Dreams within dreams, dreams containing dreams, until we come
at last, maybe, to the Dreamer of all dreams, the Being who is all

beings." This nebulous allusion to "the Dreamer of all dreams" is
one of the last traces of what Wells would later dismiss as "the
theocratic phase in my life." By the early 1930s, he was openly
regretting that he had once sought to express his political and
social beliefs in bluntly theological terms. In 1934 Wells admits
that, at least "by all preceding definitions," the God he evoked
during the period of *Britling* was "no God at all," but—more
accurately—"like a personification of, let us say, the Five Year
Plan," an "inspiring but extremely preoccupied comrade, a thoroughly hard leader." Later, in *Exasperations,* Wells puts addi-
tional distance between himself and *God, the Invisible King,*
admitting, "I am ashamed of the hysteria." But, he adds, "I cannot repudiate the intention." "I was denying," he writes—
expressing what is, perhaps, his chief ethical belief, a legacy of his
Christian training—"that such a gregarious animal as man can
live a purely self-centered life, seeking only security and sens[u]al
gratification. Thereby he defeats his own end."

In 1923, his involvement with Rebecca West at an end, Wells
began what became an often turbulent relationship with Odette
Keun, a flamboyant Frenchwoman who, after training briefly to
become a Dominican nun, took up fiction writing and journalism. Though Wells would later describe Keun as being, "from
certain points of view" a "thoroughly nasty and detestable person," he was in 1924 still sufficiently charmed by her beauty and
wit to begin residing with her in the South of France at "Lou
Pidou"—more formally, "Le Petit Dieu," Keun's name for Wells.
At Lou Pidou Wells completed *The World of William Clissold,*
his last ambitious attempt to present his philosophical and political beliefs in fictional form. Clissold is not—like Remington or
Britling or Wells—a professional writer; he is an industrialist, the
head of a large mineralogical concern. But like Wells, Clissold at
fifty-nine continues to exhibit "an inexhaustible supply of nervous energy"; he seeks "the application of the scientific method
to the whole of life." He calls for "a world state, a single terrestrial system of economic production and social cooperation,"
one that will support no army and will simply ban the manufacture of instruments of war, for it will fight "nothing but time
and space and death," its supreme goal the universal triumph of
efficiency, the utter abolition of waste. To that end, it will "orga-
nise the world production and world distribution of most staple
products"; it will construct one "interlocking system" that will
supervise the production and distribution of—among other

things—food, energy, chemicals, and steel. Clissold is Wells's version of the ideal businessman, combining Edward Ponderevo's entrepreneurial acumen with F. W. Sanderson's acute sense of social responsibility.

The World of William Clissold was regarded as something of a joke in some quarters, another predictable compendium of Wells's obsessions and peeves, an overblown monument to one man's gargantuan ego. D. H. Lawrence insisted that Clissold "is simply not good enough to be called a novel"; he called it "all chewed up newspaper, and chewed up scientific reports, like a mouse's nest," nothing but "words, words, words, about Socialism and Karl Marx, bankers and cave-men, money and the superman."[49] Arthur Thomson effectively parodied the novel in The World of Billiam Wissold (1928), assuming the voice of a narrator who is more than a little repetitive, ready to spend the rest of his life turning out torrents of prose. Wissold reports that his "youthful vigour remains unimpaired," and he is "undaunted by the outlook before me of another two million words or so."

My only anxiety is whether paper manufacturers will be able to keep pace with my demands. And even this anxiety is not an immediate one. From the floor at my side rises a 3-foot solid of clean, good square paper and on my desk is a gross of quill pens. There is probably sufficient writing material here to last me through the afternoon.[50]

H. L. Mencken, however, found merit in The World of William Clissold, correctly suggesting that much of it reveals Wells regaining his old artistic form. Not unfairly, Mencken had dismissed most of the fiction Wells produced between the years 1910 and 1920, calling The Wife of Sir Isaac Harman (1914) "500-odd pages of bosh," and The Research Magnificent "a poor soup from the dry bones of Nietzsche." Mencken considered The Soul of a Bishop (1917)—in which an Anglican clergyman comes to embrace a Wellsian vision of God—"perhaps the worst novel ever written by a serious novelist since novel writing began." Understandably, Mencken also attacked the ponderous Joan and Peter (1918), which Wells had hoped would "complement Mr. Britling Sees It Through as a study of the English spirit at war and in the face of the problems of 'reconstruction' arising out of the war." For Mencken, Joan and Peter featured little more than "uninteresting people, pointless situations, revelations that reveal nothing, arguments that have no appositeness, expositions that expose

naught save an insatiable and torturing garrulity." "Where,"
Mencken had wondered, "is the fine old address of the man?
Where is his sharp eye for the salient and significant in character?
Where is his instinct for form, his skill at putting a story together,
his hand for making it unwind itself?"[51]

As Mencken noted, *The World of William Clissold* is also plot-
less; "Clissold simply lives and dies." But he also thinks interest-
ingly. He is, as Mencken puts it, "a sort of super-Goethe, purged
of romantic illusion, and capable of visioning progress over long
periods and against all imaginable obstacles, even the obstacle of
human imbecility." As Clissold proves, Wells himself is "one of
the most remarkable personages in the England of today," with
his "bold and original" fancy, his "finger in a multitude of pies."
"Read, in *The World of William Clissold*, his chapter on sex,"
Mencken urged. "Read his several interpolated essays on money.
Read what he has to say about government, marriage, education—especially education. There is here a profoundly enterprising, competent and original mind, and I believe that it will put its
marks upon the thought of the next generation."[52]

Many of Clissold's views are restated in *The Open Conspiracy*,
which Wells designed to state "as plainly and clearly as possible
the essential ideas of my life, the perspective of my world." "My
other writings," he notes, "with hardly an exception, explore, try
over, illuminate, comment upon or flower out the essential matter
that I here attempt at last to strip bare to its foundations and
state unmistakably. This is my religion. Here are my directive
aims and the criteria of all I do."

The Open Conspiracy demonstrates again that its author was
by no means a facile optimist regarding human nature; "man,"
Wells asserts, echoing Huxley, "is an imperfect animal and never
quite trustworthy in the dark"; he is "still but half born out of
the blind struggle for existence and his nature still partakes of the
infinite wastefulness of his mother Nature." But like Huxley,
Wells points out that "man can resort to methods of escape from
that competitive pressure upon the means of subsistence, which
has been the lot of other animal species." He can abolish "the
waste of warfare and the private monopolisation of the sources of
wealth"; he can control "the increase in his numbers," and so
"escape therefore from the struggle for subsistence altogether
with a surplus of energy such as no other kind of animal species
has ever possessed." This "increasing surplus of will and energy"
is in constant danger of being thwarted or misdirected; "our

enemies," Wells declares, "are confusion of mind, want of courage, want of curiosity and want of imagination, indolence and
spendthrift egotism." These "jailers of human freedom and
achievement" cannot be effectively met by "the rank and file of
humanity," who "are accustomed to inferiority and dispossession";
who are, moreover, "disposed to childish and threatening demands upon heaven and the governments for redress and vindic-
tive and punitive action against the envied fortunate with whom
they happen to be in immediate contact, than to any reaction towards such complex, tentative disciplined constructive work as
alone can better the lot of mankind." Those educated and enlightened persons now capable of such work will remain ineffective if
their efforts are not merged, Wells contends; they must establish
an "Open Conspiracy," forming groups "in, and not only in, but
about and in relation to, the scientific world"; they must aim
mainly to advance their goals by "illumination and persuasion."
They must then ensure "the proper storage and indexing of scientific results," and strive to provide "the common intelligent man"
with summaries and analyses of the "implications and consequences of new work" in language he can readily understand.
For as scientific knowledge and clarity of vision become more
commonplace there will inevitably be more "Open Conspira-
tors"; they will comprise "a great world movement as widespread
and evident as socialism or communism. It will largely have taken
the place of these movements. It will be more, it will be a world
religion."

In 1927, Jane Wells learned she had cancer. Her death—
months later—left Wells stunned and, for a time, utterly un-
moored. He promptly undertook the publication of a collection
of Jane's previously unpublished stories and poems, calling it *The
Book of Catherine Wells* and adding an introduction full of
praise. Catherine Wells, wrote her husband, "never told a lie."
She was "before everything else gentle and sweet." She was generous, tenacious. "She stuck to me so sturdily," Wells writes,
"that in the end I stuck to myself." She "stabilized my life. She
gave it a home and dignity. She preserved its continuity." Later, in
his *Experiment in Autobiography,* Wells writes more explicitly of
the "physical and nervous incompatibilities" that became apparent in his second marriage and led, finally, to an arrangement
that allowed Wells to maintain a series of extramarital affairs. "I
do not think she believed very strongly in my beliefs," Wells
writes; her passions were, generally, less intense. According to

Wells, Catherine tolerated his amours because she simply knew "our alliance was indissoluble," and did not then demand "a monopoly of passionate intimacy"; because, too, "we had intergrown and become parts of each other." But even at home Wells and his wife saw less and less of each other; eventually, Catherine "took rooms of her own in Bloomsbury, rooms I never saw," where "quite away from all the life that centered upon me, she thought and dreamt and wrote and sought continually and fruitlessly for something she felt she had lost of herself or missed or never attained." It was here that Catherine worked on her stories, one of them—often retyped but never completed—was, according to Wells, "a dream of an island of beauty and sensuous perfection in which she lived alone and was sometimes happy in her loneliness and sometimes very lonely. In her dream there was a lover who never appeared. He was a voice heard; he was a trail of footsteps in the dewy grass, or she woke and found a rosebud at her side."

By 1928, Wells was, by his own account, "very tired of Odette," but that volatile alliance persisted until 1933, when Wells became the "open and professed lover" of Moura Budberg, an Estonian who had for some years been the companion of Maxim Gorki and apparently remained—well into her relationship with Wells—a Soviet spy. In 1934, Wells offered a highly unflattering portrait of Keun in *Apropos of Dolores,* one of the better of his later novels. *Apropos of Dolores* is not another slapdash narrative designed solely to propagate Wells's theories. It gives vent to a complex, intensely felt mixture of attraction and hate; its depiction of Dolores remains memorable because Keun herself was a vivid and memorable character, known for her caustisity and studied theatricality. The novel's narrator, Stephen Wilbeck, records that he was initially intrigued by Dolores's exotic flair and esoteric interests: her "wildly inaccurate savoir-faire about food and wine" and her curious regimen of exercises—"a combination of the best Swedish drill with the finer usages of yoga mysticism." *Apropos of Dolores* succeeds as an often-funny, often-grim story of the conflict of two willful and diverse personalities—of an erotic attraction gone gradually wrong. Unfortunately, Wells cannot simply leave it at that. He was incapable of writing about life without also hammering home a point; his characters cannot exist simply as honest portrayals of intriguing or perplexing or infuriating men and women: they must also be types, representatives of views that either support or thwart Wells's prescriptions for a more ordered world. Moreover—particularly after 1900—Wells almost never allows his readers to arrive at their own conclusions about the meanings of his books or the actions of his characters. Thus Dolores, Wilbeck instructs the reader, is "a human being stripped down to its bare egotism. She is assertion and avidity incarnate. She is the most completely, exclusively and harshly assembled individuality I have ever encountered." She is not simply Dolores in all her quirky and obnoxious splendor; she is "the Dolores type," one of a number of "sub-species, hybrids and mutations" belonging to homo sapiens; she is "a widespread, familiar type, emphatic, impulsive and implacable."

During the late twenties and early thirties Wells continued to split his time between Easton Glebe and the South of France, working on *The Science of Life,* a vast attempt to discuss everything from "Breathing" and "Birds" to "Sex Hormones" and "Slime-moulds" in terms the intelligent nonspecialist could readily grasp. The book—prepared with the help of two practicing scientists, "Gip" Wells and Thomas Huxley's grandson, Julian—sold well (though not nearly as well as *The Outline of History*), and for some years served as a textbook at various colleges and universities. A related volume, *The Work, Wealth and Happiness of Mankind* (1932) aims ambitiously to provide "a survey of the mental life of our world"; its focus is on economics and industrial planning. It earned poor sales amidst a worldwide recession and in the wake of tepid reviews. Henry Hazlitt, for one, found *The Work, Wealth and Happiness of Mankind* to be marred by rather questionable generalizations, and a certain "cocksureness," an "implication in his tone that he is addressing mental inferiors"—a tone frequently found in Wells's later writings.[53] Wells felt his health fading as he labored on *The Work, Wealth and Happiness of Mankind;* he felt "old and worn out," and troubled by "perplexing symptoms" that prompted him, finally, to seek medical counsel.

Wells discovered that he was a diabetic; and, after submitting to certain dietary disciplines (he never required the use of insulin), he found his energy restored. He began to behave "with renewed decision and steadfastness, and to see things clearly, unclouded by any morbid preoccupation with mortality." He now abandoned the large house at Easton Glebe, and (refreshed by periodic trips to the Continent) began to anchor his life more firmly in London, settling into a large flat on Baker Street, in Chiltern Court. Between 1932 and the end of 1934, Wells's publications included two novels, *The Bulpington of Blup* (1932) and *The Shape of Things to Come* (1933), as well as his huge *Experiment in Autobiography* (1934). *The Bulpington of Blup* focuses on Theodore Bulpington, whom Wells describes in his autobiography as "a very direct caricature study of the irresponsible disconnected aesthetic mentality." Bulpington is reared in what Wells portrays as a rather pretentiously arty milieu; he tends—from childhood on—to plunge deeply into a world of illusion, fashioning a series of more fascinating versions of himself. As Wells makes clear, Bulpington's fantasies and self-projections are both dangerous and infantile, the symptoms of a disordered personality unwilling to face life's hard realities, and so fearful of the future that, ultimately, he retreats into an absurdly romanticized version of the past. Bulpington not only ends up glorifying his own dubious war experiences, but plans to pen "the New Historical Romance," doing "for the nineteenth century what Sir Walter Scott had done for the eighteenth." He would "evoke its latent glamour," and make "Queen Victoria the goddess of the story, no Virgin goddess but better, almost symbolically prolific and beneficent." The world, Bulpington decides, "had had enough of realism and cynicism; how gladly would it welcome a new magician, the Wizard of the South, Captain Blup-Bulpington! Afterwards Sir Theodore Blup-Bulpington."

At least two astute critics, John Batchelor and Robert Bloom, have found much to admire in the structure and intellectual energy of *The Bulpington of Blup;* Bloom suggests that it shows Wells devising "an intriguing form—the anti-*Bildungsroman.* Instead of growing from an inadequate subjectivity to a mature consciousness of the objective world and his own place in it, the putative hero reverses the process, progressively embracing and inventing illusions, more and more resisting alternatives and voices that clash with his own."[54] But the novel passed largely unnoticed, and remains little known. Joseph Wood Krutch, reviewing *The Bulpington of Blup* in the *Nation*, found it "amazingly fluent, amazingly perspicuous and reasonable"—as well as "studded with phrases so neat and so conclusive that one would have to single them out for applause if one had not come to take them for granted in this particular author." Still, this particular author, Krutch argued—voicing what had become a consensus view—"does not bother to vary greatly the pattern of his fictions. When he feels a novel coming on he chooses either a Utopia or an imaginary biography, and after that choice has been made there remains only the task of recombining the characters and situations which he has used again and again." "One has listened before to these same conversations about science, religion, and politics," Krutch writes, suggesting too that "the enthusiasm of Mr. Wells is more nearly tireless than that of his readers. The writing may be as good as ever, and it is certainly not perfunctory, but the reading is. The mind will not follow what it has followed so many times before."[55]

When *The Shape of Things to Come* appeared, the Great Depression was deepening throughout Europe and America; and, as nationalism and militarism flourished in Germany, Italy, and Japan, the world again braced for war. Once more, Wells lazily turns to the device of a dream in order to transport his principal character entirely elsewhere; *The Shape of Things to Come* purports to be the manuscript of Dr. Phillip Raven, a diplomat and internationalist who, prior to his death, found himself drifting into a trancelike state in which he could watch the next two hundred years of human history. *The Shape of Things to Come* offers no memorably drawn characters or episodes; its textbook prose is plodding and dry: it demonstrates anew Wells's own lingering fascistic streak. It also demonstrates that Wells did possess a certain knack for accurate prediction as he describes a second European war between Britain and Germany that is triggered, in 1940, by events in the Polish corridor. Twenty years later, an uneasy peace prevails, but there are pockets of barbarism and outbreaks of disease; most of the world's population wanders numbly through empty towns, down streets "littered with gnawed bones or fully-clad skeletons."

Gradually, the world is repaired. A Wellsian World-State begins operations, helped into existence by war-hardened aviators able to descend swiftly into areas of barbarism and clean things up, bringing to an end "wars, plunderings, poverty and bitter universal frustrations." (In *The Open Conspiracy*, Wells insists that the drive for universal enlightenment and world unity "has to advance and even from the outset where it is not allowed to illuminate and persuade it must fight.") The "Modern State" Wells portrays in *The Shape of Things to Come* is committed to rule "not only the planet but the human will." To that end, it shuts down churches and religious shrines, decreeing that "there was now to be one faith only in the world, the moral expression of the one world community." This "first world government," Raven records, had to "immobilize or destroy every facile system of errors, misinterpretations, compensations and self-consolations that still survived to confuse the minds of men; it had to fight a battle against fear, indolence, greed and jealousy in every soul in the world" or inevitably "it had to lapse," thus allowing the race "to drift back again to animal individualism, and so through chaos to extinction."

Thus, what becomes known as the "Puritan Tyranny" takes hold as the airmen seek to "disinfect" the world's mental atmosphere; to ensure "the complete establishment of a code of rigorous and critical self-control, of habitual service, creative activity, cooperation." "These Puritans," we learn, "were consumed by an overwhelming fear of leisure both for themselves and others. They found it morally necessary to keep going and to keep everybody else going." It is necessary too, they decide, to destroy "the old literature and drama," which, after all, "provided patterns for behaviors and general conduct," sometimes fueling "the innate hostility and excitement caused by difference of racial type," sometimes driving "innumerable men to murders, lynchings, deliberate torture," sometimes simply perpetuating "that queer clowning with insults and repartees, that insincerely sympathetic mocking of inferiors, that denigration of superiors, which constructed 'humor' in the old days." Between 2000 and 2040, this "Air Dictatorship" also destroys or reconditions "every domicile in the world," eliminating "the huts, hovels, creeper-clad cottages and houses, old decaying stone and brick town halls, market houses, churches, mosques, factories and railway stations in which our tough if ill-proportioned and undersized forefathers assembled about their various archaic businesses." The result, Raven concedes, is "an immense loss of 'picturesqueness.' " But now come towns that are "larger, finer and more varied," where "housing blocks are grouped near stores, parks, and public clubs," combining "the idea of the English or American club with the idea of the Baths to which the Roman citizen resorted," providing too "gymnastic and sports halls, dancing-floors, conference rooms, the perpetual news cinema, libraries, reading-rooms, small studies, studios and social centers of the reviving social life." The Air Dictatorship was like a "cold bath," necessary to keep men and women "braced up" as they went about the hard business of constructing humanity's ideal habitat. "You may call it tyranny," suggests Raven, "but it was in fact a release; it did not suppress men, but obsessions." With those obsessions and confusions gone—with order and cooperation and rationality everywhere in place—the world of 2100 has eliminated disease and intelligently controls its populations; even the weather is better—thanks to enormous advances in meteorology. Knowledge is made widely accessible through the establishment of "a collective Brain, the Encyclopaedia, the Fundamental Knowledge System, which accumulates, sorts, keeps in order and renders available everything that is known." Centered in Barcelona, this "Memory of Mankind" employs millions of workers; its "tentacles" (one of Wells's favorite words, appearing both positively and negatively in his writings) "spread out in one direction to millions of investigators, checkers and correspondents, and in another to keep the educational process in living touch with mental advance." Now, finally, men and women are free to devote more and more of their time to the pursuit of knowledge and self-improvement; they associate not "for aggression or for defense," but for "a common happiness." At last, "the Martyrdom of Man is at an end." Thus:

From pole to pole now there remains no single human being without a fair prospect for self-fulfilment, of health, interest, and freedom. There are no slaves any longer; no poor; none doomed by birth to an inferior status; none sentenced to long and unhelpful terms of imprisonment; none afflicted in mind or body who are not helped with all the powers of science and the services of interested and able guardians. The world is all before us to do with what we will, within the measure of our powers and imaginations. The struggle for material existence is over. It has been won. The need for repressions and disciplines has passed. The struggle for truth and that indescribable necessity which is beauty begins now, unhampered by any of the imperatives of the lower struggle. No one need live less nor be less than his utmost.

During the spring of 1934, Wells—now one of the world's most recognizable literary figures—traveled to America, meeting with President Franklin Roosevelt, his wife Eleanor, and several top advisers, the so-called Brain Trust that had been assembled to help solve the nation's continuing economic crisis. Wells was impressed. Roosevelt, he decided, was not only brilliant and shrewd, but "unlimited," willing not only to consider radical social reforms but to put them into action, unifying "unconventional thought and practical will." In Roosevelt, Wells found nothing less than "the way thither" to the Open Conspiracy—an educated, enlightened, well-intentioned leader who "can talk on the

radio—over the heads of the party managers and newspaper pro-
prietors and so forth—quite plainly and convincingly to the ordinary voting man." In FDR, Wells found "as it were, a ganglion
for reception, expression, transmission, combination and realization, which I take it, is exactly what a modern government ought
to be."

Within weeks of leaving the United States, Wells traveled to the
Soviet Union, where he interviewed Joseph Stalin and was disappointed to discover that the Russian dictator displayed no enthusiasm for "the possible convergence of East and West," the
merging of equitable socialism with efficient capitalism along
lines proposed in *The World of William Clissold*. "The one true
faith was in Russia," Wells recalls that Stalin insisted; "there
could be no other. America must have her October Revolution
and follow her Russian leaders." Wells admits in his autobiography that while he now had access to "most of the people in the
world in key positions," he lacked "the solvent power to bring
them into unison. I can talk to them and even unsettle them but I
cannot compel their brains to see."

The publication of *Experiment in Autobiography* in 1934 was a
major literary event. Though Wells was no longer considered a
novelist of major importance, he was still very much a public figure—one with an unusually eventful past. Critics agreed: *Experiment in Autobiography* was, despite its heft, a remarkably good
read. The American critic Malcolm Cowley, for example, accurately predicted that the book would be "valued chiefly as a work
of art," calling it "a whole collection of novels, bigger and more
satisfying than most of the current trilogies and tetralogies." It
begins as "a sort of 'David Copperfield' story about a Cockney
boy who lived among all sorts of bad smells and quaint characters and managed somehow to get an education." It then becomes
"the love story of a young science instructor who married his
cousin and deserted her for one of his pupils, thereby putting an
end to his teaching career." Even better is the account of the "rising young novelist" and his "meetings with other writers and his
interchange of ideas with them." Wells, writes Cowley, "reminds
us here of something we had almost forgotten: the vigor and fer-
ment of intellectual life at the turn of the century, the passion
with which ideas were put forward and debated, the feeling that
all these projects would be realized in the better society of the
future. Those were the great days of liberalism, and Wells makes
them live again."[56]

Wells's new friend, the president of the United States, also liked the book, informing Wells in a letter that *Experiment in Autobiography* "was for me an experiment in sitting awake instead of putting the light out." "I believe," wrote Roosevelt, "our biggest success is in making people think during these past two years. They may not think straight but they are thinking in the right direction—and your direction and mine are not so far apart."[57]

As *Experiment in Autobiography* makes very clear, Wells had spent a great deal of time thinking about his life, his career, and his many relationships; he is by no means apologetic, but willing to admit, for example, that—in his Fabian days—he was sometimes guilty of "bad judgment" and "inexcusable vanity," and often antagonized his friends Bernard Shaw and Beatrice Webb with "my ill-aimed aggressiveness." He insists that "my perceptions do not seem to be so thorough, vivid, and compelling as those of many people I meet and it is rare that my impressions of things glow." "I am just a little slack," Wells writes, "not wholly and consistently interested, prone to be indolent and cold-hearted. I am readily bored." Wells also concedes that "much of my work has been slovenly, haggard and irritated, most of it hurried and inadequately revised." And much of it, he realizes, will sink into oblivion. "I come upon masterpieces by pure chance," he writes; "if sometimes I am an artist it is a freak of the gods. I am a journalist all the time and what I write *goes now*—and will presently die."

Still, one senses in reading *Experiment in Autobiography* that Wells believed that the best of his fiction had yet to be fully appreciated—while the reputations of several of his literary contemporaries were, on the whole, overblown. Thus he takes time to bash Henry James yet once more, portraying him as an artist unable to see life clearly and to see it whole—as "a strange unnatural human being, a sensitive man lost in an immensely abundant brain" who had insulated himself in "elaborations of gesture and speech" and so tended to regard the people he met "with a face of distress and a remote effort at intercourse, like some victim of enchantment placed in the centre of an immense bladder." James's novels, Wells writes, are "faintly fussy" works "from which all the fiercer experiences are excluded." Like James, Joseph Conrad was handicapped because he lacked sound training in the sciences, Wells suggests; theirs were "abundant but uneducated brains," resulting in the unfortunate lack of "a central philosophy." Conrad also possessed an "over-sensitized receptivity," which Wells believed resulted in an "oppressive" prose style, "as overwrought as an Indian tracery." "This incessant endeavour to keep prose bristling up and have it 'vivid' all the time defeats its end." "I like turning a phrase as well as any man," Wells insists, "I try my utmost to achieve precision of statement where precision is important." But, he adds, "I write as straight as I can, just as I walk as straight as I can, because that is the best way to get there."

His autobiography shows that Wells had no doubts about the legitimacy of his lifelong cause; in fact, there is a growing sense of urgency about his call for the triumph of reason and the importance of world unity—a sense too that, perhaps, his decades of effort had been in vain. "Human life as we know it," Wells repeats, "is only the dispersed raw material for life as it might be. There is a hitherto undreamt-of fullness, freedom and happiness within reach of our species. Mankind can pull itself together and take that now." But, he stresses,

if mankind fails to apprehend its opportunity, then division, cruelties, delusions and ultimate frustration lies before our kind. The decision to perish or escape has to be made within a very limited time. For escape, vast changes in the educational, economic and directive structure of human society are necessary. They are definable. They are practicable. But they demand courage and integrity. They demand a force and concentration of will and a power of adaptation in habits and usages which may not be within the compass of mankind.

Throughout the 1930s, Wells sustained a highly active pace. He gave interviews, made radio broadcasts, and traveled widely. He succeeded John Galsworthy as president of PEN (Poets, Essayists, Novelists), an organization of practicing writers established to promote literary freedom and international understanding. He worked closely with producer Alexander Korda and director William Menzies in the making of the 1936 film version of *The Shape of Things to Come* that—as George Zebrowski has noted—is today widely regarded as "the first great science fiction sound film," with its convincing use of elaborate models and extravagant sets marking a significant advance in the use of special effects.[58] Wells provided the screenplay for the film, called simply *Things to Come* and starring Ralph Richardson and Raymond Massey—the latter a chief spokesman for Wells's philosophical views. Although it has now achieved a certain cult status, *Things to Come* was not commercially successful, perhaps because it offered a few too many Wellsian arias to matinee-goers who had expected a steadier flow of action shots and battle scenes. (Posters for the film, which promised "a cast of 20,000," emphasized a racing rocket and a spaceman in dark, exotic garb.) Wells was disappointed, insisting that the film was "pretentious, clumsy and scamped. I had fumbled with it." But Menzies, he added, "was an incompetent director; he loved to get away on location and waste money on irrelevancies; and Korda let this happen. Menzies was a sort of Cecil B. de Mille without imagination; his mind ran on loud machinery and crowd effects and he had no grasp of my ideas." Wells had convinced himself, moreover, that the widely respected Korda had "produced so badly that ultimately they had to cut out a good half of my dramatic scenes." Still, at the time of his death, in 1946, Wells was planning another film with Korda— on the future of the world in the wake of the atomic bomb.

Nor was Wells pleased with Orson Welles's 1938 radio dramatization of *The War of the Worlds,* an event that sparked terror and despair among radio listeners throughout much of North America; in fact, as Hadley Cantril suggests, never had "so many people in all walks of life and in all parts of the country become so suddenly and so intensely disturbed as they did on this night."[59] Cantril, a professor at Princeton, directed a well-funded study of the phenomenon, discovering that many who heard Welles's broadcast were, understandably, unfamiliar with Wells's novel. Many were unaware that Welles had billed the mock-news event as a seasonal treat—simply a scary story for Halloween. Having tuned in late, listeners throughout the States assumed that they were in fact being attacked by vicious aliens; "they fled from home in their Studebakers and Terraplanes and Packards," Philip Klass writes, "ran and hid where they could or rioted to force mayors to break open town armories and hand out weapons against the horrors from space."[60] After hearing of the broadcast's effect, Wells cabled Welles, insisting that "totally unwarranted liberties were taken with my book," and threatening legal action. He was—as the Mackenzies note—"furious at this unexpected demonstration of the capacity of his work to terrify people," many of whom were already growing uneasy with talk, on the radio, of the imminence of yet another European war.[61]

Late in life, Wells would come to describe himself as being "of an absolutely opposite temperament to the melancholic," noting that he "preached and preached" a form of "stoical heroism"—a "cheerful fight against the odds." "I have never yet suffered so much that I have not had the spirit left to resist and attack my depression, and presently recover buoyancy." Certainly, many who knew Wells knew only a congenial, talkative man of exceptional vigor. But Wells's deeper anxieties, his darker moods, are often alluded to in his novels: in *Tono-Bungay*, for example, Wells's narrator, George Ponderevo, recalls suffering from "a sort of *ennui* of the imagination," when he found himself "without an object to hold my will together," when "my life appeared before me in bleak, relentless light, a series of ignorances, crude blunderings, degradation and cruelty." "I had," Ponderevo recalls, "what the old theologians call a 'conviction of sin.'" Stephen Stratton, who narrates *The Passionate Friends,* admits that "despair is always near to me. In the common hours of my life it is as near as a shark may be near a sleeper in a ship." Stratton has known "a sense of life as of an abysmal flood, full of cruelty, densely futile, blackly aimless." He has been "filled with self-contempt and self-disgust. I felt that I was utterly weak and vain, and all the pretensions and effort of my life were florid, fruitless pretensions and nothing more. I lost all control over my mind."

In the 1930s, Wells again writes that in his "less protected moments" his depression was intense enough to prompt him to consider suicide. He alludes to "gathering shadows of loneliness and hopelessness" he could disperse only "by a spurt of activity." Sometimes, however, "I am too fagged to work or sleep and then I have no refreshment at hand any more. I stare existence blankly in the face. I feel no incentive to action. I fear for the world then unreasonably and I am dissatisfied almost beyond endurance with everything."

Entering the 1930s, Wells was certain that he wanted to marry Moura Budberg. But Budberg refused to comply. She would be his companion, his lover; she would not, however, be his wife. The English novelist C. P. Snow recalls that during his first meeting with Wells—in the autumn of 1934—Moura was very much on Wells's mind.[62] Wells was puzzled, Snow writes, and "extremely glum." "Why," Snow recalls that Wells demanded, "had he not a wife to look after him? Why had neither of us wives to look after us? Why, in particular, would someone called Moura not marry him?" "This," Snow writes, "I found a very difficult question, since I had met him only for ten minutes and had never heard of Moura." When at last she appeared, Snow found "a woman in early middle age, handsome, dashing, strong as Mother Russia." He continues:

She sat down at the table and with gusto helped me finish the bottle of wine. She gave out well-being, she was cheerful. The temperature of the party began to rise. Wells was looking at her with love and irritation. She talked to him with down-to-earth affection. But Wells's irritation grew when she also talked to me. Wells disapproved. It was getting on for four, and he made it clear that it was time I went. 'Come back and see us soon,' said Moura. But I was not invited to Chiltern Court again, though I met him a good many times away from home.

In fact, throughout the 1930s, Wells continued to travel and lecture extensively—going as far as Australia in 1938. He remained energetic and prolific well into his seventies. In 1940, working with Lord Sankey and a committee of several others, Wells helped compile—indeed largely compose—a "Declaration of the Rights of Man" that he hoped would be "no less than a common fundamental law for the whole world, overriding any other law that it contradicts," and that did in fact provide a principal model for the Declaration of Human Rights later incorporated into the charter of the United Nations. "Every man," the so-called Sankey Declaration proclaims (meaning, by man, "every living human being without distinction of age or sex") has a right to, among other things, "Freedom from Violence" and "Freedom of Movement"; to "a Right to Knowledge" and "a Right to Work"—although all work must contribute "to the welfare of the community," and not be motivated by "the sole object of profit-making." Like all of Wells's writings, the declaration emphasizes the idea of social obligation, noting that "it is only by doing his quota of service that a man can justify his partnership in the community."[63]

By 1940, with the European war in full swing, Wells found himself confined to London, where he spent the last five years of his life refusing to seek shelter even as German bombs blew craters in the streets surrounding his Hanover Terrace flat. He continued to write and publish regularly, stressing familiar themes. In *Science and the World Mind* (1942), he again asserts that homo sapiens "cannot go on living as he has been doing in the past few score of thousands of years." There is a growing strain on the world's resources; there are ever more horrific weapons of war. He points to "the Dinosaurs and the Deinotheria. They ended on a crescendo, and went." They simply "failed to adapt." Man, Wells writes, "may be extinguished altogether, or he may undergo modification into a new species." There is "no question of his remaining as he is." He can become "a progressive superhomo, an ascendant species, or one of a series of degenerate sub-human species." He can "fail altogether to adapt" and, accordingly, "end altogether." Is there any cause for hope? "There is," Wells insists, "and it lies in his gift of speech. Almost entirely, but not entirely, in that. He can be told things. He can listen and learn." He can then "adjust himself a thousand times more rapidly than any other animal. Every generation of homo sapiens can learn the mental adaptation that has been imposed by altered conditions upon its predecessor." In other words, as late as 1943, Wells still prepared to believe in the power of knowledge and education; he is able, in the midst of war, to articulate hope.

But many of Wells's later works—including such novels as *Mr. Blettsworthy on Rampole Island* (1928) and *The Croquet Player* (1936)—reveal that his streak of pessimism regarding human nature and human possibility had not diminished since the days, three decades earlier, when he unleashed *The Island of Dr. Moreau*. In fact, *Mind at the End of Its Tether* (1945), the last work Wells published in his lifetime, is also his most bleak. "In the past," Wells writes, he was able to "think that man could pull out of his entanglements and start a new creative phase of human living." But now, in the final year of World War II—the year of Hiroshima—Wells sees ours as a jaded world devoid of recuperative power. "This World," he writes, "is at the end of its tether. The end of everything we call life is close at hand and cannot be evaded."

Wells's obsession with retelling the story of his life—with understanding, explaining, and alternately criticizing and justifying his actions and beliefs—remained strong even in his final years. In 1943, Wells published his "Auto-Obituary," describing himself as "one of the most prolific 'literary hacks'" of his generation, but one with "a flair for 'what is coming.' "[64] Wells calls himself "a Liberal Democrat in the sense that he claimed an unlimited right to think, criticise, discuss, and suggest, and he was a Socialist in his antagonism to personal, racial, or national monopolisation." He was "essentially an intellectual with an instinctive dislike for all the vehemencies, the zeals, patriotisms and partisanships, intensities and emotional floods of life"; "the question whether he was to be considered a 'humorist' was discussed but

never settled, and it need not trouble us now." In 1948, Wells—
Wells notes—was "seriously injured in a brawl with some Fascist
roughs"; "his health was further impaired by a spell in a concentration camp under the brief Communist dictatorship of 1952."
He "became a forgotten man," dying of heart failure at the age
of 97.

In fact, Wells died of liver cancer just weeks short of his eight-
ieth birthday. In 1945, a year before his death, he again took note
of the decline of his readership and reputation in "A Complete
Exposé of this Notorious Literary Humbug," a piece that—despite its air of facetiousness—reflects well the sense of incomple-
tion and gloom that informs his final years. It was, Wells muses,
The World of William Clissold, "issued in three successive volumes of rigmarole, which broke down the endurance of readers
and booksellers alike." After it, the books of H. G. Wells "vanished from the shopwindows and the tables of cultured people."
Now, "People whom once he had duped would perhaps mention
him as a figure of some significance in English literature, but the
established reply of the people who no longer read him and had
nothing to say about him, was simply the grimace of those who
scent decay. 'Oh Wells!' they would say, and leave it at that."

2

The Scientific Romances

Despite the remarkable range of his work in fiction, philosophy, and social criticism, H. G. Wells is undoubtedly best known to most readers as a writer—indeed the inventor—of "science fiction," the man who built a time machine, created an invisible man, put men on the moon, and described the destruction of much of England by hideous creatures from Mars. But of course well before Wells, writers in various times and places had already written of daring journeys to far-flung locales; Cyrano de Bergerac, for one, wrote of rocket ships and extraterrestrial life in *The History of the States and Empires of the World of the Moon*, published in 1656. In the early nineteenth century, Mary Shelley (in *Frankenstein*) and Nathaniel Hawthorne (in such stories as "The Birthmark" and "Rappacini's Daughter") evoked the eerie atmosphere of the Gothic romance as they pointed to the kind of horrific consequences that can accompany scientific experimentation—a theme that continues to recur in the science fiction of today. *Five Weeks in a Balloon*, the first of Jules Verne's highly popular novels of scientific adventuring, appeared in 1863, three years before Wells was born. With such similar novels as *Journey to the Center of the Earth* (1864) and *From the Earth to the Moon* (1865), Verne built the foundation of modern science fiction; he was, as John J. Pierce writes, "the first romancer of the future, the first to capture the spirit of scientific discovery and invention and romanticize it at a time when 'romance' was almost always associated with the past."[1] Moreover it was Hugo Gernsback, not Wells, who coined the term *science fiction* when, in 1926, he founded *Amazing Stories* magazine. Wells himself placed the most successful of his earliest fictions—including *The Time Machine* and *The War of the Worlds*—under the category of "scientific romance." He linked them to a literary tradition that includes not only *Frankenstein,* but the *Golden Ass of Apuleius,* the *True Histories of Lucian,* and *Peter Schlemihl.*[2]

Indeed, Wells's early excursions into the bizarre and the macabre often appear to owe much, structurally and thematically, to the works of other writers—as the industrious Ingvald Raknem has exhaustively shown. Raknem finds traces of Irving's "Rip Van Winkle" in Wells's short story "Mr. Skelmersdale in Fairyland"; he links Rémy de Gourmont's "D'un Pays Lointain" with Wells's "The Country of the Blind." Raknem also notes that "some incidents" in Wells's "The Story of the Late Mr. Elvesham" were "evidently suggested" by Edgar Allan Poe's "William Wilson," both of which involve "the problem of double personalities and the exchange of bodies." Raknem suggests that Wells's "The Stolen Body" has "several incidents in common" with Poe's "Tale of the Ragged Mountains"; he contends that parts of *The Island of Dr. Moreau* bear striking similarities to Poe's *Arthur Gordon Pym.*[3] Catherine Rainwater has also examined Wells's Poe connection, convincingly comparing "The Red Room" with Poe's "Fall of the House of Usher."[4]

Such examples—and there are many—seem sufficient to prove that Wells lifted routinely from writers he liked. And yet, in the making of his "scientific romances," Wells unquestionably broke new ground. He sent a man into the future via a machine, not a dream; he brought an unprecedented sense of plausibility to his treatment of extraterrestrial life—and thus, for better or worse, inspired a continuing series of novelistic and cinematic accounts of the earth's invasion by hostile forces from space. As importantly, Wells structured such works as *The Time Machine, The War of the Worlds,* and *The Invisible Man* to do far more than amuse and divert; he used them to air his most basic biases and beliefs—to warn of the dangers of man's latent animality, to call for a world made safe for reason, free inquiry, and lasting peace. By treating these early novels seriously, by mixing the weirdness and playfulness of the romance with the sense of veracity found in the best "realistic" fiction, Wells—more than Verne—helped forge the way for the such writers as writers as Olaf Stapledon, Brian Aldiss, Isaac Asimov, and Ursula K. Le Guin, who have similarly brought art and respectibility to the making of narratives that combine strange incidents and settings with the serious treatment of ethical issues and scientific themes.[5]

By examining *The Time Machine* in its first and final published versions, one can watch Wells giving significant shape and

direction to what would become modern science fiction. Its earliest version, "The Chronic Argonauts" shows that, at twenty-
one, Wells was still more concerned with evoking an eerie atmo
sphere than in making a point—or even a viable plot. "The
Chronic Argonauts" reads like an unintended parody of early
nineteenth-century Gothic fiction, the work of a young writer
still under the sway of such authors as Poe, Nathaniel Hawthorne, and Mary Shelley. Its opening paragraphs lengthily describe a rotting "manse" complete with draughts, cobwebs, and
"creeping things innumerable"; its current tenant, a scientist
called Dr. Moses Nebogipfel, has a "phenomenally wide and high
forehead" and "lank black hair" as well as "temporal arteries
that pulsated visibly through his transparent yellow skin"—traits
that have somehow not blocked his entry into the Royal Society.
His many years of secret labor on "The Chronic Argo"—a ship
that sails through time—have left Nebogipfel with nothing but
"silence and suffering" and much hostility from the Welsh village
where he resides. Wells fills these opening pages with mists,
clouds, cobwebs; he throws in toadstools, black gables, "blotchy
toads," a hunchback. The story is stilted and affected and goes
nowhere.[6] "I still jumbled both my prose and my story in an entirely incompetent fashion," Wells admits, recalling this piece in
his *Experiment in Autobiography*. "If a young man of twenty-one
were to bring me a story like 'The Chronic Argonauts' for my advice
to-day I do not think I should encourage him to go on writing."

In its finished form, *The Time Machine* features a central character, the "Time Traveller," who is not a ghoul; he is congenial,
refined—precisely the sort of figure that Sir Richard Gregory had
in mind when he praised Wells's ability to present "scientific
workers" as "human beings and not as the travesties in which
they figure in novels and romances written without his intimate
knowledge of them and their impulses."[7] After declaring that
"time is only a kind of space"—and as traversable as any high-
way—the Time Traveller reveals that he has constructed, in his
London laboratory, a rather elegant vehicle of nickel and ivory
that can cruise "in any direction of Space and Time, as the driver
determines." At first, the Time Traveller's friends—settled, rather
skeptical professional men—are reluctant to accept such claims.
But one evening they find the Time Traveller looking worn and
pale, announcing that he has just taken his amazing device for its
inaugural ride. Strapped to its saddle—a kind of cosmic bicyclist

shot through the surreal landscape of a dream—he recalls watching night follow day "like the flapping of a black wing" and seeing the sun "hopping swiftly across the sky." He tells of emerging, finally, in an apparently serene world filled with small, smooth, androgynous people, "strict vegetarians" who wear sandals and robes and spend their days "speaking in soft cooing notes to each other," in "playing gently, in bathing in the river, in making love in a half-playful fashion, in eating fruit and sleeping."

Weena, one of these "delicious people" becomes fond of the Time Traveller, and grows anxious when he leaves her sight, especially at nightfall. As the Time Traveller relates, Weena "dreaded the dark, dreaded shadows, dreaded black things." He soon learns why. Weena and her kin, the Eloi, are not alone; their world is far from paradise. Below them, in caves, are Morlocks—blanched, chinless, simian creatures for whom the Eloi are simply "fatted cattle," a steady source of protein. The Time Traveller is himself attacked by the Morlocks, fending them off with an iron crowbar that he swings with gusto, discovering a certain elation when, striking the faces of some of these "human rats," he feels "the succulent giving of flesh and bone." Later, the Morlocks bait the Time Traveller, but again he flees, speeding thousands of years into the future, and encountering yet another chilling scene.

Now, the sky is "inky black," the terrain bleak; the air is "rarefied," filled with a "harsh scream." The Time Traveller sees "a thing like a huge white butterfly go slanting and fluttering up into the sky"; he sees, approaching, "a crab as large as yonder table," its mouth "alive with appetite," its eyes "wriggling on their stalks," its claws "smeared with an algal slime." The Traveller elects to depart, speeding millions of years ahead, "drawn on by the mystery of the earth's fate." Stopping, he finds a dying planet. There is only bitter cold and utter quiet, little left of life except yet another of Wells's gross, tentacled things—this one "the size of a football perhaps" and "hopping fitfully about" a desolate shoreline.

The Time Traveller stands for much that Wells would consistently praise: he is resourceful, intrepid, and intensely curious about the world he occupies; he is then linked to a long line of literary heroes, to Ulysses and Aeneas, bravely facing a series of hard tests and gaining wisdom as he goes. To a large extent, then, *The Time Machine* is—like many of Wells's later works—an in-

vitation to adventure and discovery, a celebration of human courage and ingenuity. But it is also a cautioning tale, a political
tract—the first in a long line of Wellsian attacks on the kind of
crude industrial capitalism he watched operate in the closing decades of the nineteenth century. The Eloi, as the Traveller himself
comes to realize, are the descendants of landowners, aristocrats—
the nation's elite. Cultivating leisure while increasingly abhorring
all forms of physical and intellectual labor, they became, over the
centuries, soft; like "the Carlovingian kings," they "had decayed
to a mere beautiful futility." The Morlocks' forerunners were society's drudges, the tenders of its vast machines: they worked end-
lessly, mindlessly, without dignity—out of sight and out of mind.
Eventually, they wound up permanently below ground, where—
cut off from the more humanizing effects of civilization—they
continued to regress, becoming night-prowling cannibals, quite
literally devouring the enfeebled class that once demanded their
subjugation.

The Time Machine thus illustrates Wells's realization, expressed repeatedly in his writings, that while the death of the
earth is—in the long run—inevitable, there are choices involved
in the making of human society. We could cease to strive, to will,
to care about progress and community, and grow self-indulgent,
morally obtuse, and mentally slack, like the etiolated Eloi; we
could give in to animalistic tendencies and become, like the Morlocks, little more than rather clever but terribly brutal apes. We
could exercise reason and will and commit ourselves to the intellectual and ethical progress of all our citizens, or persist in economic and social warfare and create a world where the struggle
for existence still involves perpetual conflict, one group exploiting—even murdering—the other. "I am neither a pessimist nor an
optimist at bottom," writes Wells in his introduction to *The Scientific Romances of H. G. Wells* (1934); "this is an entirely indifferent world in which willful wisdom seems to have a perfectly
fair chance."

Wells's next scientific romance, *The Island of Dr. Moreau,* ex-
plores similar themes. Prendick, the novel's protagonist, is, like
the Time Traveller and several of Wells's later protagonists, a
middle-class Englishman who suddenly finds himself in harsh and
harrowing surroundings. He is shipwrecked, facing death in the
restless South Seas. Saved by a passing schooner, Prendick ends up
on Noble's Isle, mingling with a population of weird, unsettling
figures who, like the ship's crew, display "the strangest air about

them of some familiar animal." One has a decidedly apelike face, another ears "covered with a fine fur"; another is "covered with a dull grey hair almost like a Skye terrier. What was it?" Prendick wonders. "What were they all?"

As Prendick eventually learns, these "grotesque caricatures of humanity" are the results of experimentations conducted by one Dr. Moreau, who, some years earlier, had been a "prominent and masterful physiologist" respected throughout Europe for his work on "morbid growths" and "the transfusion of blood." But Moreau, as Prendick recalls, "was simply howled out" of England when "a wretched dog, flayed and otherwise mutilated" fled from the scientist's house on the same day a newspaper linked him to the unsavory practice of vivisection. Now, far from the scrutiny of the press and the censure of his peers, Moreau seeks to fashion humanlike beings from various animals—including dogs, horses, monkeys, pigs. It is, he concedes, a procedure that produces grotesque results and considerable pain. But he is gripped "by an intellectual passion." "You cannot imagine," he tells Prendick, "the strange colourless delight of these intellectual desires." They cause him to conclude that "the thing before you is no longer an animal, a fellow-creature"—simply "a problem." Once, years earlier, Moreau knew "sympathetic pain," but now, increasingly driven, he wants only to learn "the extreme limit of plasticity in a living shape."

After Moreau is killed by a puma he has mutilated, Prendick assures the island's grotesque and pathetic residents that their master lives on, watching them from the sky. But as Prendick fears, Moreau's disappearance prompts the "Beast People" to revert gradually to their instinctively animalistic ways. Like the Traveller in *The Time Machine*, Prendick must concentrate entirely on staying alive in a thoroughly hostile environment; he must face—among others—the "Hyaena-Swine," who, after eating the friendly "St. Bernard creature," is shown with "red-stained teeth," the last trace of its uneasy humanity irretrievably gone. Prendick does manage to escape from Noble's Isle, and is "only glad to be quit of the foulness of the Beast Monsters." But, like Swift's Lemuel Gulliver at the close of the *Travels*, Prendick finds it difficult to readjust to human society. He is constantly distracted by the traces of animality he sees everywhere, in "prowling women" and "gibing children"—in the "blank expressionless faces of people in trains and omnibuses." "I could not persuade myself," Prendick relates, "that the men and women I met were not also another, still passably human, Beast People, animals half-wrought into the outward image of human souls; and that they would presently begin to revert, to show first this bestial mark and then that." Now, sometimes, "it seemed that I, too, was not a reasonable creature, but only an animal tormented with some strange disorder in its brain, that sent it to wander alone, like a sheep stricken with the gid."

The Island of Dr. Moreau is complex as well as disturbing; it can be read innumerable ways. Moreau is, perhaps, a symbol for the world of Nature that Wells consistently portrays as more vicious than benign; he kills and tortures as he creates, as indifferent to the waste and pain of the process as he is to the muddled results. He is, arguably, God—or, more precisely, a bitterly satirical portrayal of God as invented by primitive peoples accustomed to rough paternalistic rule and kept alive in certain texts and myths of fundamentalist Christianity. This "Thunder God" of Wells's own childhood is of course nothing like the God Wells came to revere in such works as *Mr. Britling Sees It Through*. The latter is a mysterious force, at one with the powers of goodness and creativity. The former is despotic and fickle, demanding unthinking adoration from creatures to whom he grants a legacy of confusion and keeps in line with blunt commands and threats of unending agony. The Beast People, in turn, represent in large part Wells's view of tormented humanity, creatures stuck uneasily between the rule of the jungle and the demanding codes of civilization. "Before they had been beasts," Prendick observes,

their instincts fitly adapted to their surroundings, and happy as living things may be. Now they stumbled in the shackles of humanity, lived in a fear that never died, fretted by a law they could not understand; their mock-human existence began in an agony, was one long internal struggle, one long dread of Moreau—and for what? It was the wantonness that stirred me.

Given his cruel and dubious experimentations, Moreau can also be viewed as Wells's indictment of stark, relentless, selfish ambition—an indictment that of course remains relevant in the wake of the evil investigations of Josef Mengele and his fellow Nazi doctors, and at a time when unprecedented powers of creation and destruction have been assumed by genetic engineers. He stands, then, as a particularly effective reminder of the horrors that await humankind if scientific knowledge should proceed without a similar growth in ethical sensitivity—if Huxley's "Kingdom of Man" were to develop devoid of ethical considerations.

Whatever its messages, *The Island of Dr. Moreau* is a particularly bleak book, demonstrating again that Wells, like Prendick, often found it difficult to identify with other members of his species; that a large part of his imagination was attracted to morbid and depressing subjects, and to images of violence and horror—much as certain boys are irresistibly compelled to study the roadside remains of small animals struck by cars. Understandably, reviewers who found much to praise in Wells's other work found much to dislike in *The Island of Dr. Moreau*; Chalmers Mitchell—himself a zoologist and biographer of Thomas Huxley—had admired "the simple delight" of Wells's story telling, his ability to combine "the emotions of an artist and the intellectual imagination of a scientific investigator." But Mitchell read *The Island of Dr. Moreau* with disgust and "the frankest dismay." "Mr. Wells," he declared, "has put out his talent to the most flagitious usury," seeking out "revolting details with the zeal of a sanitary inspector probing a crowded graveyard."[8] "The book," concurred the *Guardian*, an Anglican weekly, "is one no one could have the courage to recommend, and we are not inclined to commend it either. It is certainly unpleasant and painful, and we cannot find it profitable."[9]

In *The Invisible Man*, his next scientific romance, Wells again depicts an egotistical scientist whose intellectual obsessions produce grotesque results. Griffin, the title character, is a young physicist, an albino, who uncovers "a general principle of pigments and refraction" that enables him to become wholly transparent to the human eye. When he fails to find a way to reverse the process, Griffin begins to panic. Deciding that his invisibility equals invincibility, he embarks on a "Reign of Terror," vowing to murder those who would seek to block his drive to unlimited power. Kemp, another scientist, urges Griffin not to become "a lone wolf," to stop "playing a game against the rule." But Griffin persists in his violence and his quest for power before he is cornered—and lethally throttled—in the Sussex village where Kemp resides. As he dies, "naked and pitiful on the ground," Griffin regains his fleshly form, revealing that "his hands were clenched, his eyes wide open, and his expression was one of anger and dismay."

Like Moreau, Griffin possesses plenty of will, a quality Wells repeatedly celebrates. But Griffin's will, like Moreau's, is utterly disordered, yielding nothing, ultimately, but confusion and crime.

The Invisible Man is, in a sense, Huxley's "primitive man," standing for all that Wells would repeatedly condemn, for what Kemp calls "pure selfishness" and "brutal self seeking." As Griffin himself discovers, such ruthless egotism can never bring lasting satisfaction. "The more I thought it over," he tells Kemp, "the more I realized what a helpless absurdity an Invisible Man was." Invisibility promised him "a thousand advantages," but, ironically, "made it impossible to enjoy them when they are got." Like Faust, Griffin finds that his quest for power has led to his own destruction, left him permanently beyond the pale. He becomes "a wrapped up mystery, a swathed and bandaged caricature of a man."

There is some satire, certainly, in Wells's depiction of the villagers whom Griffin befuddles and torments. But The Invisible Man has little of the black bitterness found in The Island of Dr. Moreau; like two of Wells's lesser, more overtly humorous novels, The Wheels of Chance (1896) and The Sea Lady (1902), it owes more to Dickens than Swift. In Thomas Marvel—a beery tramp who functions briefly, if unwillingly, as Griffin's adjutant—Wells presents one of his most memorable creations, "a person of copious, flexible visage, a nose of cylindrical protrusion, a liquorish, ample, fluctuating mouth, and a beard of bristling eccentricity." Marvel's figure "inclined to embonpoint; his short limbs accentuated this inclination. He wore a furry silk hat, and the frequent substitution of twine and shoelaces for buttons, apparent at critical points of his costume, marked a man essentially a bachelor." With its blend of suspense, careful characterization and comic relief, The Invisible Man was more warmly received than The Island of Dr. Moreau. W. T. Stead, for example, called Moreau a book "which ought never to have been written," but found much to admire in The Invisible Man, including its convincingly detailed depiction of small-town English life. Wells, Stead pointed out, "has caught the trick of describing events which only exist in his imagination with the technical precision of a newspaper reporter."[10] It is a "trick" Wells executes no less effectively in The War of the Worlds.

Wells begins The War of the Worlds by detailing—in Chapter 3—the "little crowd" that surrounds the large hole where a strange gray cylinder has come to rest, having crashed with the force of a meteorite the night before. The gawkers include "Gregg the butcher and his little boy, and two or three loafers and golf caddies who were accustomed to hang about the railway station."

There are a pair of cyclists and a girl with a baby, as well as the shopkeeper's son sent over to hawk apples and ginger beer. There are "four or five boys sitting on the edge of the pit" and pitching stones at the cylinder, which resembles "a rusty gas float," a thing "no more exciting than an overturned carriage or a tree blown across the road." For in those days, the narrator notes, "few of the common people in England had anything but the vaguest astronomical ideas."

But curiosity soon gives way to repulsion and fear. The cylinder opens: a woman shrieks. "I think everyone expected to see a man emerge," the narrator recalls, "I know I did." Instead, "a big greyish rounded bulk" emerges, "the size, perhaps, of a bear." It is tentacled; its lipless mouth "quivered and panted, and dropped saliva." Its skin is "oily brown," and "glistened like wet leather." The narrator is a sober, well-read man and the author of philosophical essays, including a recent "series of papers discussing the probable developments of moral ideas as civilization progresses." But as he contemplates these hideous creatures he too finds himself feeling "helpless, unprotected, and alone. Suddenly, like a thing falling upon me from without, came—fear."

It proves well founded. The creatures in the cylinder have not come in peace. They are Martians driven from a dying planet, a place of shrinking oceans and thinning air. They have come to conquer—and their comrades soon arrive, bringing weapons that shoot beams of heat fierce enough to melt steel. As the narrator explains, the Martians are "heads—merely heads." They do not then eat or digest; they use "the fresh, living blood of other creatures," preferably humans, injecting it into their veins "by means of a little pipette."

Despite the best efforts of the British military, it soon appears that the Martians will succeed in securing a fresh food supply. Driving toward London, they produce panic, confusion, and—occasionally—philosophical speculation. An artillery man, assuming a Martian victory, tells the narrator of his plan to live underground, in tunnels and drains, storing up books—"not novels and poetry swipes, but ideas, science books." He plans to form a band of "able-bodied, clean minded" men and women who will carry on, defying the aliens. Like Wells himself, the artilleryman prizes will, valor, resolve—qualities he suggests are not widespread in the human population, with its ample supply of "damn little clerks," men who, before the invasion, could be seen scurrying to work, "bit of breakfast in hand," working "at businesses they were afraid to take the trouble to understand; skedaddling back for fear they wouldn't be in time for dinner; keeping indoors for fear of the back streets." Such men, the artilleryman reckons, will actually cheer the Martian victory, with its prospect of "nice roomy cages, fattening food, careful breeding, no worry." Indeed, "they'll wonder what people did before there were Martians to take care of them."

But the Martians fall short, destroyed by a common earthly bacteria against which they have no immunological defense. In London, as he moves amid scenes of destruction and despair, the narrator sees a dog prance off with a piece of Martian flesh, an appropriately grisly image in yet another Wellsian fiction meant to drive home the message that ours is an utterly indifferent world that, like the "little wood" in Tennyson's "Maud," is "a world of plunder and prey." Everywhere he looks the narrator sees shock, smoke, and the "blackened skeletons" of buildings that had once seemed permanent fixtures in what was then the strongest nation on earth, a colonial power accustomed to using its own force to subdue and exploit less technologically sophisticated nations. Of course, such scenes eerily prefigure the very real destruction that befell Europe in the twentieth century's two world wars, the first of which was just beginning to take shape—in a climate of name-calling and saber-rattling—when Wells wrote *The War of the Worlds*. In fact, the novel points bluntly not only to the earth's vulnerability in the vast blackness of space, but to humanity's own savagery, still flourishing after centuries of supposed cultural and ethical refinement. The narrator recalls the "ruthless and utter destruction" that supposedly civilized men brought to, for example, "the bison and the dodo"; he alludes to the Tasmanians, who "were swept out of existence in a war of extermination waged by European immigrants, in the space of fifty years. Are we such apostles of mercy as to complain if the Martians warred in the same spirit?"

The narrator is able to find some benefit in the alien attack. It "robbed us of that serene confidence in the future which is the most fruitful source of decadence, the gifts to human science it has brought are enormous, and it has done much to promote the conception of the commonweal of mankind." Now "we see further. If the Martians can reach Venus, there is no reason to suppose that the thing is impossible for men, and when the slow cooling of the sun makes this earth uninhabitable, as at last it must do, it may be that the thread of life that has begun here will have streamed out and caught our sister planet within its toils."

Wells's ability to sustain readability and suspense was noted by several early critics of *The War of the Worlds*. John St. Loe Strachey, for one, praised as "most original" the book's "main design."[11] "As a rule," Strachey noted, writers who "deal with non-terrestrial matters take their readers to the planets or the moon." Wells, however, ingeniously "brings the awful creatures of another sphere to Woking Junction, and places them, with all their abhorred dexterity, in the most homely and familiar surroundings." As a result,

When the Martians come flying through the vast and dreadful expanses of interplanetary space hid in the fiery womb of their infernal cylinders, and land on a peaceful Surrey common, we come to close quarters at once with the full horror of the earth's invasion. Those who know the valleys of the Wey and the Thames, and to whom Shepperton and Laleham are familiar places, will follow the advance of the Martians upon London with breathless interest. The vividness of the local touches, and the accuracy of the geographical details, enormously enhance the horror of the picture.

Wells's next scientific romance, *The First Men in the Moon* is the carefully paced, often comical account of two Englishmen who sail to the moon from the Kent countryside, their small sphere fueled by an anti-gravitational substance called Cavorite. Cavor, its inventor, is "a short, round-bodied, thin-legged little man," and one of the unlikely astronauts; the other, Bedford, the novel's narrator, is a businessman far more interested in building a fortune than in forging new scientific pathways. Bedford is convinced that—if marketed properly—Cavorite could make him exceedingly rich. "If one wanted to move a weight," he explains, "however enormous, one had only to get a sheet of this substance beneath it and one might lift it with a straw." He sees its uses in "shipping, locomotion, building, every conceivable form of human industry"; he envisions, then, "a parent company and daughter companies, applications to right of us, applications to left, rings and trusts, privileges and concessions spreading and spreading, until one vast stupendous Cavorite Company ran and ruled the world."

Wells's powers of description—among the best in English fiction—are strikingly displayed in *The First Men in the Moon*.

From the start, the lunar journey of Bedford and Cavor is wonderfully detailed and, in its way, wholly convincing. After blast-
off, the two men and their various bits of equipment float loosely
in the little sphere as it speeds into space; "now the star of the
electric light would be overhead, now under foot," Bedford recalls. "Now Cavor's feet would float up before my eyes, and now
we would be crosswise to each other." They land, finally, in a
crater shrouded by darkness and fog; Bedford, eager to glimpse
the moon's surface, grabs a blanket and wipes a window, but "it
became opaque again with freshly-condensed moisture, mixed
with an increasing quantity of blanket hairs." At last the lunar
sunrise arrives, and Wells's depiction of it is, as T. S. Eliot would
recall, "quite unforgettable."[12] The sun, tinged with amber, casts
"deeply purple" shadows on the crater's walls. Exploring, Cavor
and Bedford find vegetation, "bundle-like buds" that "swelled
and strained and opened" in the morning light, "thrusting out a
coronet of red sharp tips, spreading a whorl of tiny, spiky,
brownish leaves, that lengthened rapidly, lengthened visibly even
as we watched." They see other "bristling" bits of "spiky and
fleshy" vegetation, and "banks of bluish snow." They are slowed
by the moon's atmosphere, experiencing nausea and vertigo; they
dine on lunar fungi that warms the throat and induces "an irrational exhilaration." And, at last, they observe lunar life in the
form of "mooncalves," huge, wormlike creatures that are "almost
brainless," simply "animated lumps of provender" herded about
by Selenites, curiously antlike, rather comical creatures whom
Wells endows with his trademark tentacles as well as "very short
thighs, very long shanks, and little feet."

Bedford and Cavor are seized by the Selenites, who live below
the ground in elaborately designed caverns that Wells describes
with relish and brilliance, filling them with a phosphorescent blue
light and "metallic or livid-white creatures" who pay continual
homage to the Grand Lunar, the "Master of the Moon"—a being
with a "dwarfed body" and a huge brain who sits "brooding on
his glaucous throne," surrounded by "tiers of attendants and
helpers" who pet and sustain him, and keep his "purple glowing
brain-case" continually bathed with "a cooling spray." Cavor,
ever the scientist, seeks cordial "intercourse" with these curious
creatures; Bedford, ever the entrepreneur, notes only that most of
the metal goods in Selenite civilization are, amazingly, made of
gold. Bedford does escape, but narrowly, striking in his flight one
Selenite who "smashed like some sort of sweet meat with liquid

in it," splashing "like a damp toadstool." Cavor, however, is re-
captured, left behind as Bedford returns to earth, clutching his
gold. Later Bedford learns that Cavor has not been killed, but is
holding discussions with his captors and sending back to earth
telegraphic accounts of Selenite life. Their society, Cavor reports,
is "a kind of super ant-hill," its inhabitants meticulously bred to
perform optimally in specific tasks. There are, for example, "extremely swift messengers with spider-like legs." Those who perform "delicate chemical operations" possess "a vast olfactory
organ; others again have flat feet for treadles with anchylosed
joints"; others, glassblowers, "seem mere lung-bellows." Cavor
also describes young Selenites held in jars from which "only the
fore limbs protruded": they are literally "compressed to become
machine-minders of a special sort." This process, Cavor learns, is
painful; that "wretched-looking hand sticking out of its jar," he
observes, "seemed to appeal for lost possibilities." Still, he concludes, contorting at birth is "in the end a far more humane proceeding than our earthly method of leaving children to grow into
human beings, and then making machines of them."

The First Men in the Moon is, in part, a satire of human greed,
here represented by the otherwise likable Bedford with his itch for
easy profits, his automatic impulse to use force if necessary to
enrich himself with lunar booty. In effect, Bedford reappears as
the similarly materialistic Edward Ponderevo in Tono-Bungay,
Wells's most complete picture of profit mongering and cynical
self-seeking run amok. In fact, in his portrait of the Selenites'
highly rigid society, Wells seems to be not only mocking the process of overspecialization he complains against elsewhere—as in,
briefly, The World Set Free (1914)—but continuing the attack on
industrial capitalism he had recently offered in When the Sleeper
Wakes, with its legions of workers in underground work zones
functioning as little more than mindless machines.

But there is ambivalence in Wells's depiction of Selenite society.
Such works as Anticipations and A Modern Utopia make plain
Wells's passion for social systems that are logically run and scrupulously planned. Indeed, William Clissold—an articulate es-
pouser of Wellsian attitudes—advocates "the organisation of all
mankind into one terrestrial anthill," calling it imperative, "the
necessary, the only possible continuation, of human history."
Moreover, at the close of The First Men in the Moon, Wells allows the Grand Lunar to express his own astonishment at the
chaotic way in which the planet earth carries on, with its division

into competing nations and its lack of a common tongue. After hearing Cavor talk at length of "invasions and massacres, of the Huns and Tartars, and the wars of Mahomet and the Caliphs and the Crusades," the Grand Lunar "was so incredulous," Cavor reports, that "he interrupted the translation of what I had said in order to have my verification of my account." The Selenites have eliminated war as well as inefficiency; as Cavor notes, "they particularly doubted my description of the men cheering and rejoicing as they went into battle."

By 1900, Wells's interest in producing scientific romances had begun to wane; by 1904 he was complaining in print that "I do not see why I should always pander to the vulgar appetite for stark stories." Published in 1904, *The Food of the Gods* is one of Wells's last ambitious scientific romances; it is in many ways fascinating—and in several respects flawed. It describes the social consequences of a scientific discovery, a form of nutriment that produces spectacular growth in animals and plants. Carelessly handled in the English countryside, this "Herakleophorbia"—or "Boomfood" as it is more commonly called—inadvertently enters the stomachs of various vermin, including some rats, which expand to the size of big game cats and must then be tracked and "bagged." Indeed, Wells's description of a rat hunt, presented in a chapter entitled "The Giant Rats," is remarkably well done, an adroit blending of humor and suspense. The hunt ends successfully, with the band of hunters—local men, some of them huffing and puffing, because unaccustomed to such exertions—soaking the rats in paraffin before leaving them to burn in a fire that also destroys the "Experimental Farm" where the Boomfood was first produced.

The novel's early chapters suggest that it will focus on the efforts of a harassed citizenry fending off gigantic rodents and bugs—rather in the manner of, say, *The Attack of the Killer Tomatoes*, itself a parody of countless science fiction films of the 1950s and 60s in which hapless men and women suddenly find themselves menaced by once harmless but now overgrown life forms. But *The Food of the Gods* shifts somewhat awkwardly, coming to focus on the activities of a group of children who also consumed the food, and now must struggle to live comfortably in what has become for them an absurdly undersized world. They become "mighty forms, forty feet high the least of them." They live in a "great single-storeyed house" that is "Egyptian in its massiveness." They become known as the "Children of the Food"

and their mere presence presents problems for the town's "little
people," unaccustomed as they are to sharing parks and road-
ways with people the size of trees. As one villager complains, the
footprint of even a single giant can cause all sorts of problems,
being "a pitfall for horses and rider, a trap to the unwary." The
giants, he gripes, trample rose bushes and uproot grass. They
bring destruction "all over the world, all over the order and decency the world of men has made."

The conflict between the Children of the Food and those they
call "pygmies" continues to intensify—particularly when one of
the giants is killed by police. Though greatly outnumbered (they
total "not half a hundred"), the young giants refuse to accept the
decree that they stop multiplying, and live out their lives some-
where a bit less close by—in Africa, say. For as one of the leaders
of the giants asserts, the "little people" may

fight against greatness in us who are the children of men, but can they
conquer? Even if they should destroy us every one, what then? Would it
save them? No! For greatness is abroad, not only in us, not only in the
Food, but in the purpose of all things! It is the nature of all things, it is
part of space and time. To grow, and still to grow, from first to last that
is Being, that is the law of life. What other law can there be?

As their spokesman makes clear, the giants are not driven by a
desire to "oust the little people from the world." They fight because, like the "New Republicans" of Wells's *Anticipations* and
his later cadres of far-seeing elites, they regard themselves as rep-
resenting spirit and adventure—the power of growth—and thus
can never rest content with the stagnating security of things-as-
they-are. "We fight," then, "not for ourselves—for we are but
the momentary hands and eyes of the Life of the World."
"Through us," he asserts, "and through the little folk the Spirit
looks and learns. From us by word and birth and act it must
pass—to still greater lives. This earth is no resting place; this
earth is no playing place." "We fight," he proclaims, "for
growth, growth that goes on forever. To-morrow, whether we live
or die, growth will conquer through us."

This blaring celebration of progress, of humankind's relentless
push toward a universal enlightenment born of knowledge and
will, begins to recur regularly, almost formulaically, at the close
of Wells's imaginative writings. It is there, for example, in the
final scenes of one of his last major projects, the screenplay for

Things to Come. John Cabal—a principal figure in the film—stands firmly for will, risk, growth; he responds decisively when another character—unsettled by the prospect of a forthcoming flight to the moon—asks: "Is there never to be an age of happiness? Is there never to be rest?" "Rest enough for the individual man," Cabal replies, echoing Wells and Winwood Reade. "Too much of it too soon, and we call it death. But for MAN no rest and no ending." First, he must conquer

this little planet and its winds and ways, and all the laws of mind and matter that restrain him. Then the planets about him, and at last across immensity to the stars. And when he has conquered all the deeps of space and all the mysteries of time—still he will be beginning.

Wells refers only passingly to *The Food of the Gods* in his autobiography, pointing to the way it "begins in cheerful burlesque and ends in poetic symbolism." In their biography of Wells, Norman and Jeanne Mackenzie aptly describe *The Food of the Gods* as "a run-of-the-mill book."[13] In his perceptive—and sympathetic—study of Wells's early novels, V. S. Pritchett calls *The Food of the Gods* "the poorest" of Wells's scientific romances, and suggests, not unfairly, that its love scenes—played out among the ponderous giants—are "the most embarrassing in English fiction."[14]

In the Days of the Comet, Wells's next scientific romance, is a much better book; in fact—like *The Time Machine* and *The War of the Worlds*—it remains a compelling read from its first chapter to its last. Willie Leadford, the novel's narrator, is a man of seventy recalling the many social changes that have taken place over the course of his life—changes that occurred when a comet, passing close to the earth, spewed forth a green gas that triggered an extraordinary shift in human behavior. Before the comet, as Leadford recalls, "we British, forty-one million of people," were enmeshed "in a state of almost indescribably aimless economic and moral muddle that we had neither the courage, the energy, nor the intelligence to improve." Leadford was reared in an industrial section of the country where landlords and factory owners lived contentedly and well, but working people were "herded together, ill clothed, ill nourished, ill taught, badly and expensively served at every occasion in life, uncertain even of their insufficient livelihood from day to day." In the town that had "borne me and dwarfed and crippled and made me," there were,

Leadford remembers, a "jumble of mines and homes, collieries and pot-banks," a "vast irregular agglomeration of ugly smoking accidents in which men lived as happy as frogs in a dustbin." But in the comet's wake, after the universal inhalation of this remarkable gas, love and tranquillity and a shared yearning for perfection began to bloom. "Nothing was lost from my nature," Leadford remembers, "nothing had gone, only the power of thought and restraint had been wonderfully increased, and new interests had been forced upon me." These "Green Vapours" left the minds of people everywhere "swept and garnished."

As Wells pointed out, *In the Days of the Comet* "deals more with character and conduct than any of its imaginative predecessors, and in spirit it is a transitional book to the series of novels that chiefly occupied the writer's attention for the next seven years"—including *Kipps, Tono-Bungay,* and *The History of Mr. Polly.* "The people in it are real," Wells writes, "it is only the scenery which remains on the fantastical side." Certainly, Leadford's early environment resembles Wells's own. Leadford grows up in ignorance as well as ugliness and grime; he was "stifled in the darkness, in a poisoned and vitiated air," learning very little of the realities of life and love. For, toward the young, "the world maintained a conspiracy of stimulating silences." There were books, he recalls, that "insisted on certain qualities in every love-affair and greatly intensified one's natural desire for them, perfect trust, perfect loyalty, lifelong devotion." However, "the complex essentials of love were altogether hidden"; thus, "we were like misguided travellers who had camped in the dry bed of a tropical river. Presently we were knee deep and neck deep in the flood." "Ashamed" but "full of desire," we "drifted in the most accidental way against some other blindly seeking creature, and linked like nascent atoms."

In one of the novel's most memorable passages, Wells gives voice to the ambivalence—the intense irritation and love—that Wells elsewhere implies characterized his own feelings toward the badgering but beleaguered Sarah. Leadford's mother, like Wells's, adheres to a dour religious creed, one that often denounced "the wicked lusts of the flesh," expecting the faithful to believe that "most of our poor unhappy world was to atone for its muddle and trouble here by suffering exquisite torments for ever after, world without end, Amen." As a youth, Leadford is often irritated by his mother's warnings and solicitations; "there were times," he recalls, "when that dumb beseeching of my mother's face irritated me unspeakably. . . . I felt I had to struggle against it, that I could not exist if I gave way to its pleadings, and it hurt me and divided me to resist it, almost beyond endurance." "It was clear to me that I had to think out for myself religious problems, social problems, questions of conduct, questions of expediency, that her poor dear simple beliefs could not help me at all—and she did not understand!" For Leadford's mother, as for Sarah Wells, social adjustment was simply a series of "blind submissions to the accepted order—to laws, to doctors, to clergymen, lawyers, masters, and all respectable persons in authority over us, and with her to believe was to fear." As Leadford observes, his mother

had been cowed into submission, as so many women of that time had been, by the sheer brutality of the accepted thing. The existing order dominated her into a worship of abject observances. It had bent her, aged her, robbed her of eyesight so that at fifty-five she peered through cheap spectacles at my face and saw it only dimly, filled her with a habit of anxiety, made her hands—Her poor dear hands! Not in the whole world now could you find a woman with hands so grimy, so needle-worn, so misshapen by toil, so chapped and coarsened, so evilly entreated.

There is poignance in Leadford's recollection of his mother; there is power and beauty in his closing description of the wonderful new world the comet—and a renewed collective will—had made. Where, Leadford rhetorically wonders, "is white-lime Paris," with its "smartly organised viciousness, and the myriads of workers, noisily shod, streaming over the bridges in the grey cold light of dawn?" Where is Chicago, "with its interminable bloodstained stockyards, its polyglot underworld of furious discontent?" They are gone forever, and "the lives that were caught, crippled, starved, and maimed amidst their labyrinths, their forgotten and neglected maladjustments, and their vast, inhuman, ill-conceived industrial machinery have escaped—to life." In their place stand cities of spires and theaters, cities "laced with avenues of cedar," full of "roses and wonderful flowers and the perpetual humming of bees"—cities "planned and made," made "by the loving hands of men for living men, cities men weep to enter, so fair they are, so gracious and so kind." No longer must "our sons" turn into "servile clerks and shopmen, plough drudges and servants"—no longer must their sisters become "anaemic

drudges, prostitutes, sluts, anxiety-racked mothers or sere, repin-
ing failures." Now, they too "go about this world glad and brave,
learning, living, doing, happy and rejoicing, brave and free."

Coming of age in an eat-or-be-eaten society rife with inequity,
Leadford is much given to fits of uncontrollable jealousy; before
"the Change" he burns to possess a young woman, Nettie Stew-
art, who is similarly desired by another man, the wealthier Edward Verral. When Nettie settles on Verral, Leadford so loses his
grip that he buys a gun and comes close to committing murder:
"I was going to kill Nettie," he recalls, "Nettie who had smiled
and promised and given herself to another, and who stood now
for all the conceivable delightfulness, the lost imaginations of the
youthful heart, the unattainable joys in life; and Verral, who
stood for all who profited by the incurable injustice of our social
order." In a closing scene Wells renders with suspense and skill,
Leadford comes quite close to killing the pair. At that point, however, he finds himself walking through a thick green haze; it is the
comet passing, cleansing men and women of their brutal drives.
Now, Leadford does not regard Nettie as "a goddess" but as a
"fellow-creature"; his craving to worship and possess her is simply gone. Leadford and Nettie can now love each other more ma-
turely, the novel suggests, and in the meantime love others too;
for in the new world "love is unstinted; it is a golden net about
our globe that nets all humanity together." *In the Days of the
Comet* thus introduces a theme that Wells would take up more
thoroughly in *The Passionate Friends* and *The Wife of Sir Isaac
Harman*; in fact, it becomes a central tenet of his work that a
social system built upon envy and greed will, inevitably, breed
more envy and greed—poisoning human relationships in numerous spheres.

The sexual theme that achieves prominence at the close of *In
the Days of the Comet* was, not surprisingly, widely noticed—
and did much to contribute to Wells's reputation as a daring
writer during a period when a growing number of artists and intellectuals were calling for a reexamination of sexual attitudes
that prevailed—at least officially—during the Victorian era. The
1890s, Cunningham notes, saw the appearance of such crusading
publications as *The Adult*, which "offered a social conscience in
place of pornography," and "presents us with a remarkable
picture of sexual liberation in the late nineteenth century." As
Cunningham records, the editors of *The Adult* wrote of the
" 'paramount right of the individual to self-realisation in all non-

invasive directions' "; they backed " 'the absolute freedom of two individuals of full age, to enter into and conclude at will, any mutual relationships whatever, where no third person's material interests are concerned.' " The "ringing calls for Free Love which echo through almost every number" of the *Adult* were often illustrated, Cunningham writes, "by case histories of couples who can speak for its efficacy as a cure for all social ills."[15] Seen in this context, *In the Days of the Comet* is very much a work of its time, and—some might suggest—even more a work of fantasy.

As Wells notes, both *The War in the Air* (1908) and *The World Set Free* are "cast" similarly to his earlier scientific romances. Both were "written with a very different intention," to offer "an imaginative play" with a particular idea—namely, that "flying would release war from its former restrictions to a 'front' and a 'seat of war' and destroy the distinctions of combatant and non-combatant, and that it would then become socially disintegrative to an extent quite beyond any historical precedent." In *The War in the Air*, Wells's central character is a bicycle repairman called Bert Smallways, a "vulgar little creature, the sort of pert, limited soul that the old civilization of the early twentieth century produced by the millions in every country of the world." The son of a coach driver from Kent, Smallways comes to adulthood when "flying machines" of various kinds were starting to fill the skies; when—as the narrator of *The War in the Air* points out—"the development of Science had altered the scale of human affairs." Through an odd series of events, Smallways finds himself the lone passenger in a hot air balloon that floats across the English Channel and into German territory, where it is shot from the sky. German military men—preparing to invade North America—mistake Smallways for another Englishman, an inventor whose more advanced type of flying machine they have been secretly seeking to buy. With the Germans, Smallways witnesses the ghastly fighting that ensues. He watches the sinking of battleships and the saturation bombing of New York City, which soon becomes "a furnace of crimson flames." The war escalates, expands. "Think of it, Smallways," one of the Germans exclaims, "there's war everywhere! . . . Everywhere! Down in South America even they are fighting among themselves! No place is safe—no place is at peace. . . . The war comes through the air, bombs drop in the night. Quiet people go out in the morning, and see airfleets passing overhead—dripping death—dripping death!"

Throughout *The War in the Air*, Wells drives home the point that the next war will not be confined to far-flung battle zones; the next war, he asserts—with chilling accuracy—will in effect make infantrymen of infants and invalids. And it will persist, causing "the whole fabric of civilization to bend and give" before coming to the state of collapse that Wells describes in the latter chapters of *The War in the Air*. Wells foresees famine, random violence, raging disease. He makes the novel's key points resoundingly clear. Men and women, cozy in prosperous Europe, had grown lazy and obtuse. They "did not realize that this age of relative good fortune was an age of immense but temporary opportunity for their kind. They complacently assumed a necessary progress towards which they had no moral responsibility." They lacked vision and will. "What mankind could achieve with a different will," observes the narrator of *The War in the Air*, "is a speculation as idle as it is magnificent."

As Jefferson Hunter points out, *The War in the Air* stands as another example of Wells's tendency to borrow from other writers. In fact, he "modelled much of his science fiction on the productions of George Chetwynd Griffith, the late-Victorian author of imperial, adventure and scientific romances, including *The Outlaws of the Air* (1895), which had a direct effect on Wells's *The War in the Air*. Wells confessed the debt, by having his heroes read Griffith." Wells, as Hunter puts it, "turned to books when his imagination, resourceful and free-ranging as it was, could not keep pace with his compulsion to publish—a compulsion producing some seventeen books during the Edwardian years."[16] Wells would also confess, in *Exasperations*, that *The War in the Air* reveals that—despite his "reputation for successful prophecy"—he had made "some extraordinary bad guess about things to come." "An excellent Cambridge mathematician" had at the time convinced him that "no aeroplane driven by a screw behind could fly. It was bound to cock up its nose into the air and topple backwards on itself." Thus, in *The War in the Air*, "the great German raid on America is done by gas bag affairs, and gas bags rule the story. It is exasperating to realise how I went wrong about that, but there is no recalling it now."

The antiwar message that informs *The War in the Air* is stated no less directly in *The World Set Free*. This work, like *The War in the Air*, cannot be counted among Wells's best. It lacks polish and depth; it is as subtle as a billboard. But it also features one of

Wells's more startling predictions. *The World Set Free*—published more than thirty years before the destruction of Hiroshima and Nagasaki—is above all else an account of atomic warfare. "Reading the book today," J. R. Hammond writes, "it is difficult to realise that it was written before the First World War, before the discovery of artificial radioactivity, before the potentialities of the aeroplane as a military weapon had been fully realised. Wells could not have forseen that 'artificial radium' would be produced by Irène and Frédéric Joliot-Curie, the daughter and son-in-law of Madame Curie, but he was uncannily accurate in forecasting that this discovery would be made in 1933."[17]

The war that rages in *The World Set Free* begins in 1956, largely because the leadership of the world has once again fallen into the hands of "short-sighted, commonplace" types who were "blind to the new possibilities and litigiously reliant upon the traditions of the past." This meant that nationalism and militarism continued to flourish; that, still, "the memory of the empires of Rome and Alexander squatted, an unlaid carnivorous ghost, in the human imagination—it bored into the human brain like some grisly parasite and filled it with disordered thoughts and violent impulses." Triggered by an economic crisis, the war—with its wide use of atomic weaponry—levels the world's centers of civilization before peace begins and a Wellsian "World Republic" is born. One of its leaders, Marcus Karenin, talks at length in the novel's closing sections, telling an audience of women and men "how he thought and felt about many of the principle things in life"; about, for example, women, whom he hopes will assume key roles in the world to come. "I want to abolish the woman whose support is jealousy and whose gift possession," Karenin asserts, announcing the principal theme of *The Passionate Friends,* published a year before. "I want to abolish the woman who can be won as a prize or locked up as a delicious treasure." Indeed, he tells his listeners,

I do not care a rap about your future—as women. I do not care a rap about the future of men—as males. I want to destroy these peculiar features. I care for your future as intelligences, as parts of and contributions to the universal mind of the race. Humanity is not only naturally over-specialised in these matters, but all its institutions, its customs, everything, exaggerate, intensify this difference. I want to unspecialise women. No new idea. Plato wanted exactly that. I do not want to go on as we go now, emphasising this natural difference; I do not deny it, but I want to reduce it and overcome it.

Wells tags Karenin with a couple of distinctive traits: he is old, a cripple; he moves with great difficulty. He is not, however, a great character: he is barely a character at all—merely a talking head for Wells's views. As such, he signals a trend. Like most writers of science fiction, Wells comes to reveal repeatedly that he is far more interested in the struggles and successes of the human species than with the trials and triumphs of individuals, whose perceptions (as he seeks to show in such works as *The Bulpington of Blup*) are generally limited, often illusory, and enormously influenced by prevailing social and cultural attitudes. As a result, one comes away from Wells's later fictions knowing precisely what he believes about God, economics, and social organization, but with the regret that carefully, vividly rendered figures like Thomas Marvel have all but disappeared. Like Karenin, Wells's later characters tend more and more to display clear views but no clear profile; lacking true individuality, they linger indistinctly in the memory, like so many ducks on a pond.

3

The Edwardian Novels

Although he is widely regarded as the quintessentially modern man, his name inevitably linked with rockets, airplanes, and time machines, it is worth remembering that H. G. Wells came to intellectual maturity in the Victorian era, and in many respects he remained firmly rooted in the nineteenth century. His worldview was shaped overwhelmingly by Winwood Reade and Thomas Huxley, both of whom were publishing key works in the 1860s; certainly, aesthetically speaking, Wells's contemporaries are not James Joyce and Virginia Woolf, but more nearly Charles Dickens and William Makepeace Thackeray.

This fact is made particularly clear in the 1914 essay "The Contemporary Novel," Wells's most complete expression of his artistic beliefs. At the time of its composition, Wells had been publishing book-length fiction for nearly two decades—a fact that "made me think a good deal about the business of writing novels, and what it means, and is, and may be." The word *business* is itself revealing: Wells's income came entirely from his writing; he was notorious among London's publishers for haggling over royalties and demanding that his works be aggressively pushed.[1] ("I expect my publishers," Wells told Frederick Warburg, "to bankrupt themselves on my behalf.") Still, as "The Contemporary Novel" shows, Wells was firm and consistent in his principles: the novelist, he believed, has strong social responsibilities. The novel should be more than a "cooling refreshment," a "harmless opiate for the vacant hours of prosperous men." It is a "powerful instrument of moral suggestion," an "important and necessary thing indeed in that complicated system of uneasy adjustments and readjustments which is modern civilisation." It is a "social mediator," a "vehicle of understanding," its range necessarily huge. The novelist "demands," then, "an absolutely free hand"—the right to write about, among other things, "political questions and religious questions and social questions." "If I may presume to speak for other novelists," Wells writes,

I would say it is not so much a demand we make as an intention we proclaim. . . . We are going to write about it all. We are going to write about business and finance and politics and precedence and pretentiousness and decorum and indecorum, until a thousand pretences and ten thousand impostures shrivel in the cold, clear air of our elucidations. We are going to write of wasted opportunities and latent beauties until a thousand new ways of living open to men and women. We are going to appeal to the young and the hopeful and the curious, against the established, the dignified, and defensive. Before we have done, we will have all life within the scope of the novel.

The novelist should be pardoned, then, if aiming for such comprehensiveness he or she is less than finicking about form. Wells has no patience for critics and scholars who, "with profound gravity," discuss novels as if they were sonnets, obliged to meet a "definitive length and a definitive form." The novel is "a discursive thing," Wells writes; it should engage readers "first by this affection and curiosity, and then by that." He is particularly fond of the novels of Dickens, finding them "long as they are, too short for me." "I am sorry," Wells writes, that Dickens's novels "do not flow into one another more than they do. I wish Micawber and Dick Swiveller and Sairey Gamp turned up again in other novels than their own, just as Shakespeare ran the glorious glow of Falstaff through a group of plays." Wells calls for "a return towards a laxer, more spacious form of novel-writing," towards "the rambling discursiveness, the right to roam, of the earlier English novel, of *Tristram Shandy* and of *Tom Jones*"—novels Wells particularly likes because they are "saturated in the personality of the author," delightfully full of "unaffected personal outbreaks."[2]

Such attitudes do not prevail in, say, James Joyce's *A Portrait of the Artist as a Young Man* (1916) or Virginia Woolf's *Mrs. Dalloway* (1925). But they are amply displayed in *Kipps, Tono-Bungay* and, to a somewhat lesser extent, in *The History of Mr. Polly,* three of Wells's best novels, all of them published during the first decade of the twentieth century. In fact, *Kipps* might well have become the most "discursive" novel in English; as Wells would recall, "a whole introductory book was written before Kipps himself came on the scene"—before Wells realized that he had planned his task "upon too colossal a scale" and that a book so spectacularly sprawling could not be practically serialized, even published. Still, *Kipps* does proceed leisurely—and bristles with Wells's personality. It is lively, often funny; it features, in Arthur Kipps, one of Wells's most appealing central characters. It has remained among Wells's most successful books, providing the basis for two popular feature films, most recently a 1966 musical, *Half-a-Sixpence*.

Kipps is illegitimate; he is reared by an anxious aunt and an untidy uncle with several chins; they are dull, humorless people, shop keepers, and, Wells implies, typical of the lower middle class with their suspicions, inhibitions, and exaggerated sense of propriety. Kipps attends a grandly named "Academy for Young Gentlemen" with its "worn desks" and "out-of-date maps." Its principal "had paid certain guineas for a bogus diploma": his lectures are punctuated with "bitter mockery and blows." Not surprisingly, Kipps learns little here, later associating his school days with "an atmosphere of stuffiness and mental muddle," and with "being bullied"—something he must endure again when, in early adolesence, he is apprenticed to a draper in Folkestone. It is not, Kipps decides, enthralling work. Daily he "plumbed an abyss of boredom, or stood a mere carcass with his mind far away, fighting the enemies of the empire, or steering a dream-ship perilously into unknown seas." He begins to believe that "the great stupid machine of retail trade had caught his life into its wheels, a vast, irresistible force which he had neither strength of will nor knowledge to escape.

Kipps possesses "a social disposition" and in Folkestone manages to acquire a few friends, one of whom, Chitterlow, knows something about books and has his own literary ambitions. Another, Helen Walsingham, hails from a family accustomed to culture and wealth; she dresses, the narrator notes, in the sort of "soft and tempered shades that arose in England in the socialistic-aesthetic epoch, and remain to this day among us the badge of those who read Turgenev's novels, scorn current fiction, and think on higher planes." As narrator, Wells steps repeatedly into *Kipps,* stopping the action to offer a wry crack or air a pet peeve, or, more frequently, to explain or assess the actions of his characters, once even shouting out in outrage: "The stupid little tragedies of these clipped and limited lives! . . . See what I can see! Above them, brooding over them, I tell you there is a monster, a lumpish monster, like some great, clumsy griffin thing . . . like all that is darkening and heavy and obstructive in life. It is matter and darkness, it is the anti-soul, it is the ruling power of this land, Stupidity." Such intrusiveness greatly irked the American novelist William Dean Howells, who reviewed *Kipps* for the *North American Review*. Howells, an admirer of James's more discreet approach to writing novels, respected Wells's "manifold" mind. But like James, Howells had begun to regret that Wells had maintained the Thackeray-like habit of "coming forward in person" and disrupting the flow of his fictions; that he was plotty and preachy, a member of "that bad English school of fictional art, whose teachings he ought to have forgotten."[3]

Much in the tradition of popular Victorian fiction, Artie Kipps experiences a dramatic change in situation, unexpectedly inheriting, from his paternal grandfather, a large house in Folkstone and twenty-four thousand pounds. Kipps now gains entry to more rarefied circles, but knows that he needs polish, his accent a particularly stark indication of his modest roots. Despite Helen's efforts to school him in the social graces, Kipps is ill at ease among the well-to-do; he breaks his engagement to Helen and marries Ann Pornick, a childhood friend who now works as a maid. Later, Kipps learns that Helen's brother has bilked him of much of his fortune; that he has just enough left to start up a bookshop and pursue life's simpler joys. Kipps persists in this more modest life after he learns that he is once again wealthy; for Chitterlow's play, *The Pestered Butterfly*—in which Kipps had heavily invested—becomes a roaring success. At the close of *Kipps*, Wells shows Artie rowing with Ann on the nearby Hythe canal. The sun is setting "in a mighty blaze"; the water is "shining bright" and the world is "warm, and very still." Kipps is content, "touched by the wonder of life," by "the wonder of the beauty, the purposeless, inconsecutive beauty, that falls so strangely among the happenings and memories of life."

As this closing passage shows, Wells could be exceptionally good at communicating an intense pleasure for life's delights and splendors. (Consider, too, the closing paragraphs of one of his best short stories, "The Country of the Blind." Its central character, after living among a tribe of sightless people, finds himself newly sensitized to nature; "the mountain summits around him" become "things of light and fire, and the little details of the rocks near at hand were drenched with subtle beauty—a vein of green mineral piercing the grey, the flash of crystal faces here and there, a minute, minutely beautiful orange lichen close beside his face. There were deep mysterious shadows in the gorge, blue deepening into purple, and purple into a luminous darkness, and overhead was the illimitable vastness of the sky.") Surely the life-affirming ending of *Kipps* added much to its appeal, perhaps allowing many readers to overlook its darker political themes.

These Wells conveys principally through the figure of Masterman, one of Kipps's acquaintances—a gaunt, consumptive man embittered because he was simply too poor to afford access to a decent education. As Masterman tells Kipps, he was, at thirteen, "forced into a factory like a rabbit into a chloroformed box." Now, nearing forty, he is "beaten and wasted"—"crushed, trampled, and defiled by a drove of hogs," by the callous rich who wallow greedily in the power and wealth they have, in many cases, so effortlessly gained. "God," Masterman complains, "gives them a power like the motorcar, and all they can do with it is to go careering about the roads in goggled masks, killing children and making machinery hateful to the soul of man!" They possess "means of communication, power unparalleled of every sort, time, and absolute liberty!" And yet, "they waste it all in folly!" "Under their feet, . . . under their accursed wheels," Masterman tells Kipps, "the great mass of men festers and breeds in darkness, darkness those others make by standing in the light." The wealthy, he insists,

grudge us our schools, they grudge us a gleam of light and air, they cheat us, and then seek to forget us. . . . There is no rule, no guidance, only accidents and happy flukes. . . . Our multitudes of poverty increase, and this crew of rulers makes no provision, forsees nothing, anticipates nothing!

"The world," according to Masterman, "is out of joint, and there isn't a soul alive who isn't half waste or more." "You'll find it the same with you in the end," he tells Kipps, "wherever your luck may take you." Indeed, the attentive reader of *Kipps* is likely to conclude that Kipps too has been wasted, left to career about in a social system run by accident and cash. Kipps got his one shot at social approbation not because he was Kipps, but simply because he one day found his bank balance hugely enhanced. And as *Kipps* makes clear, money—particularly in a world so chaotically run—can vanish as quickly as it comes. "Wait for the lean years," warns Masterman, who foresees only "universal confusion" ahead, with "every fool in the world panting and shoving. We're all going to be as happy and comfortable as a household during a removal," he predicts. "What else can we expect?"

In *Tono-Bungay*, Wells expands on political ideas put forth not only in *Kipps*, but such works as *First and Last Things* (1908), written when Wells had *Tono-Bungay* much on his mind. In *First and Last Things*, Wells records his despair at the thought of "the grimy millions who slave for industrial production," of "peasants living in wretched huts knee-deep in manure, mere parasites of their own pigs and cows"—a despair that deepens as he thinks too of those "extravagant and yet contemptible creatures of luxury," those "tens of thousands of wealthy people wasting lives in vulgar and unsatisfying trivialities, hundreds of thousands meanly chaffering themselves, rich or poor, in the wasteful byways of trade." In *First and Last Things* Wells condemns "trading that is merely speculative"—"in fact all trading and manufacture that is not a positive social service." He attacks "every act of advertisement that is not punctiliously truthful;" he condemns "the dealer who sells and pushes an article because it fits the customer's folly," "the journalist who writes against his personal convictions," and "the solicitor who knowingly assists the schemes of rogues"—calling them "prostitutes of mind and soul if not of body, with no right to lift an eyebrow at the painted disasters of the streets."

In *Kipps*, Wells draws freely upon his travails as a draper's trainee; in *Tono-Bungay* he recalls life at Uppark—and, later, South Kensington. George Ponderevo, the novel's narrator, first becomes familiar with upper-class life because his mother is housekeeper at Bladesover, a large country estate; his relatives, firmly situated on the lower end of the social scale, include an uncle, "a baker in a back street," who bears the Dickensian moniker of Nicodemus Frapp, and who "presented the servile tradition perfected": he is a shy, muddled, obsequious man who "made no fight against the world at all," often "floundering in small debts that were not so small but that finally they overwhelmed him." As an adolescent, George cuts his ties to Christianity, telling his stunned cousins that "there's no hell, . . . and no eternal punishment. No God would be such a fool as that." Studying hard, George earns a scholarship that enables him to study science in London, where he discovers an interest in politics and a passion for women—a penchant "to fall in love faintly with girls I passed in the street, with women who sat before me in trains, with girl fellow students, with ladies in passing carriages, with loiterers at the corners, with neat-handed waitresses in shops and tea-rooms, with pictures even of girls and women." Quite accidentally, he finds himself keeping company with a real woman, Marion, with whom he has little in common.

But Marion was "the unconscious custodian of something that had gripped my most intimate instinct," Ponderevo recalls; she "embodied the hope of a possibility, was the careless proprietor of a physical quality that had turned my head like strong wine."

Restless and distracted, Ponderevo finds himself "falling away from all the militant ideals of unflinching study" that had heretofore marked his educational career. As a result, his scholarship expires and he leaves school quite aware that "without a degree or any qualification, one earned hardly a bare living and had little leisure to struggle up to anything better." But George copes. Eager for success and the chance to impress Marion, he begins working for his uncle, Edward, a paunchy provincial chemist whose hero is Napoleon Bonaparte. Uncle Edward, full of bluster but not without charm, sets out to conquer the world of commerce, concocting a worthless tonic—"Tono-Bungay"—which George promotes. "My special and distinctive duty," he explains, "was to give Tono-Bungay substance and an outward and visible bottle, to translate my uncle's great imaginings into the creation of case after case of labelled bottles of nonsense, and the punctual discharge of them by railway, road, and steamer towards their ultimate goal in the Great Stomach of the People." George's marriage to Marion founders—but Tono-Bungay thrives. As it enters growing numbers of stomachs, Uncle Edward's product line begins to expand. Soon, there are Tono-Bungay lozenges and Tono-Bungay chocolates. There is a Tono-Bungay hair dressing that promises to stop baldness by activating hair follicles that, after years of sprouting away, have simply grown "fagged."

These products are also successful, owing largely to George's promotional skills. The lozenges appear in ads that show "a dreadfully barristerish barrister, wig, side-whiskers, teeth, a horribly life-like portrait of all existing barristers, talking at a table, and beneath, this legend: 'A Four Hours' Speech on Tono-Bungay Lozenges, and as fresh as when he began.' " "That," George notes, "brought in regiments of school-teachers, revivalist ministers, politicians and the like." There "really" was, he adds, "an element of 'kick' in the strychnine in these lozenges, especially in those made according to our earlier formula." For of course "we altered all our formulae—invariably weakening them enormously as sales got ahead."

Eventually, even clever advertising fails to save Uncle Edward: he loses out in a world of business and industry that, in Wells's depiction, is as ruthless as any jungle. But before he falls, the elder Ponderevo amasses "unmanageable wealth and power and real respect," all for creating and peddling what George calls "the one reality of human life—illusion. We gave them a feeling of hope and profit; we sent a tidal wave of water and confidence into their stranded affairs." At the peak of his success, Uncle Edward communes with dukes and lords and prominent politicians, with other members of the nouveaux riches—men and women who, George notes, plunge into shopping as one "plunges into a career," who "talk, think, and dream possessions," for whom "acquisition" has become "the substance of their lives." Just prior to his collapse, Uncle Edward begins to construct a mansion, Crest Hill, as massive and vulgar as the Xanadu of Orson Welles's *Citizen Kane*. The house, never completed, involves squads of "stonemasons, sanitary engineers, painters, sculptors, scribes, metal-workers, wood-carvers, furniture-designers, ceramic specialists, landscape-gardeners"; it features a "delirium of pinnacles and terraces and arcades and corridors," as well as "a swimming bath thirty feet square" and a "ten-foot wall, glass-surmounted," installed to hold Edward's "dominions together, free from the invasion of common men."

There is considerable humor in *Tono-Bungay*, much of it conveyed in breezy dialogue, comical names, and characters with amusing quirks; the novel is enlivened by the witty observations of Ponderevo's eccentric friend Ewart, who—particularly in his lengthy diatribe against Victorian attitudes toward sex—voices views that run close to Wells's own. Certainly, Ponderevo often speaks for Wells himself, revealing, for example, that "I don't like things so human"—"I'm in earnest in warp and woof." In fact, as the novel proceeds, a more sobering sense of social injustice and disarray becomes prominent, conveyed for example in a scene in which George, newly prosperous but increasingly self-aware, observes a long procession of unemployed men, "a silent, foot-dragging, interminable, grey procession," some of them carrying "wet, dirty banners," others rattling "boxes for pence." These, George notes, are "the gutter waste of competitive civilisation."

As in Thomas Pynchon's cult classic *The Crying of Lot 49* (1966), much of the effectiveness of *Tono-Bungay* derives from Wells's brilliant blend of the comic and the apocalyptic; from his ability to portray disorder and decay in images and symbols that are unusually vivid and memorable.[4] The most effective of these is "Quap," which Uncle Edward insists on pulling out of Africa for use in the manufacture of cheap filaments for lamps. It is a "festering mass of earths and heavy metals, polonium, radium, ythorium, thorium, cerium, and new things too"; all of it "mucked up together in a sort of rotting sand." It is "the most radio-active stuff in the world," and for Wells the perfect symbol of the rampant chaos and destruction that stems from human disorganization, stupidity, and greed. George likens Quap to a disease; indeed, *Tono-Bungay* is imbued by images of disorder and decay, emphasizing not only Wells's sense of the harshness of nature, but the spirit of anarchy that—in modern society—dominates the affairs of women and men. "It spreads," George observes darkly, and "I am haunted by a grotesque fancy of the ultimate eating away and dry-rotting and dispersal of all our world. . . . Suppose, indeed, that is to be the end of our planet; no splendid climax and finale, no towering accumulation of achievements but just—atomic decay!"

Along the way, George succeeds in becoming a major figure in the fledgling field of aeronautics—a fact that enables him, at thirty-seven, to become a member of the Royal Society. But more important, as the novel makes plain, is George's flight from social and intellectual anarchy, from the warped system of values in which he was once so tightly enmeshed. He matures, coming to see himself and his society with a clarity of vision that his selfish pursuits had temporarily concealed. He sees the full horror and stupidity inherent in a society that is committed to nothing more than the crass pursuit of power and wealth; that is titillated by an endless series of cheap thrills and cleverly packaged lies, by a vast network of illusions symbolized by Tono-Bungay itself. George returns to his intellectual roots, to "Science," which he equates with "Truth"—the ultimate reality, the continuum of knowledge, "the one enduring thing" to which "men and nations, epochs and civilisations" can contribute before, inexorably, they fade. In this light—the light of Wells's own religion—George sees the awfulness of his own egotism fully exposed; he is prepared to accept the fact that, like all living things, he is but a small part of a vast, fascinating, and ultimately unfathomable mystery. "We are all things that make and pass," he observes in the novel's final line, "striving upon a hidden mission, out to the open sea."

But George is also regretful, drained, and aware that, given their greedy scheming, their brazen pushing of spurious goods, he and his uncle were "no more than specimens of a modern species of brigand, wasting the savings of the public out of the sheer wantonness of enterprise." "I see now ... a story of activity and urgency and sterility," he notes, looking over his manuscript, "I have called it *Tono-Bungay*, but I had far better have called it *Waste*." For much of modern life, he realizes, "is all one spectacle of forces running to waste, of people who use and do not replace." In "the even evening sunlight" he studies the hulking shell of his uncle's unfinished mansion, seeing an "utter absurdity," a thing "as idiotic as the pyramids"—and "the compactest image and sample of all that passes for Progress, of all the advertisement-inflated spending, the aimless building up and pulling down, the enterprise and promise of my age." Arguably, it is here, as George meditates upon the vast and garish Crest Hill, that one finds the essential Wells—his sense of social outrage and cosmic despair quite vividly combined:

For this armies drilled, for this the Law was administered and the prisons did their duty, for this the millions toiled and perished in suffering, in order that a few of us should build palaces we never finished, make billiard-rooms under ponds, run imbecile walls round irrational estates, scorch about the world in motor-cars, devise flying-machines, play golf and a dozen such foolish games of ball, crowd into chattering dinner parties, gamble and make our lives one vast dismal spectacle of witless waste! ... This was Life! It came to me like a revelation, a revelation at once incredible and indisputable of the abysmal folly of our being.

At the close of *Tono-Bungay*, George is designing naval vessels—destroyers. The ending has tended to puzzle readers, including Mark Schorer, who found it odd that "science, power and knowledge, are summed up at last in a destroyer. As far as one can tell Wells intends no irony, although he may have come upon the essence of the major irony in modern history." According to Schorer, *Tono-Bungay* "ends in a kind of meditative rhapsody which denies every value that the book had been aiming toward."[5]

The novel's closing paragraphs are ambiguous. Ponderevo does make clear that this ship, the X2, "isn't intended for the empire, or indeed for the hands of any European power"; England he equates with "greedy trade, base profit-seeking, bold advertisement"—with an old world order that, ineluctably, will pass. And he only vaguely implies that the destroyer, "stark and swift," is a symbol of science—a potent tool placed at the disposal of those prepared to put an absolute end to waste and absurdity before building the world anew. In other novels and nonfictional writings, Wells does in fact portray war as the ultimate absurdity; but he also sometimes suggests—quite directly in such works as *The World Set Free* and *The Shape of Things to Come*—that war itself might be a preliminary, a necessary catalyst to global change. For a time, Wells believed that what came to be called World War I might have those regenerating possibilities; in 1914 he published a collection of essays called *The War That Will End War.*

Tono-Bungay is a vast, sprawling, vigorous work; at its outset George makes clear he is not attempting a "novel" that will win praise for its sharp prose or its perfect construction. (Of course, since *Tono-Bungay* is supposed to be the accurate story of Ponderevo's life, he—or, more precisely, Wells—ought not call it a "novel" at all.) "I have got an unusual series of impressions," he announces, "that I want very urgently to tell." He thus warns that "this book is going to be something of an agglomeration"; it "is my first novel and almost certainly my last." He will aim, then, to include "all sorts of things that struck me, things that amused me and impressions I got—even although they don't minister directly to my narrative at all." In other words, Ponderevo's aesthetic views are Wells's aesthetic views; like Wells himself, he is comprehensive, catalogic—driven to clarify, justify, explain; he is preoccupied with understanding the dynamics of his own life while coming to grips with the way the whole world works, and setting forth his discoveries, all of them, between the covers of a book. The principles that Wells would defend in "The Contemporary Novel"—and that animate his entire novelistic career—are already very clearly illustrated in *Tono-Bungay.*

Like *Kipps* and *Tono-Bungay, The History of Mr. Polly* is marked by narrative digressions and authorial intrusions, by bits of memorable humor and wit. As J. R. Hammond suggests, *The History of Mr. Polly* has "taken its place alongside *Three Men in a Boat* and *The Diary of a Nobody* as one of the quintessential expressions of English humour."[6] Its central character, Alfred Polly, is a shopkeeper; his wife, Miriam, "combined earnestness of spirit with great practical incapacity"; she cooks "because food had to be cooked, and with a sound moralist's entire disregard of the quality or the consequences." As a result, as with Sarah Wells, "the food came from her hands done rather than improved, and looking as uncomfortable as savages clothed under duress by a missionary with a stock of out-sizes." Like Sarah, Miriam is frequently cross; she tends to tune out her husband's talk and had long since "ceased to unwrinkle the kink in her brow at his presence, giving herself up to mental states that had a quality of preoccupation." She particularly objects to the fact that Polly spends so much of his time with his books, books with "torn covers and broken covers, fat books whose backs were naked string and glue—an inimical litter to Miriam."

Polly, more than Kipps, is intellectually alert, and enthralled by life's endless curiosities. But like Kipps he has been wretchedly educated; his mind, the novel's narrator notes, "was in much the same state that you would be in, dear reader, if you were operated upon for appendicitis by a well-meaning, boldly enterprising, but rather overworked and underpaid butcher boy, who was superseded towards the climax of the operation by a left-handed clerk of high principles but intemperate habits—that is to say, it was in a thorough mess." It left Polly with little confidence, his potentially fine mind in "a jumbled and thwarted condition." Thus, by the time his schooling is complete, Polly "thought of the present world no longer as a wonderland of experiences, but as geography and history, as the repeating of names that were hard to pronounce, and lists of products and populations and heights and lengths, and as lists and dates—oh! and Boredom indescribable."

Polly is also bored by the chores associated with the apprenticeship he must serve in "one of those large, rather low-class establishments which sell everything from pianos and furniture to books and millinery." Here, in Port Burdock, Polly discovers the delights of close friendship, falling in with a boy, Parsons, who is also keen on books. Through Parsons, Polly encounters "an Italian writer, whose name Mr. Polly rendered at 'Bocashieu.' " He discovers "the glorious revelation of that great Frenchman whom Mr. Polly called 'Rabooloose.' " Parsons and Polly and their friend Platt "thought the birth-feast of Gargantua the most glorious piece of writing in the world—and," the narrator remarks, "I am not certain they were wrong; and on wet Sunday evenings, when there was danger of hymn-singing, they would get Parsons to read it aloud."

Dreamy, imaginative, moody: Polly is not likely to triumph in the rough world of retail trade. But, like Kipps, he finds few other clear options; he bumbles into running a clothing shop in Fishbourne—just as he had bumbled into wedlock. Not surprisingly, Polly comes to realize he "hated the whole scheme of life—which was at once excessive and inadequate of him. He hated Fishbourne, he hated Fishbourne High Street, he hated his shop

and his wife and his neighbors—every blessed neighbor—and
with indescribable bitterness he hated himself." "Why did I ever
get into this silly Hole?" he keeps asking himself. "Why did I
ever?" Living on Miriam's food, he has become chronically dys-
peptic; doing little but selling swimsuits and socks has left him
soured, distressed, vividly aware that, for fifteen years, his life has
"not been worth living, that it had been in apathetic and feebly
hostile and critical company, ugly in detail and mean in scope,
and that it had brought him at last to an outlook utterly hopeless
and grey."

Thus, at thirty-seven, seeing nothing before him but more "toil
and struggle, toil and struggle," Polly resolves to end his life,
leaving his wife with "the full benefit of both his life insurance
and his fire insurance." For Polly's loathing for Miriam "vanished directly the idea of getting away from her for ever became
clear in his mind," and he had "not the remotest intention of
leaving her unprotected, with a painfully dead husband and a
bankrupt shop on her hands." Polly succeeds in burning down his
shop—but fails in his attempt at suicide. In fact, Polly emerges
from the blaze a hero, having led a neighbor's aged mother-in-law
safely away from the flames. The woman is feisty but deaf; Polly's efforts to coax her through the smoke and down a long ladder are among the book's best scenes. "Not for jumpin' I don't,"
the old woman keeps asserting. "Not a bit of it. I bain't no good
at jumping, and I *wun't*."

Polly clears out when his insurance money comes through. He
becomes a tramp, strolling the countryside, discovering that—for
the first time in his life—he is leading a healthy life, "a healthy
human life, living constantly in the open air, walking every day
for eight or nine hours, eating sparingly, accepting every conversational opportunity, not even disdaining the discussion of possible work." Eventually, he finds employment at a rural inn, and
settles in with its landlady, a fat woman who knows how to cook.
At the Potwell Inn, Polly continues to ponder "the mystery of
life"—but now his mood is mellow and his digestion sound, enabling him to savor especially "those evenings serenely luminous,
amply and atmospherically still, when the river bend was at its
best." "Sometimes I think I live for sunsets," Polly tells the fat
woman as swans float by and "everything lay securely within a
great, warm, friendly globe of crystal sky."

Polly, Wells would note, "is compounded from life." He "is my
dear elder brother, he is various others, and he is a very typical

Englishman. Kipps and Polly, in their sensitiveness, diffidence, want of push . . . are very English." But of course, in their determination to live life on their own terms, they are very like Wells himself. Polly, like Wells, had come to see that "his soul had been cramped and his eyes bandaged from the hour of his birth." And he realizes, like many of Wells's central characters, that no personal satisfaction, no sustained happiness, can be gained without, first, risk. Polly comes to ask himself: "Why had he lived such a life? Why had he submitted to things, blundered into things? Why had he never insisted on the things he desired, never sought them, fought for them, taken any risk for them, died rather than abandon them?" "He had been a fool," he realizes, "a coward and a fool; he had been fooled, too, for no one had ever warned him to take a firm hold upon life, no one had ever told him of the littleness of fear or pain or death." "Safety," Polly realizes, coming upon a theme that runs from *The Time Machine* to *Things to Come*, "did not matter. A living did not matter unless there were things to live for." Elsewhere, the novel's narrator asserts:

If the world does not please you, *you can change it*. Determine to alter it at any price, and you can change it altogether. You may change it to something sinister and angry, to something appalling, but it may be you will change it to something brighter, something more agreeable, and at the worst something much more interesting. There is only one sort of man who is absolutely to blame for his own misery, and that is the man who finds life dull and dreary.

In *The History of Mr. Polly*, writes Vincent Brome, "Wells was back for the moment in the full-blooded Dickens tradition, rebelling against the frustrations of the human personality in the petty bourgeois world, kicking hard at the dumb elephant of education, but possessed more than anything with the essence of Polly, the man as a man."[7] When the novel first appeared, H. L. Mencken noted similarly that Dickens "would have loved Mr. Polly—loved him for his helplessness, his doggish joys, his calflike sorrows." In fact, on the strength of such works as *Kipps* and *Mr. Polly*, Wells found himself being increasingly praised for having stepped into Dickens's "long vacant boots," for Wells, the Anglophobic Mencken notes, had "staked out for himself" the same lower class that Dickens "knew so intimately and loved with such shameless sentimentality—that hunkerous, uncleanly, tea swilling *garde du corps* of all the more discusting virtues, traditions, superstitions and epidemic diseases of the Anglican people."[8]

But as Mencken points out, *The History of Mr. Polly* reveals that, in the end, "despite a good deal of likeness," Dickens and Wells were "as far apart as the poles"—a fact that becomes even more apparent in Wells's subsequent novels. Dickens, writes Mencken, "regarded his characters as a young mother regards her baby; Wells looks at his as a porkpacker looks at a hog." Wells, in other words, is far less prone to sentimentality; he clearly likes Polly, but keeps him at a distance, sometimes treating him less like an individual than what Mencken calls a "biological specimen." According to Mencken, the first part of the book can be read simply as an analysis of the root causes of Mr. Polly's indigestion; its later chapters recount "the gradual salvation of Mr. Polly's stomach, and through it, of Mr. Polly's immortal soul."

Mencken's remarks are a bit strong. Polly's intellectual cravings are no less intense than his physical wants; he has the artist's ability to delight in sights, sounds, and smells—to be moved deeply by the deft arrangement of words. He is very probably Wells's best-drawn character, made particularly attractive because he is very perceptive and verbally inventive, able to savor the mere sound of "floriferous," say, and—with a relish at once charming and pathetic—come up with curious verbal formations of his own. Polly "loved laughter," asserts the novel's narrator; he had "a capacity for joy and beauty at least as keen and subtle as yours or mine." To be marooned in Fishbourne nearly kills him. And there is courage as well as desperation in his decision to escape and then secure his place at the Potwell—something he can achieve only by first facing up to a particularly unsavory character called Uncle Jim.

Still, Wells does place considerable emphasis on the digestive factors contributing to Polly's unhappiness; in works ranging from *The War of the Worlds* to *Mr. Blettsworthy on Rampole Island,* he reveals a tendency to view life in thoroughly biological terms. As a result, it is likely many readers will find that even the fullest of Wells's characters lack dimension; that many seem little more than attempts to verify Ludwig Feuerbach's observation that, quite simply, "Man is what he eats." Indeed, a reader willing to slog his or her way through all of Wells's fictional efforts, to press on past *The History of Mr. Polly* and through *The Undying Fire* (1919)—one of the bleakest novels of the century— might well conclude that Graham Greene was perhaps right when, in an essay on Somerset Maugham, he suggested that, com-

monly, it is difficult for the absolute materialist to endure successfully as a novelist. "Rob human beings of their heavenly and their
infernal importance," Greene writes, "and you rob your characters of their individuality." "It has never been Maugham's characters that we have remembered," he adds—in words that often
seem applicable to Wells—"so much as the narrator, with his
contempt for human life, his unhappy honesty."[9]

4

Wells and Women

In *The New Machiavelli*, published in 1911, H. G. Wells allows his highly autobiographical protagonist, a political journalist called Richard Remington, to speak for H. G. Wells on a wide range of social and political issues. Remington wants to reform a Britain he finds full of disorder and waste; he wants to use science to cast a searing light upon a lingering "nineteenth-century darkness"; to "foster literature, clarify, strengthen the public consciousness, develop social organization and a sense of the State." And he wants "this coddling and brow-beating of women to cease." "I want to see women come in, free and fearless, to a full participation in the collective purpose of mankind," Remington asserts. "I confess myself altogether feminist. I have no doubts in the matter."

But was Wells, in fact, a feminist? Some critics have reflected their own doubts in the matter, noting for example that Wells's second marriage represented anything but a break with male attitudes dominant during the Victorian era. Wells seemed quite content to regard Amy Catherine, writes Nancy Steffen-Fluhr, "as if she were a piece of porcelain depicting the Victorian 'Angel of the Home,' " a "perfected good-housekeeping version of Wells's own mother, without any of his mother's domination"—a point perhaps strengthened by the fact that, after their first child, Wells took to calling his wife "little Mummy."[1] According to Victoria Glendinning, Wells's various relationships with other women, including West, show repeatedly that he simply "found it impossible to think of women except in relation to men, and considered 'independent women' ridiculous and pathetic." The only freedom Wells really wanted for women, Glendinning writes, "was sexual freedom, which meant in practice sexual availability."[2] In any event, Steffen-Fluhr adds, Wells was simply not interested "in the otherness of other people"; he was, in all of his affairs, "acting out a pyschomachia—chasing the shadow cast by his own heart."[3]

Such criticisms were anticipated by Wells himself. Wells admits that "I have preyed upon people more generous than myself who have loved me gave life to me." He was often afflicted by a "strain of essential vulgarity about sex," which showed itself when he swapped stories of his conquests with other "codpiece-minded males." In the posthumously published postscript to his *Experiment in Autobiography*, Wells writes that his affairs were generally friendly and refreshing, the "fairly equal" meeting of "two libertines." But he also reveals, with characteristic contradiction, that his continuing pursuit of "the Lover Shadow"—his name for one's ideal mate, one's perfect romantic and sexual complement—left him, by late middle age, flustered and drained.[4] "My story of my relations with women," Wells writes, "is mainly a story of greed, foolishness and great expectation." "I am," he quite remarkably admits, "an insufficient and often irritable 'great man' with an infantile craving for help."

Certainly, much in Wells's writing would strike the contemporary feminist as far less than enlightened. In *The Work, Wealth and Happiness of Mankind,* for example, he takes time to point out that women "have yet displayed qualities and initiatives to put them on a level with the best of men in any such department of activity"; even in "literature, in art, in the scientific laboratory"—where, Wells suggests, women "suffer no handicap"—"none has displayed structural power or breadth, depth and steadfastness of conception, to compare with the best work of men." In several of his novels, including *Ann Veronica,* he strongly implies that motherhood, the fulfillment of woman's biological destiny, is imperative to the meaningfulness of her life. And yet, it is likely that no major male writer of the twentieth century wrote so frequently and with such consistent sympathy about women's concerns. In *Ann Veronica* and elsewhere Wells sets forth to expose the sexist attitudes of his male contemporaries. He argues against the notion that women were simply meant to remain the subordinate gender, and had no business testing their talents in the world of men. Wells's principal female characters are regularly bright, determined, self-assertive; they show resilience as they challenge stereotypes meant to confine their roles. Like Thomas Huxley, Wells believed that increased educational and social opportunities for women were long overdue. "Women," wrote Huxley in 1865, "are meant neither to be men's guides nor their playthings, but their comrades, their fellows and their equals."[5] It is a conviction that Wells's novels often endorse.

Ann Veronica appeared in 1909, when throughout Britain and America the suffragette movement was gaining momentum and talk of the "New Woman" was everywhere. Its central character, Ann Veronica Stanley, is an intelligent young woman who studies biology—and dissects well. As the novel opens, Ann is eager to join some friends on a weekend trip to London that will include a costume ball and an unchaperoned night in a Soho hotel. But Ann still resides in a sedate London suburb under the vigilance of her widowed father, a prosperous businessman whom Wells gives a hard mouth, a sharp nose, and the conviction that "women are made like the potter's vessels, either for worship or contumely, and are withal fragile vessels." Stanley believes that a daughter is simply a father's "absolute property, bound to obey him, his to give away or his to keep to be a comfort in his declining years, just as he thought fit." He disapproves of Ann's plan to further her studies with a scientist well-known for his agnosticism and his spirited defenses of Darwinian views. And he refuses to allow her to attend the art students' ball. "You have begun to get hold of some very queer ideas about what a young lady in your position may or may not venture to do," Mr. Stanley informs his daughter. "You have no grasp upon the essential facts of life (I pray God you never may), and in your rash ignorance you are prepared to dash into positions that may end in lifelong regret." "The life of a young girl," he concludes—accurately, as the novel shows—"is set about with prowling pitfalls."

Defying her father, Ann does move to London and takes a small flat. Soon after arriving, she finds herself followed about the city's streets by a silk-hatted man with "desire and appraisal in his eyes," reminding her of "this supreme, ugly fact of pursuit—the pursuit of the undesired, persistent male." In London, Ann passes the "myriad fronts" of offices and shops, assuming that behind them "there must be a career or careers." She is wrong. There are only low wages paid to shop girls who must put up with the "smirking men in frock coats who dominate these establishments." Ann's brother arrives to tell her to "go home and wait a century" when "you *may* have a bit of a chance"; other males appear armed with advice. One of them, a civil servant called Hubert Manning, is yet another example of the obtuse male hindering the progress of women: he is a sentimentalist with a penchant for producing poems that read like bad imitations of Dante Gabriel Rossetti in his most fervid flights. Manning tells Ann: "You're like some splendid Princess in Exile in these Dreadful Dingy apartments!"

To this Ann responds effectively, asking Manning to consider if his "sentiment" accords "with the realities." "Are women truly such angelic things," she says, "and men so chivalrous?" "You men," she continues, "have, I know, meant to make us queens and goddesses, but in practice—well, look, for example, at the stream of girls one meets going to work of a morning, round-shouldered, cheap, underfed! They aren't queens, and no one is treating them as queens. And look, again, at the women one finds letting lodgings. . . . Everywhere I went and rapped at a door I found behind it another dreadful dingy woman—another fallen queen, I suppose—dingier than the last, dirty, you know, in grain. Their poor hands!"

In her frustration, Ann starts to take part in Britain's young feminist movement; she is arrested after joining a suffragette raid on the House of Commons and is sentenced to a month in jail. But here, with ample time for reflection, Ann decides that, on the whole, she quite likes men; that what "a woman wants" is, in fact, "a proper alliance with a man, a man who is better stuff than herself." A woman, Ann Veronica decides, "wants to be legally and economically free, so as not to be subject to the wrong man; but only God, who made the world, can alter things to prevent her being slave to the right one." "It may not be just," she concludes, "it may not be fair, but things are so. It is just how things happen to be."

Ann realizes that her right man is one Godwin Capes—a professor of biology and yet another of Wells's idealized self-portraits, the skilled teacher, the lucid thinker, the writer of "easy and confident" prose. Separated but not yet divorced, he tells Ann that he was recently caught in "a friendship with the wife of a friend," a "gratification of an immense necessity" that left him "smirched," a focus for gossip in London's social circles. But Ann responds to Capes's brilliance, and finds him sexually exciting— "the magic man whose touch turned one to trembling fire." "I want you," Ann tells Capes. "I want you to be my lover. I want to give myself to you. I want to be whatever I can to you."

Capes does not refuse. He quits his teaching post and joins Ann in Switzerland, where—under a pseudonym—he starts writing what would become highly successful plays. Here, amid the Wagnerian scenery, the "towering sunlit cliffs," the "valleys of haze and warm darkness," Ann and Capes exult in each other's company; in one of her arias, Ann—"glowing with heroic love"—declares that "I know now what it is to be an abandoned female. I *am* an abandoned female." Wells would later concede that *Ann Veronica* suffers from "an excessive use of soliloquy"; in fact, the novel is replete with problems. It begins, after all, with a biting portrayal of male stolidity in the form of Ann's father; it implies strongly that—given support and opportunity—Ann would continue to develop intellectually, revealing a first-rate scientific mind. But by the novel's close Mr. Stanley is completely defanged: he is now, as Ann calls him, "Dear old daddy," the B-movie curmudgeon who, beneath the bluster, is a fellow with a heart of gold, ready to accept his daughter's elopement with Capes and to pronounce serenely, "All's well that ends well" and "the less one says about things the better." Ann, meanwhile, scraps her scientific ambitions now that she has grown cozy with Capes in a house stuffed with new furniture. "We've had so splendid a time," she asserts in the novel's concluding scene, "and fought our fight and won."

Oh, I've loved love, dear! I've loved love and you, and the glory of you; and the great time is over, and I have to go carefully and bear children, and—take care of my hair—and when I am done with that I shall be an old woman.... All this furniture—and successes! We are successful at last! Successful!

Amid the cascade of exclamation marks, one can virtually hear the violins. The detached, satiric tone that Wells effectively employs at the start of *Ann Veronica* has slowly dissolved; he now sounds like Barbara Cartland. Along the way, the novel's explicitly feminist slant is superseded by a condescending—and often mocking—view of feminists themselves. One of them, Nettie Miniver, is unattractive as well as dotty, punctuating her confused discourses with "weak little gestures with her hands." She has "bent shoulders," a "physical insufficiency"; "maternity," she asserts, "has been our undoing." She will not then partake in what Wells often makes clear is an intelligent woman's most basic obligation—the bearing of healthy children whose superior genes will, he implies, further enhance the progress of the race.

Ann Veronica bears more than a few similarities to Grant Allen's 1895 novel, *The Woman Who Did*. Both works feature heroines who openly challenge prevailing sexual mores; both lapse into melodrama and aromatic prose. And one finds in *Ann Veronica* much the same message that Gail Cunningham finds in Allen's novel, where—despite a good deal of talk about the need for female autonomy—there "lurks an almost entirely traditional ideal of femininity." As Cunningham points out, Allen writes that his heroine, Herminia Barton, " 'was woman enough to like being led,' " realizing that " 'it is a woman's ancestral part to look up to the man; and she is happiest in doing it, and must long remain so.' " Cunningham notes that, in an 1889 article published in the *Fortnightly Review*, Allen declared himself "an enthusiast on the Woman Question," but proceeds to "set out a programme of reform which would effectively shackle her forever." "Higher education for women is a most desirable thing, he says, so long as what they are taught is 'to suckle strong and intelligent children, and to order well a wholesome, beautiful, reasonable household.' "[6] This sounds quite like the Wells of *Ann Veronica*.

The Passionate Friends is similarly concerned with the position of women in the modern world. But it is far more artistically controlled; in fact, for Vladimir Nabokov, *The Passionate Friends* was his "most prized example of the unjustly ignored masterpiece." "Today at seventy-seven," wrote Nabokov in 1977, "I clearly remember how affected I was by the style, the charm, the cream of the book, while not bothering about its 'message' or 'symbols' if any."[7]

The novel's narrator, Stephen Stratton, is a rector's son; at twenty-one he joins the army and takes part in the Boer War—an event that leaves him with a loathing for bloodshed and a commitment to work unceasingly toward the creation of a more rational "World Republic of civilised men," calling it "not a dream" but "a manifestly reasonable possibility." He also begins to pursue Lady Mary Christian, whom he knew in his youth. She is the daughter of an earl—a fact that puts her a bit beyond Stratton's social reach. Mary is similarly attracted to Stephen, but chooses instead to become Lady Mary Justin, the wife of a wealthy financier. It proves an unfortunate match. Justin is plodding, possessive. Mary continues to meet with Stephen, who is uncomfortable in his role as her furtive lover and persists in his attempts at gaining her complete allegiance—thus incensing Justin and causing Mary much distress. "Why," Mary tells the two of them, "must I choose between two men? I want neither of you. I want myself. I'm not a thing. I'm a human being. I'm not your thing, Justin—not yours, Stephen. Yet you want to quarrel over me—like two dogs over a bone."

Although Wells clearly intends to allow Stephen to sound astute on matters pertaining to the running of the world, it is clear from the start of *The Passionate Friends* that he has had to learn much about women, and what Wells portrays as the real meaning of love. Only belatedly—after Mary's suicide—does he realize the full harm of his increasingly raging jealousy. "I had always wanted to own Mary," Stratton concedes, "and always she had disputed that. That is our whole story, the story of an instinctive subjugation struggling against a passionate desire for fellowship." "It rankled," he adds, "that she could still go on living a life independent of mine." Indeed, unlike Ann, the more mature and consistently drawn Mary refuses to accept the theory that a woman's happiness ultimately depends upon her bonding with the proper man; she comes to resent the fact that a proper marriage was made to seem the only possible outlet for her talents and energies. Lady Mary knows many women who feel similarly but are reluctant to speak, preferring for the sake of domestic peace and security to remain "pretty silken, furry, feathery jewelled *silences*." "All their suppression doesn't keep them orthodox," she adds, "it only makes them furtive and crumpled and creased in their minds—in just the way that things get crumpled and creased if they are always being shoved back into a drawer." She feels trapped by both social expectation and her biological role; she resents the fact that "men have shifted the responsibility for attraction and passion upon us and made us pay in servitude and restriction and blame for the common defect of the species." But like Ann, Mary cannot relate to a feminist movement that Wells again portrays as being chaotically run and ideationally disorganized; she compares "those suffrage women" to "agitated geese upon a common." But "something," she tells Stephen, "has to be done for women."

Stratton gets the message. After Mary's death, induced by frustration and despair, he realizes that she was "destroyed, not merely by the unconsidered, undisciplined passions of her husband and her lover, but by the vast tradition that sustains and enforces the subjugation of her sex." She was, he now knows, "the very prototype of that sister-lover who must replace the seductive and abject womanhood, owned, mastered and deceiving, who waste the world to-day." It is a point Wells returns to frequently in his writings, arguing—in the *Work, Wealth and Hap-*

piness of Mankind, for example—that the modern woman must become "less a gaudy incentive to man," less "a prize in the competition"—and far more "of a companion and collaborator."

This will not be easy, as *The Wife of Sir Isaac Harman* reveals. Harman's wife, Ellen, marries at eighteen and soon finds herself thoroughly stifled, a mere ornament to a man who has made much money in the baking industry and whose chief passions in life remain profits, possessions, and social respectability. Harman has "little eager eyes, a sharp nose, gaunt gestures and a leaden complexion"; he regards his employees with indifference and is angered by Ellen's suggestions that he do more to bring safety and dignity to their working conditions. He dislikes too her increasingly desperate attempts to lead a more independent life, initially evidenced in her simple desire to select her own friends and go off alone to various meetings and teas. Sir Isaac understood that a woman "had to be wooed to be won, but when she was won, she was won." He was obliged, he knew, "to keep her, dress her, be kind to her, give her the appearances of pride and authority." But in return he expects full "powers of control." "You're losing your bearings," he shouts at one point. "You don't seem to be remembering where you are. You come and tell me you're going to do this and that. Don't you know, Lady Harman, that it's your wifely duty to obey, to do as I say, to behave as I wish."

Wells makes certain attempts to bring dimensionality to his portrayal of Sir Isaac, pointing for example to his early struggle for acceptance and success in an economic and social system that tends to breed covetousness and cruelty. But Sir Isaac is, for the most part, a stereotypical figure in a novel that—like most of Wells's later works—fails as a fully satisfying work of art, as Walter Lippmann suggested when he reviewed *The Wife of Sir Isaac Harman* in 1914. "Since he wrote *The New Machiavelli,*" Lippmann observed, "Wells seems like a man who has retired to live in the country on the proceeds of his accumulated spiritual capital. Where formerly each book had been a fresh adventure and a new conquest, these later ones seem like creations from an armchair which cost little and give little." Lippmann found the novel "hasty, imitative"—a "somewhat querulous" addition to "the stock of the popular novel."[8]

Still, Wells does succeed in bringing sympathy and consistency to his depiction of Ellen, and deftly paces the events that contribute to her continuing self-growth. He gives her believability and—in the end—full autonomy, declining to suggest that, in the wake of Harman's death, she can only find completion in yet another marriage, to Mr. Brumley, a well-meaning author who is avid to make Ellen his wife. Brumley is very well drawn, an appealing if rather comical combination of sensitivity, earnestness, and naïveté. He is anything but a lout; Ellen clearly likes him a great deal. But, luckily, she has not been disinherited by her husband, and at the novel's close she calmly declines Brumley's proposal, even suggesting that she will never marry, choosing instead, much in the manner of Arthur Kipps and Alfred Polly, to savor a sense of independence she has never known. "You see," she tells Brumley, "I have become a human being—owning myself." "It has been," she tells him, "like falling out of a prison from which one never hoped to escape. I feel like a moth that has just come out of its case,—you know how they come out, wet and weak but—released. For a time I can do nothing but sit in the sun."

5

The Later Novels

With *Mr. Britling Sees It Through,* Wells's popularity as a novelist reached an all-time high. *The Times Literary Supplement* was
not alone in regarding the book "a remarkable event," a "true
and fine" portrayal of Britain's middle class during a period of
increasingly horrid warfare.[1] *Mr. Britling* achieved huge sales; "it
became," Patrick Parrinder writes, "the most widely-read serious
novel of the war years."[2] In *Exasperations,* Wells writes that the
success of *Mr. Britling* during a period of wide suffering contrib-
uted to his decision to undertake *The Outline of History.* "My
wife and I were distressed," Wells writes, "to think that we had
made a good thing of a war that had hurt so many of our friends,
and, finding that there was a tremendous amount of foggy thinking about the necessity, biological value and outlook for war, we
determined to devote a year to earning no money at all while we
put together a summary of the whole human story." Ironically,
this "story" proved to be Wells's most immediately successful
publication. As Robert Bloom writes, the book "helped fix his
identity as a sage rather than a novelist"; once "the most gifted
imaginative writer of his generation," Wells now "emerged as a
guardian of civilization itself."[3] During the 1920s, Wells lectured
widely. He wrote newspaper columns and ran twice for parliament: he concentrated ever more intently on the production of
nonfictional prose.

Still, a fresh Wells novel appeared almost yearly throughout
the twenties and thirties. *Christina Alberta's Father* (1925) is
among the better of these: its title character, Albert Preemby, has
a lifelong penchant for revery; he decides, after the death of his
wife—one of a series of domineering mother-figures to appear in
Wells's fictions—that he is rather more than an eccentric little
man who once ran a laundry. He is the reincarnation of Sargon,
"the King of Kings"—ruler of Sumeria "thousands of years ago."

As such, Preemby begins a search for disciples, seeking to teach them, and the world, that this is "the Beginning of an Age." He has come to bring "Peace and not War among the Nations. Peace and not War among individuals. Peace in the street—in the work-room—in the shop. *Peace*." Preemby is less than successful, and soon finds himself confined to a mental asylum in Kent, "handed over to the nearly autocratic control of under-educated, ill-paid, ill-fed, and overworked attendants," to "a medical staff with no special training in mental science." Preemby's confinement here allows Wells, as narrator, to comment critically on the wretched-ness of mental health care in the first decades of the twentieth century, showing it to be inexcusably underfunded, and con-cerned more with confinement and control than with enlightened care. As a result, unfortunates like the harmless Preemby are "roughly handled" and "coarsely clothed"; they have "no other familiar company than the insane." They "have no privacy; no escape from those others; no peace. Our world herds these dis-cards together out of sight, walls them up, spends so little upon them that they are neither properly fed nor properly looked after, and does its brave hopeful best to forget all about them."

Such comments do of course accord with the hatred of disorder and social injustice that informs most of Wells's writing. But they are also informed by a sense of empathy and compassion that is not common in his earlier writings (and certainly not in *Antici-pations*); they stem, perhaps, from Wells's own growing aware-ness that he was himself susceptible to periods of depression and anxiety severe enough to leave him quite unable to function as steadily and efficiently as one of his strong-minded Samurai. (Rebecca West would recall that, in the early twenties, Wells's nervous despair was often especially intense, leaving him rest-less and vulnerable, and going "round and round like a rat in a maze.")[4]

Preemby's daughter, Christina Alberta, is herself more lucidly self-directed, another of Wells's attempts to portray sympatheti-cally an intelligent and ambitious young woman at odds with reigning social attitudes that would keep her silent and subdued. She is interested in science and the world of ideas; she hopes for "a world-wide social revolution." She is not, perhaps, a very well-realized character (few of Wells's later characters are), and reminds one of Ann Veronica Stanley, Wells's earlier portrait of youthful frustration and thwarted energy. In the course of the novel, Christina Alberta does, however, convincingly mature; her father's plight makes her question the belief in "the social framework" that had previously been at the core of her "radicalism and rebellion." She

> had assumed without thinking very much about it that hospitals were places of comfort and luxury, doctors in full possession and use of all existing science, prisons clean and exemplary places, that though laws might still be unjust that the administration of the law was untouched by knavery or weakness. She had had the same confidence in the ultimate integrity of social life that a little child has in the invincible safeness of nursery and home. But now she was awakening to the fact that the whole world was insecure. It was not that it was a wicked or malignant world, but that it was an inattentive and casual world. It dreaded bothers. It would do the meanest, most dangerous, and cruellest things to escape the pressure of bothers, and it would refuse to be bothered by any sufferings or evil it could possibly contrive to ignore. It was a dangerous world, a world of bothered people in which one might be lost and forgotten while one was still alive and suffering.

By far the most ambitious of Wells's final fictions is *The World of William Clissold,* which—at nearly eight hundred pages— made it one of the longest novels of the decade, comparable to James Joyce's *Ulysses.* Of course, Wells does not equal Joyce's intricate, painstaking artistry. *The World of William Clissold* contains little humor and relatively few memorable characterizations. Much of it covers ground that Wells had covered before. Occasionally, it drags. And yet, *The World of William Clissold* is, in its way, a work of some distinction--and remains among the most thoroughly readable of Wells's later novels. Its prose is often beautifully graceful; its tone relaxed, spacious, refined. In the main, it manages to convey Wells's attitudes on a wide array of subjects without sounding like a mere anthology of political tracts. Moreover, Clissold is himself an attractive figure, a blunt-talking businessman capable of frank self-analysis and continuing self-discovery. He is alert, perceptive, prodigiously well-informed. Nearing sixty, he regards himself "a fairly fortunate and happy man, glad to have lived and very glad still to be alive." He is vigorous, eager to lend his talents and experience to an enormous project—the making of a World Republic, a "scientifically organised world unity" that will fully release humanity's intellectual and creative powers.

In his preface to *The World of William Clissold,* Wells attempts to distance himself from his narrator, insisting that "this is not a

roman à clef," but "a work of fiction, purely and completely."
Clissold is simply Clissold, he writes, a "study of a modern type
seeking modes of self-realisation." Clissold does, however, share
certain general traits with Alred Mond, who ran the huge chemical company ICI. Mond—later Lord Melchett—was, as Krishan
Kumar explains, "one of the new breed of scientist-industrialist,"
the socially enlightened head of a successful conglomerate at a
time when "both the left and the right were hailing the conglom-
erates enthusiastically as the latest and most progressive organiza-
tional form in the modern world: the right because they were a
move towards 'rationalization,' the left because they were a half-
way house to 'nationalization.' "[5] Indeed, Mond had previously
expressed many of Clissold's more basic biases and beliefs in a
series of articles and addresses collected, in 1928, in *Industry and
Politics*. Mond distances himself from socialism; he is a "progressive" industrialist, seeking to create "an atmosphere of greater
confidence and comradeship between the co-partners of industry." Mond's own experience has taught him to avoid labor dis-
putes not by "waiting for claims to be made and then yielding to
them reluctantly," but by "forseeing reasonable demands and in
granting them even before they were asked." He seeks more careful industrial planning, and more cooperation between related in-
dustries; writing some thirty years before the establishment of the
Common Market, he points to growing competition from North
America and urges the nations of Europe to forge closer economic
bonds. Mond is not suspicious of scientists; indeed, "it is to the
chemist, the physicist, the biologist and the engineer that we have
to look to recreate our economic conditions, for it is only by the
better utilisation of the forces of nature, by more economical use,
by a greater efficiency in processes in existence, and by the creation of processes yet to come, that the wealth of the world, and
consequently the prosperity of its population, can be increased."[6]
  Clissold has achieved eminence with Romer, Steinhart, Crest
and Co., a worldwide minerological concern committed to earning profits without exploiting its workers, recognizing that "we
cannot afford to use our premises as a social battlefield." Thus
Clissold's company grants its workers generous salaries as well as
cultural and recreational facilities; it seeks their input in opera-
tional decisions, financing two weekly newspapers that explain
"what is going on in our business and what becomes of our products." The company's founder, Clissold notes, was a disciple of
Robert Owen, the British social theorist and die-hard optimist

who, in the early nineteenth century, designed and constructed model industrial towns that reflected his belief in careful social planning—in the kind of benign paternalism that Clissold himself comes to extol. "I won't pretend," Clissold admits, "that our virtue has had to struggle against our interests; old Steinhart's good intentions happen to have yielded the very best policy for us." Clissold does go beyond Mond on many points; he seeks not only more global economic cooperation and the more careful combining of science and industry; he calls for a "world directorate" capable of "actively organising the world production and world distribution of most staple products," including food, chemicals, steel. "It will in fact be the gigantic world-plant of which Romer, Steinart, Crest and Co., their allies, subsidiaries and associates, are the germ. It will be not a world kingdom nor a world empire nor a world state but a world business organisation."

Clissold is not the son of a shopkeeper and a housemaid. He does not serve time as a draper's apprentice. His father had become wealthy and influential before being caught in a series of suspicious financial dealings that led to scandal and his eventual suicide. But Clissold does have much in common with his creator. He studies science in South Kensington, and finds in Thomas Huxley "a great hero." He has known many women, and declines "to put a fig-leaf upon my account of myself"; indeed his ruminations on the rewards—and exasperations—of sex closely resemble those put forth by Wells in his later autobiographical writings. Clissold admits that, despite an "entire lack of personal splendour," he has been "what the eighteenth century called a rake"—but one who "never cheated, made dishonest promises, nor wilfully inflicted humiliation," who often found in his encounters "an exquisite sense of personal reception, a vividness of being," and who sought, far more than "bodily desire," a "kind of brightness, an elation, a material entanglement with beauty," the "other half of my androgynous self I had lost and had to find again." But elsewhere Clissold notes that "I have not seen much sexual happiness either in my own life or in the lives of those around me"; he acknowledges that his unending pursuit of his other, complementary half has never been achieved. "I have never found that completion," Clissold states. "For me, at any rate, it has been no more than a sustaining illusion."

Clissold also has thought much about God, deciding that he does not "find any necessity for religious phraseology to express my own apprehension of the drama of human existence." That apprehension is, however, fundamentally life-affirming; Clissold refers to "The Adventure of Life," and "The Adventure of Mankind"; he often notes with great delight the beauty of the land surrounding his home, which—like Wells's "Lou Pidou"—sits near Grasse, in the South of France. And Clissold's life, like Wells's, is imbued with religious impulses: he seeks wholeness and inner peace for himself and for all of humanity, a "comprehensive mental community" characterized by "fuller self-knowledge and self-direction." Clissold has grown "less self-centered, year by year," caring "more and more for the republic of mankind." This sense of selflessness he equates with "the fully adult life," which he believes can be universally obtained only when "man" is freed from "traditions, economic usages, social injustices, mental habits, encumbering institutions, needless subserviences and puerile interpretations, that dwarf, confuse and cripple life upon this planet, that divide it, impoverish it, keep it in a continual danger from the wasting fever of war and threaten him with extinction." Clissold believes that in the "salvation of the species lies the salvation of the individual." And because of continuing, ever improving advances in communications, education, and industrial technology, that belief will—he believes—prevail: people everywhere will "put away childish things, childish extravagances of passion and nightmare fears." Then:

Our minds will live in a living world literature and exercise in living art; our science will grow incessantly and our power increase. Our planet will become like a workshop in a pleasant garden, and from it we shall look out with ever diminishing fear upon our heritage of space and time amidst the stars.

To get there, Clissold insists, neither Marxism nor parliamentary democracy will ever suffice. It is "an aristocratic and not a democratic revolution" that Clissold hopes to foster; for, "I believe that the multitude, when it is suitably roused, can upset anything, but I do not believe it can create anything whatever." It will be then a "deliberate," not a "convulsive" process, blooming forth from the ever widening dissemination of scientific knowledge. It will be an "Open Conspiracy," the combined effort of "exceptional types," men and women "of experience, who have learnt about human affairs by handling them." They will ensure that their uncompromising vision will "radiate into the general mass"; they will be patient, aware that their enemy is the well-entrenched "egoist and fool in man, the ancestral, instinctive brute"; that opposition comes "as much in the suspicious and angry mob below as in the timid, mean, and violent propertied classes above."

The sense of qualified hopefulness that marks *The World of William Clissold* is echoed at the close of *Mr. Blettsworthy on Rampole Island* (1928), when a bookseller named Graves reminds the novel's principal character, Arnold Blettsworthy, of the "reconstruction in human affairs" that looms ahead. Graves envisions world peace; the last war, he believes, "*was* a war to end war and it will end war. There will never be a war so huge and silly as that last war." He notes too that, because of somewhat better schooling and the slow spread of civilizing ideas, even "business people are less grabbing, distrustful and competitive. The quantity of spite per head of population isn't a quarter of what it was in the days of Dickens and Thackeray." But such comments seem loosely glued to the conclusion of the novel, which—in structure and tone—makes one think of Voltaire. In it, Blettsworthy floats into a prolonged fantasy that places him on an island populated by cannibals who revere gigantic sloths, the *Megatheria* which Wells describes at length, and with the kind of precision and comic gusto that made such early works as *The First Men in the Moon* such a pleasure to read. The hide of these wonderfully ugly creatures is "a disagreeable pink, but mostly hidden by long coarse hairs that are almost quills, the colour of old thatch and infested not only with a diverse creeping population, including the largest black ticks I have ever beheld, but with a slimy growth of greenish algae and lichens that form pendent masses over the flanks and tail." The beast "usually moves forward in rheumatic jerks, usually with a grunt of self-preoccupation"—" 'Galumphing' would be quite a good word to express its paces." It looks about "with peculiar sniffing perturbations of a very flexible snout, and occasionally opens its mouth and emits a noise like that of a broken-hearted calf, but louder and more sustained." Despite such amusing interludes, *Mr. Blettsworthy on Rampole Island* is quite grim; it is, like *Candide*, a study in human illusion and barbarism, and another of Wells's sustained reminders of the humankind's less ennobling traits.

The Autocracy of Mr. Parham (1930) satirizes the sort of jingoistic, militaristic mentality that Wells felt was a principal impediment to his "Open Conspiracy." Parham is an academic who holds extremely right-wing views; like Blettsworthy—like too many of Wells's later characters—he one day enters a dreamlike state in which he believes himself engaged in palpably real events. In his fantasy, Parham turns into Lord Paramount, Britain's supreme commander, an unabashed imperialist with grand designs. He antagonizes both the Soviet Union and the United States; he seeks the development of a super weapon—a highly poisonous gas. Parham's militant actions lead to a confrontation between British and American fleets in the North Atlantic and bring on civil unrest in Britain itself. But he remains unapologetic. "What the devil are fleets and armies for," he proclaims, "if we are never to use them? What other ways are there for settling national differences? What's a flag for if you're never going to wave it?" The novel is predictable and flat, and is probably most notable for its splendid illustrations, provided by the well-known political cartoonist, David Low. It also contains a highly effective portrait of Mussolini, who appears briefly as an Italian dictator called Paramuzzi. When Paramount visits the pompous Paramuzzi in Rome, he is greatly impressed by the "tremendous saluting by serried Fascisti. They were patterned across to the Piazza Venetia. Never was saluting carried to higher levels than in Italy under Paramuzzi," comments the novel's narrative voice, which is linked closely with what Paramount himself thinks and observes. "They did marvellous things with their hands, their chests, their legs and knees, their chins and noses. They brought down their hands with a slap so unanimous and simultaneous that it was as if the sky had cracked." "London," the voice adds, "cannot do things in this style."

In *The Croquet Player* (1936), Wells presents, in the figure of Frobisher, another of his disliked types—another far more typical impediment to human progress. Frobisher is anything but ambitious: he is a bland, complacent member of the upper class, quite content to pass his days solving crossword puzzles and playing croquet. He describes himself as "indolent, self-indulgent" and having "an ineffective will." Christina Alberta would quickly recognize him as a man who simply does not wish to be bothered. He is, at thirty-three, the antithesis of Clissold's "fully mature" adult.

Frobisher's calm routine is ruined when—at a resort hotel in Les Noupets—he meets an English physician, Finchatton, with a weird tale to tell. Finchatton asserts that his hometown, Crainmarsh, is under siege by "grisly ghosts." They are, he is certain, the spirits of human ancestors of long ago, cavemen bent on inciting fear and violence in Crainmarsh's heretofore peaceable citizenry. Frobisher then meets Finchatton's psychiatrist, Dr. Norbert, who resembles "the old Punch pictures of the Grand Old Man, or Henry Irving, or Thomas Carlyle." Norbert assures Frobisher that Finchatton is, in fact, imagining things. There are no ghosts in Crainmarsh. There is something far worse—something Finchatton, like most people, would prefer to ignore, or attribute to some mysterious or supernatural force. There is growing violence in Crainmarsh and throughout the world only because human beings are not, after all, fully developed. "Man is still what he was," Norbert points out. "He is bestial, envious, malicious, greedy." "Man," he reminds Frobisher, is

the same fearing, snarling, fighting beast he was a hundred thousand years ago. These are no metaphors, Sir. What I tell you is the monstrous reality. The brute has been marking time and dreaming of a progress it has failed to make. Any archaelogist will tell you as much; modern man has no better skull, no better brain. Just a cave man, more or less trained. There has been no real change, no real escape. Civilisation, progress, all *that* we are discovering, was a delusion. Nothing was secured. Nothing. . . . It was artificial, it was artistic, fictitious. We are only beginning to realize *how* artificial. . . . It is breaking down all about us and we seem unable to prevent it.

Men like Finchatton, Norbert suggests, are unable "to face a world so grim and great as the world really is." And the world of as it really is—the world, in 1936, of Hitler and Mussolini, a world of tanks and airplanes being readied once more for war— is, Frobisher notes, "pretty black." There "is a rather unusual amount of massacre and torture going on nowadays." "But," Frobisher asks, "what am *I* to do about it?" He has certainly never given much thought to restructuring human society. He is willing, he supposes, to "fall in with anything that seems promising"; he is, in a vague kind of way, "for peace, order, social justice, service, and all that. But if I'm to *think!* If I'm to find out what to do with myself! That's too much." After listening to Norbert's catalogue of horrors, Frobisher decides that he "had enough of this apocalyptic stuff." "I don't care," he tells the psychiatrist. "The world *may* be going to pieces. The Stone Age may be returning. This may, as you say, be the sunset of civilisation. I'm sorry, but I can't help it this morning. I have other engagements."

The Croquet Player is a novella—running less than one hundred pages. Because of its clean, lean construction, it is one of the most effective of Wells's later fictions. It is also very representative of his later worldview. By the middle of the 1930s, Wells was finding it increasingly difficult to maintain a Clissold-like faith in world reform brought about by public-spirited people of influence and wealth. By then, he was fully aware of the steady slippage of his own influence and his literary reputation; he began to fear that his own life's work had been largely for naught—noting, in *Exasperations,* for example, that while *The Outline of History* sold millions of copies, "I do not think that more a minute percentage of that tremendous issue was ever more than glanced at." "I doubt," Wells writes, "if more than two or three thousand were ever attentively read. It was bought because it was the thing to buy it. It was bought and stowed away. When the topic of this H. G. Wells who was trying to tell the world something, came up, the good Anglo-Saxon world could say: We know all about H. G. W. We've got an illustrated copy of his *Outline* in the library and the Christmas before last we made it our gift book to all our friends."

The sense of exasperation that flavors *The Croquet Player* lingers on in *You Can't Be Too Careful,* Wells's final novel. Its central character, Edward Albert Tewler, is born into what Wells portrays as a stifling lower-middle-class environment; his mother likes to remind him that "you can't be too careful," to avoid all sorts of daily dangers, including dogs and cats. Cats, she tells him, "have pins in their toes, and sometimes these can be very poisonous pins. Lots of people have caught things from a cat's scratches. They bring measles into the house. They don't love you even when they purr." Tewler is orphaned in his early adolescence; unfortunately, he meets other adults of his class who similarly teach him to approach life with suspicion and fear. Thus by the time Tewler reaches adulthood he is, Wells sets out to show, woefully stunted—prepared only to muddle and bumble along. Tewler's wedding night proves particularly disastrous, and ends with his angry and embarrassed bride calling him, among other things, a "foul, disgusting young hog."

Tewler never achieves enlightenment; he ends up passing along his fears and prejudices to his son, warning him of the great danger posed by books, most of which are dangerously full of "ideers," and composed by "some cleverish *clever* chap who isn't reely anybody at all. Somebody who'd just jump at the chance of getting a 'undred pounds for writing a book to depress people and not mind what happens." "I was never a great reader," Tewler boasts, "and when I did read I stuck to safe books." After all, he notes, echoing his own mother, "you can't be too careful about those books."

For Wells, Tewler is all-too-typical, "a contemporary specimen man." *You Can't Be Too Careful* is, too, typical of Wells's later novels, featuring a few strong scenes and long, often tedious sections of social preaching. Wells of course hopes for the extinction of the Tewler type; but he is not optimistic. "Now that the environment of *Homo Tewler* has begun to change," he observes at one point, "and to an extent that would have been absolutely incredible fifty years ago, a ruthless energy calls upon him to adapt his mind and his way of living to these vast demands and become *Homo sapiens* indeed, before utter disaster overwhelms him. Can he? And will he?" Probably not, Wells concludes. Instead, he sees ahead "inquisitions" and "violent persecutions," and "storms of taboo terrorism." "Nature is a sloven," he adds, underlining the point he emphasized in *The Croquet Player*; "she never cleans up completely after her advances, and so we abound in vestigial structures, and our beings are haunted by the ghosts of rhythms that served her in the past."

In "Some Novelists I Have Known," Somerset Maugham notes that Wells "had a fluent pen and too often it ran away with him"; that, as a novelist, he increasingly put forth characters, like Tewler, who "are not individuals, but lively and talkative marionettes whose function it is to express the ideas he was out to attack or to defend." Maugham suggests that, in the main, Wells's later novels "are difficult to read with delight. You begin to read them with interest, but as you go on you find your interest dwindle and it is only by an effort of will that you continue to read."[7] And Maugham is right.

6

The Reputation

As Odette Keun remarked in 1934, H. G. Wells built his career exhorting and attacking the world; the world, in turn, repaid him "with an exorbitant lavishness; it rewarded his talents, his labor, his personality, with a responsiveness that is anything but the general rule."[1] By the early 1920s Wells had wealth, credibility, and access to the most powerful people of his age. His books were prominently displayed and carefully reviewed. Until his death, in 1944, Wells could count among his most ardent admirers many prominent literary names, including Sinclair Lewis, who praised Wells in a new American edition of *The History of Mr. Polly.* "There is no such thing as a 'greatest' novelist," Lewis wrote, "for how can you compare Lewis Carroll with Proust or Willa Cather with Dreiser? But it seems to me that just now, in 1941, there is no *greater* novelist living than Mr. H. G. Wells."[2]

But by the late 1920s, Wells's critical reputation had begun what would become a marked decline. Though his *Experiment in Autobiography* was widely praised, it became increasingly common for reviewers to point to the structural laxity and thematic predictability of Wells's latest offerings—and for other authors, like Aldous Huxley, to question seriously the moral validity of Wells's views. In 1932 Huxley published *Brave New World,* a much-acclaimed novel widely recognized as being, among other things, an attack upon Wellsian thinking—at least as conveyed in the more sanguine sections of Wells's utopian writings. As *Brave New World* demonstrates, Huxley was not convinced that science plus sex plus central planning would equal paradise. In *Brave New World,* a cool, rational ruling elite guarantees ample leisure and an abundance of food. Drugs that bring on euphoria are plentiful; orgies are State-approved. But it is a chilling place that Huxley portrays. Life is certain and safe—and it is sterile, appallingly hollow. As he later explained, Huxley did not doubt that "organization is indispensable; for liberty arises and has meaning only within a self-regulating community of freely co-operating individuals." But of course "organization can also be fatal."[3] In Wells's work, Huxley perceived—just beneath the promise of prosperity and release—a system of social organization and conditioning that could easily be abused, turning "men and women into automata," and choking off not only creativity but, ultimately, the very desire for freedom itself. Quite simply, Huxley argued, "it is unsafe to allow power to be concentrated in the hands of a ruling oligarchy"—particularly at a time when growing knowledge in the fields of psychology and chemistry have brought new refinements to methods of mind-control. "There seems to be no good reason," Huxley writes, "why a thoroughly scientific dictatorship should ever be overthrown."

In 1934, in a series of pieces published in the British journal *Time and Tide*, Keun herself dealt Wells a damaging blow.[4] Keun praised Wells's "imaginative powers," his "incomparable mastery of words," his "half a century of ceaseless creative toil." But her former lover was, she announced, less a social reformer than a self-promoter; in the final analysis, nothing interested him more than the forward thrust of his own career. Wells, according to Keun, was hypersensitive and vain. As thinker—and man—he was unsettled, capricious: he had no core. As a result, Wells shifted frequently from cause to cause, from grand scheme to grand scheme, often leaving many of his admirers and potential followers utterly confused. Once, Keun notes, Wells was a Fabian, but "before we knew what he was about, he was doing his best to discredit that patient body of generous and disinterested pioneers—and he consummated his ingratitude in *The New Machiavelli*." Wells worked intently for the League of Nations, but just as that organization had "begun to draw its first feeble breath," he declared it not worth his while. He ran twice for Parliament as a member of the Labour Party, but wound up pitching into that organization as well, "jibing and jeering at its door like a picket in a strike, and abandoning it at last in a gale of vituperation. In Wells's writings, Keun suggests, one can trace an erratic pattern of enthusiasms as they crest and wane. "In *God the Invisible King* he foists *tout do go* upon us a Wells-made and Wells-minded deity"; "in *The World of William Clissold,* it is not only Big Business and the Press that will set us straight, but Big Advertisement as well"; "in *Joan and Peter* Education is our escape." Keun concedes that Wells had "stimulated man with such torrential vigor that he was instrumental in bringing about our modern mentality." He "lifted minds in every country, and blazingly drove them along new paths and new vistas." And yet, "he never made a movement—not even the core of a movement." Why? Because Wells was "hasty and impulsive," regarding his intellectual and political activities as little more than a private game; because, despite his repeated assailing of self-absorption, he was himself "egotistic" and prone to pettiness—to turning "intellectual debates into a private quarrel." Over and over Wells called for concerted, collective action, but "put his shoulder to no steadily revolving wheel; he organized no group that might lead to an unswerving aim."

Keun does manage to catalogue a number of Wells's quirks and flaws; but many of her condemnations require qualification—and were undoubtedly colored by the fact that her once-intimate relationship with Wells came to a nasty, rancorous end. A more influential and cogent attack on Wells and his work appeared four years later, in Christopher Caudwell's *Studies and Further Studies in a Dying Culture*.[5] Caudwell was a Marxist writing at a time when an interest in Marxism among younger intellectuals in Britain and America ran high; when, as George Orwell would recall, "the Communist Party had an almost irresistible fascination for any writer under forty."[6] Wells, Caudwell writes, had clear artistic gifts, but proved again and again that he viewed art "as a means to success and the best road to cash." Indeed, according to Caudwell, Wells stands exposed as "the typical *petit bourgeois*," repeatedly, if unintentionally, revealing his ignorance of and loathing for the working class. Wells, the shopkeeper's son who spent the balmiest days of his youth grazing in a well-stocked library on a country estate, is "unable even to imagine what workers are like"; for "all he has of them is childhood memories of the proletarian abyss below the *petit bourgeois,* the dreadful Morlocks whom one must kill blindly when revolting they come up to the light of day." Moreover, he fails to transcend "his *petit bourgeois* reverence for the big bourgeois—the Roosevelt, the farseeing capitalist visualised as a Samurai." Thus Wells can only create "bourgeois dream-Utopias," with "characterless, commercialised, hygienic, eugenic, Aryan-Fascist uniformity." Wells, argues Caudwell, should begin to see the proletariat not as "passive inferior brutes," but as "the sole creative force of contemporary society." "This class," writes Caudwell, which Wells "comes to comfort and set free and relieve, has on the contrary the task of comforting and releasing and reviving him." "These sufferers afflicted by war and capitalist anarchy and slumps are to fight and destroy these very evils," Caudwell thunders; the world of Wells's youth, "whose ruins he sees tumbling on them, is to be rebuilt and more largely planned by them. This humiliating knowledge, which can only be won against his instincts, by an insight into the structure of the social relations in which he lives, is the most difficult of all wisdoms for the bourgeois to attain. Wells is a hundred miles from it."

Orwell had long admired Wells; in fact, in several of Orwell's own novels—in *Keep the Aspidistra Flying* (1936), for example, or *Coming Up for Air* (1939)—it is not hard to detect the influence of Kipps and, more particularly, *The History of Mr. Polly*. In "Wells, Hitler, and the World State," published as war in Europe raged, Orwell recalls fondly that, forty years earlier, "it was a wonderful experience for a boy to discover H. G. Wells," a "wonderful man who could tell you about the inhabitants of the planets and the bottom of the sea"; who knew that men would fly "because he himself *wanted* to be able to fly, and therefore felt sure that research in that direction would continue."[7] But now, Orwell too was ready to lodge a complaint, provoked by Wells's recent glib dismissal of Hitler as "that screaming little defective in Berlin"—with its implication that the German dictator was something less than a rather shrewd military commander who had managed to amass "an army of millions of men, aeroplanes in thousands, tanks in tens of thousands" and had successfully convinced "a great nation" to "overwork itself for six years and then to fight for two years more." Against this "criminal lunatic," Wells—Orwell writes—sets "the usual rigmarole about a World State, plus the Sankey Declaration."

Like too many left-leaning intellectuals, Wells, Orwell argues, had "for ten dreadful years" acted as if Hitler were little more than "a figure out of comic opera." Preaching "a commonsense, essentially hedonistic" vision of life and the world, he had proven himself "quite incapable of understanding that nationalism, religious bigotry and feudal loyalty are far more powerful forces than what he himself would describe as sanity." History, Orwell observes, is more than "a series of victories won by the scientific man over the romantic man"—as Germany itself had recently proved. "Modern Germany," he points out, "is far more scientific than England, and far more barbarous." Indeed, "much of what Wells has imagined and worked for is physically there in Nazi

Germany. The order, the planning, the State encouragement of science, the steel, the concrete, the aeroplanes, are all there, but all in the service of ideas appropriate to the Stone Age. Science is fighting on the side of superstition." It is this fact that Wells simply cannot accept—for it flies in the face of "the world-view on which his own works are based." According to Wells, "the war-lords and witch-doctors must fail," Orwell writes, "the common-sense World-State, as seen by the nineteenth-century Liberal whose heart does not leap at the sound of bugles, must triumph." That Hitler should eventually win "would be an impossible reversal of history, like a Jacobite restoration."

Comments like these angered Wells, who—in a letter to Orwell— snapped: "I don't say that at all. Read my early works, you shit." Indeed, though Orwell was one of the most perceptive writers of his generation, the summary he presents here and elsewhere of Wells's worldview is, in several key respects, flawed. For of course Wells had repeatedly warned that—given humanity's animalistic impulses—the march of progress is anything but absolute; that science without reason and tolerance could well turn the entire planet into the island of Doctor Moreau. Still, in the dark days of 1941, Orwell's savaging of one of his literary heroes is understandable. The existence of basic political freedoms, of free speech, and unfettered intellectual inquiry—the very things that Wells himself had defended—were now in grave jeopardy, threatened by a figure of monstrous evil and cunning. Suddenly, the sunnier of Wells's projections—a serene world full of cerebral nudists—must have seemed especially absurd, and anything but imminent. "What has kept England on its feet during the past year," Orwell writes, is in part "some vague idea about a better future, but chiefly the atavistic emotion of patriotism." "For the last twenty years," he notes, "the main object of English left-wing intellectuals has been to break this feeling down, and if they had succeeded, we might be watching the S.S. men patrolling the London streets at this moment."

Prior to the 1940s, the most trenchant and perhaps best-known criticism of Wells's skills as a novelist belonged to Virginia Woolf, who wrote dismissively of both Wells and his friend Arnold Bennett in one of her best-known critical essays, *Mr. Bennett and Mrs. Brown* (1928). Woolf argues "that it is to express character—not to preach doctrines, sing songs, or celebrate the glories of the British Empire, that the form of the novel . . . has been evolved."[8] The serious novelist (and, Woolf implies, the only sort of novelist worth taking seriously) will then consistently reveal an intense interest in the varieties and subtleties of human character—male or female, rich or poor, young or old. Woolf produces a prime candidate for such careful characterization—a small, prim, apparently impoverished woman of sixty or so with whom she chanced to share a compartment on a train traveling from Richmond to Waterloo. Woolf insists that neither Bennett nor Wells would be capable of rendering the fullness, the reality— the richness—of such a character; in fact, asking either of these men to create realistic characters "is precisely like going to a bootmaker and asking him to teach you how to make a watch." They could sketch her; they could describe her wardrobe and her bits of jewelry and the details of her surroundings, the carriage in which she rode, "the advertisements; the pictures of Swanage and Portsmouth; the way in which the cushion bulged between the buttons." But Wells "would instantly project upon the windowpane a vision of a better, breezier, jollier, happier, more adventurous and gallant world, where these musty railway carriages and fusty old women do not exist; where miraculous barges bring tropical fruit to Camberwell by eight o'clock in the morning; where there are public nurseries, fountains, and libraries, dining-rooms, drawing-rooms, and marriages; where every citizen is generous and candid, manly and magnificent, and rather like Mr. Wells himself." For "there are no Mrs. Browns in Utopia. Indeed I do not think that Mr. Wells, in his passion to make her what she ought to be, would waste a thought upon her as she is."

Equally damaging to Wells's literary reputation were the criticisms of Mark Schorer, a respected American academic writing in 1948, when the triumph of literary modernism—at least in departments of English—had cast an aura of sanctity around Jamesian attitudes to art. In his essay "Technique as Discovery," Schorer argues that Wells had "no respect for the techniques of his medium," producing in *Tono-Bungay* a work that, structurally speaking, is little more than chaos and pastiche.[9] According to Schorer, *Tono-Bungay* shows Wells floundering "through a series of literary imitations—from an early Dickensian episode, through a kind of Shavian interlude, through a Conradian episode, to a Jules Verne vision at the end." Worse, because he declined to apply even "a minimum of attention to the virtues of technique," Wells failed to establish "a point of view and a tone" that would have better clarified his artistic and intellectual intentions. Wells, Schorer writes, simply failed to grasp the revolution in fiction that James and Conrad and Joyce had brought about—one based upon the recognition "that technique is not the secondary thing that it seemed to Wells, some external machination, a mechanical affair, but a deep and primary operation" that "*contains* intellectual and moral implications" even as "it *discovers* them." According to Schorer, Joyce's *A Portrait of the Artist as a Young Man*, another "autobiographical" novel, stands as the antithesis to *Tono-Bungay*, for it "analyzes its material rigorously" and defines "the value and the quality of its experience not by appended comment or moral epithet, but by the texture of the style."

One of the century's great writers, Jorge Luis Borges, recorded his deep appreciation for Wells—and particularly his scientific romances—in an essay, "The First Wells," published in 1946.[10] These works, Borges notes, are not only ingenious, but universal in their appeal. Like all "work that endures," they are rich in symbolism, and "capable of an infinite and plastic ambiguity," reflecting "the reader's own traits" while providing, too, "a map of the world." They are "ambiguous in an evanescent and modest way"—in a way that suggests that Wells himself was "ignorant of all symbolism," writing with a kind of "lucid innocence." In fact, Borges has no doubt that such works will survive; that Wells, "like Quevedo, like Voltaire, like Goethe, like some others," is "less a man of letters than a literature," producing—among other things—"garrulous books in which the gigantic felicity of Charles Dickens somehow reappears," while constructing encyclopedias and enlarging "the possibilities of the novel." Borges writes:

Of the vast and diversified library he left us, nothing has pleased me more than his narration of some atrocious miracles: *The Time Machine, The Island of Doctor Moreau, The Plattner Story, The First Men in the Moon.* They are the first books I read; perhaps they will be the last. I think they will be incorporated, like the fables of Theseus or Ahasuerus, into the general memory of the species and even transcend the fame of their creator or the extinction of the language in which they were written.

During the 1940s, Borges was still relatively unknown in English-speaking countries; his assessment of Wells—translated and published in the United States in 1964—was not then widely noticed. It was probably Bernard Bergonzi who did most to initiate the more recent appreciation for Wells as literary artist. In *The Early H. G. Wells* (1960), Bergonzi makes clear that he has little interest in Wells's later writings, which reveal that Wells "had a temperamental strain of impatience that made him incapable of tolerating the difficulties and problems and disappointments that are inextricably part of the texture of normal life. He wished, in short, for a world where nothing would ever go wrong; or, in other words, a world where no one need ever grow up." "For all their elaborate apparatus of applied science and social engineering," writes Bergonzi, "Wells's utopias are the projection of a radically immature view of human existence."[11]

Bergonzi's *The Early H. G. Wells* focuses then on Wells as "an imaginative writer rather than a purveyor of ideas," on the stories and novels he published during the 1890s and the first years of the twentieth century. Bergonzi persuasively shows that these early romances "are something more than the simple yarns they are generally taken to be"; they often reflect many of "the dominant preoccupations of the *fin de siècle* period" in which they appeared. As Bergonzi notes, there was then common a keen sense, shared by artists and intellectuals of varying styles and temperaments, that "the nineteenth century—which had contained more events, more history than any other— had gone on too long, and that sensitive souls were growing weary of it." It was also, however, a period of doubt and uncertainty, of "foreboding about the future," of "*fin du globe,* the sense that the whole elaborate intellectual and social order of the nineteenth century was trembling on the brink of dissolution." The *fin du globe* myth is, as Bergonzi shows, "a dominant element in Wells's early work," perhaps most noticeably in *The War of the Worlds,* which—as Bergonzi points out—"first appeared as a magazine serial in 1897, the year of the second Victorian jubilee, when national complacency and self-righteousness had reached such a peak that even Kipling felt obliged to deliver a warning in his 'A Recessional.'" Bergonzi was able to shed new light on Wells's works by discussing them in their cultural context; he stirred particular interest in the symbolic and mythic complexities of *The Time Machine,* showing it to reflect, among other things, "an opposition between aestheticism and utilitarianism, pastoralism and technology, contempla-

tion and action, and ultimately, and least specifically, between
beauty and ugliness, and light and darkness."

David Lodge similarly helped return Wells's fiction to critical
respectability by demonstrating how, in *Tono-Bungay*, Wells had
created "an impressive, and certainly coherent work of art."[12]
True, it does contain "examples of loose grammar and careless
punctuation which obscure meaning and serve no perceptible ex-
pressive function." But then, Wells's undertaking here "does not
require the elegant, harmonious intricate kind of language
adopted by James, but a language that is hurried, urgent, groping." Lodge locates *Tono-Bungay* in the tradition of the "Condition of England novel" common to the nineteenth century—
novels like Disraeli's *Sybil* (1845) and Charles Kingsley's *Alton
Locke* (1850), which focus similarly on "the changing nature of
English society in an era of economic, political, religious, and
philosophical revolution." Lodge points to "the web of description and commentary by which all the proliferating events and
characters of the story are placed in a comprehensive political,
social, and historical perspective"; in fact, "it is the language of
the novel that binds it into a unified whole, setting up verbal echoes that establish connections between the many disparate subjects of George's discourse, and giving that discourse a consistent
and individual tone of voice." Wells, as Lodge shows, also
"chooses his pathological metaphors with care in *Tono-Bungay*;
he offers descriptions that are brilliantly vivid, creating an image
of London that remains remarkably accurate, and stays long in
the mind."

In more recent years, such critics as John Batchelor, J. R. Hammond, David Smith, and John R. Reed have looked insightfully
and objectively at Wells's work, pointing to its weaknesses without denying its obvious strengths—its vitality, clarity, and often
surprising complexity. "Wells," writes Batchelor, "is a great artist, and those of us who enjoy his work need not feel ashamed of
the pleasure that we take in reading him."[13] Peter Kemp, in *H. G.
Wells and the Culminating Ape* (1982), an extremely insightful
and entertaining book, is less concerned with revealing Wells'
artistry than in tracing the "biological themes" that pervade his novels, the "powerful obsessions" that stem from Wells's scientific
training, his sense that humanity is—in Wells's own words—"animal rough-hewn to a reasonable shape."[14] "Wells writes not just
as a biologist," Kemp notes, "but as a highly idiosyncratic personality whose very individual menagerie of hobby-horses and

bêtes noires is unleashed at every opportunity." Hence, the constant treatment of "food, sex, habitat" in Wells's fictions—and the odd preoccupation with, among other things, tentacles.

As Kemp portrays him, Wells is less interesting for the bulk of his art than the complex and often tormented nature of his personality. Much of his fiction is, after all, "very second hand"; Wells regularly recycles material, even entire books. As Kemp notes, *Babes in the Darkling Wood* (1940), "seems a virtual rewrite of *Joan and Peter*." The central female character in *Christina Alberta's Father* is, Kemp adds, "really Ann Veronica reincarnated." As Kemp accurately observes, in Wells's later books,

> life is not so much portrayed as theorised about; inventiveness yields to the doctrinaire. The early works are constantly enriched with unexpected detail scooped from life by deftly imaginative phrases. In the later ones, predictable generalisations are ponderously laid down across pages of prosy *longueurs*. Wells's imagination is increasingly tethered by his sense of self-importance.

Wells did squander much of his enormous talent. Despite calling repeatedly for selflessness and the transcendence of ego, Wells was thoroughly self-absorbed; he could find few human beings as fully fascinating as himself—obviously a major shortcoming in a novelist with serious artistic aspirations. Wells was able, then, to write again and again of the life of H. G. Wells, casting himself variously as Arthur Kipps, Arthur Polly, Richard Remington, William Clissold and Hugh Britling—even as Ann Veronica Stanley, with her youthful passion for science and her impatience with unexamined social assumptions. Like Dickens, Wells had a fine sense of comedy, an unusually good ear for the patterns and rhythms of speech, and the rare ability to blend detail and atmosphere in the making of highly memorable descriptions and scenes. Like Dickens, he had no trouble constructing a compelling narrative, or maintaining the kind of rigorous writing routine that enabled him to publish prolifically and profitably. But because of his increasing self-absorption, Wells could not, like Dickens, continuously create characters like Bob Cratchit or Esther Summerson, like Pickwick or Peggoty or Micawber or Pip—characters who are not only fully realized but richly varied, and maintain a universal appeal.

And of course, as Wells himself admitted, the ability to maintain a steady writing routine is itself no guarantee of consistent quality. In the beginning of his career, as he worked desperately to survive both professionally and economically, Wells produced his very best work. But he was always susceptible to distraction, and once he found himself with ample opportunities to play the part of the famous prophet and sage, he found it increasingly difficult to sustain the kind of intense concentration that is essential for the steady production of first-rate work. Artistically, Wells ceased to stretch and chose to coast. True, there is almost always something to admire in even the least of Wells's fictions; often, there is intellectual power, lively dialogue, stylistic grace. But, as frequently, there is little more than garrulousness and pontification, symptoms of an unusually gifted man operating on automatic pilot, repackaging characters and plots and justifying this practice by insisting, disingenuously, that he never aspired to artistic greatness anyway. *The Shape of Things to Come, Brynhild, The Holy Terror*: such works are, as H. L. Mencken might have put it, as dead as Baalam's ass. They are likely to appeal, today, to only the most ardent of Wells's devotees.

As his strongest admirers tend not to note, Wells did possess a highly unappealing totalitarian streak; as a writer on philosophical and social matters he was frequently riveting, convincing, and moving, but neither particularly original nor profound. Indeed, there are very few key Wellsian ideas that cannot be traced directly to Thomas Huxley or Winwood Reade. As Odette Keun rightly observed, Wells could be remarkably contradictory, revering God in one work while proclaiming atheism in another, often undercutting his sane and powerful pleas for social justice and world peace by his own shouts of intolerance and belligerency. And though he regularly attacked bourgeoise values, Wells was himself something of a Philistine. He had relatively little interest in any art that did not, like his own, further social reform. Thus late in his life, as the war in Europe dragged on, Wells could be found urging the Allies to begin the heavy bombing of Rome, and particularly the Vatican, suggesting that the preservation of paintings and frescoes was, after all, a trifling concern. For were there not copies and photographs of these masterpieces readily available everywhere? ("For the better part of three centuries," writes Wells in *Exasperations,* "these 'art treasures' have been copied, studied, engraved and made familiar to our eyes." They "can be recalled exactly as they were—directly we recover sufficient world equanimity to set about it. That is the answer to all this 'art treasure' balderdash.") In fact, it is in his later fulminations against the Catholic Church, most crudely displayed in

Crux Ansata (1943), that one can observe Wells in his least attractive light. The tone of tolerant truth-seeking that informs *Mr.
Britling Sees it Through* (and, to a lesser extent, *God the Invisible
King*) is quite gone, replaced by boorish bigotry. Reading *Crux
Ansata*, one realizes that, in many ways, Wells remained Sarah's
boy, curiously rooted in a brand of fundamentalist Protestantism
that was ever alert to the dark machinations of Rome. One thinks
not of William James, but Ian Paisley.

Still, it remains a fact that nearly one hundred years after their
publication such works as *The Time Machine, The War of the
Worlds, The Invisible Man* continue to sell well throughout the
world, reminding yet another generation of readers of Wells's
imaginative powers and narrative skills, his brilliant ability to
combine humor with suspense, to make bring an air of plausibility to the utterly impossible. Other works—including *Kipps,
Tono-Bungay,* and the *History of Mr. Polly*—also remain health-
ily in print, kept alive by well-made plots and the most satisfying
of Wells's characterizations. Such novels as *The New Machiavelli*
and *The Passionate Friends* have recently been reissued in paper-
back, further indicating that, nearly fifty years after his death,
much of what Wells wrote has proven to be more durable—and
influential—than he himself had foreseen. Indeed, as the twentieth century comes to a close, there is a growing sense that a new
generation of leaders in both the East and West have come to
understand that war is inevitably more of a curse than a cure.
More and more one hears talk of continued world unity through
cultural and scientific exchanges and increased global trade. The
sort of rabid nationalism that brought on two world wars
has been diminishing for decades; a kind of "United States of
Europe"—an utter impossibility when Wells wrote *The War of
the Worlds* and *The War in the Air*—now appears all but inevitable, a going concern by the twenty-first century. In Europe, and
throughout much of the world, science is respected and informa-
tion is plentiful, accessible; because of growing governmental ex-
penditures, educational options have broadened enormously for
people of all ages and classes; opportunities for women continue
to expand. Human beings have walked on the moon and now
probe the depths of space; satellites fill the skies. For several decades, Wells was one of the world's most widely read serious authors. Clearly, he played a crucial role in helping create the
mental and social environment in which such events could, however belatedly, take place.

Of course, in other respects, the world that Wells had exhorted and excoriated at the turn of the century remains little changed. There is everywhere fear, violence, illiteracy, poverty, greed. In much of the world, population growth remains dangerously unchecked; cities choke in pollution made possible because of governmental indifference and, too frequently, a total lack of respect for the idea of careful social planning. Indeed, it is impossible to read, in *Tono-Bungay*, of poisonous, ever-spreading Quap and not think of leaking power plants and fouled oceans, of ravaged tropical forests and growing holes in the layer of ozone that protects the earth's atmosphere and, thus, all of earthly life. There is strong and mounting evidence that, in fact, decades of unceasing carelessness and waste could well produce, soon, a change in the earth's climate severe enough to bring on a wide range of horrors—including massive drought and famine and coastal floods that will wipe out cities and create new geographical outlines. Without wide and immediate action—without, for example, systematic cuts in the use of those fuels that produce carbon dioxide—it is quite possible that Wells's vision of the apocalypse could materialize. His image of a bleak and barren earth will no longer be merely a chilling image in a haunting fiction. Our world is not likely to made better by squads of Wells's pious airmen leveling buildings and burning books. But that it could still use far more education and anticipation—and far less illusion—would be hard to deny. At his best, Wells stood for the best in humanity: for reason, foresight, courage, cooperation, hope. And it is at his best that he deserves to be remembered and read.

Notes

Chapter 1: The Life

1. George Orwell, "Wells, Hitler and the World State," in his *Collected Essays* (London: Secker & Warburg, 1961), p. 164.

2. George Bernard Shaw, "The Man I Knew," *The New Statesman and Nation* (August 17, 1946): 115. Although they were friends, and shared similar political views, Wells and Shaw often exchanged criticisms. In *The Work, Wealth, and Happiness of Mankind* (pp. 533–34), for example, Wells suggests that Shaw possessed "an essentially scientific mind that has never undergone mental discipline, it is a scientific mind that was found and brought up by musicians and artists, and it has been greatly depraved by his irresistible sense of fun and his unsurpassed genius for platform effect. His is a fine intelligence which is always going off on the spree . . . His indolence is about fundamentals. He betrays an unwillingness to scrutinize the springs of his opinions, and these springs arise, more directly than is usual among minds of his calibre, from personal attachments and reactions." Wells's focusing on Shaw's lack of proper scientific training is typical; he would level similar charges against Henry James and Joseph Conrad, among others.

3. Rebecca West, review of *Marriage, Freewoman* (September 19, 1912), in Patrick Parrinder, ed., *H. G. Wells: The Critical Heritage* (London: Routledge & Kegan Paul, 1972), p. 207.

4. Norman and Jeanne MacKenzie, *The Life of H. G. Wells: The Time Traveller*, revised edition (London: The Hogarth Press, 1987), p. 33.

5. Winwood Reade, *The Martyrdom of Man* (New York: The Truth Seeker Company, n.d.), p. 491. The quotations that follow are found in the book's final chapters; see especially "The Future of the Human Race" and "The Religion of Reason and Love." Although not widely known, *The Martyrdom of Man* has remained consistently in print in numerous editions. George Orwell, reviewing the book in 1946, called it "that queer, unhonored masterpiece," a "vision, or epic, inspired by the conception of progress." See Sonia Orwell and Ian Angus, eds., *The Collected Essays, Journalism and Letters of George Orwell*, Volume 4 (London: Secker & Warburg, 1968), pp. 116–20.

6. As Owen Chadwick writes, "*The Life of Jesus* was a landmark; no landmark in theology, where its influence was negligible or neglected, but in the attitude of the middle class to religion. It was the first time that a biography of the man was written, which excluded the supernatural and at the same time was aimed at the

general reader and written by a master of the evidence." Renan's book "shows a person moving through primitive stories of wonders and exorcisms. If we could get behind these layers of piety to find the man, we should not only understand him better for ourselves but make him intelligible again to all men. The Christ we have received is a Christ who stands outside history, and anyone who stands outside history is not a man. Therefore we must put him back into history." Renan's Jesus is a "self-sacrificial genius of ethical understanding, who by the union between moral person and moral teaching changed the world"; he is an "incomparable man, admirable teacher." See Chadwick, *The Secularization of the European Mind in the Nineteenth Century* (Cambridge: Cambridge University Press, 1975), pp. 219–21.

7. Charles Darwin, *The Origin of Species* and *The Descent of Man* (New York: The Modern Library, n. d.), pp. 98–100. See chapter 4, "Natural Selection; or the Survival of the Fittest."

8. Matthew Arnold, *Culture and Anarchy* (Ann Arbor: The University of Michigan Press, 1965), pp. 90–114. See chapter 1, "Sweetness and Light."

9. George Eliot, "Oh May I Join the Choir Invisible," in *The Poetical Works of George Eliot* (New York: Thomas Y. Crowell, n. d.) pp. 441–42. Eliot translated two controversial studies of Christianity, D. F. Strauss's *Life of Jesus*, which appeared in 1846, and Ludwig Feuerbach's *The Essence of Christianity*, published eight years later. As Owen Chadwick writes, for Feuerbach, "God is an idea which makes personal the infinite aspect of man's nature. Man is divine, and so projects this divinity into supernatural Being. Knowledge of God is knowledge of the self, or rather of all human selves." See Chadwick, p. 54.

10. See Thomas Huxley, "The Struggle for Existence in Human Society," in Alburey Castell, ed., *Selections from the Essays of Thomas Huxley* (New York: Appelton-Century-Crofts, 1948), pp. 59–69. This essay, one of Huxley's best known, has been widely reprinted. For a particularly thorough discussion of Huxley's influence on Wells, see Roslynn Haynes, *H. G. Wells: Discoverer of the Future* (New York: New York University Press, 1980).

11. Hugh Kenner, *A Sinking Island: The Modern English Writers* (New York: Knopf, 1988), p. 47.

12. James M. Barrie, *When a Man's Single* (New York: William L. Allison, n. d.), pp. 118–19.

13. Israel Zangwill, review of *The Time Machine,* *The Pall Mall Magazine* (September 1895), in Dennis Poupard, ed., *Twentieth Century Literary Criticism*, volume 12 (Detroit: Gale, 1984), p. 487. See also Parrinder, *H. G. Wells: The Critical Heritage*, pp. 40–42.

14. In Parrinder, *H. G. Wells: The Critical Heritage*, p. 60.

15. Kingsley Amis, *New Maps of Hell: A Survey of Science Fiction* (New York: Arno Press, 1975), p. 41.

16. Quoted in Parrinder, *H. G. Wells: The Critical Heritage*, p. 83;

17. Rebecca West, *The New Meaning of Treason* (New York: The Viking Press, 1967), p. 147.

18. William Lyon Phelps, *The Advance of the English Novel* (New York: Dodd, Mead and Company, 1916), p. 253.

19. See Anthony Burgess, "Inexhaustible Wells," in *But Do Blondes Prefer Gentelmen?* (New York: McGraw-Hill, 1986), pp. 378–82. In his review of Wells's *Mankind in the Making* (1903), Havelock Ellis had similarly pointed to Wells's "parochialism." "The evolution of man," writes Ellis, "if it means anything, must affect the whole species, and not a single section. Mr. Wells confines himself exclusively to the English-speaking lands, and through a great part of his book he is very much occupied with tinkering at some of our cherished institutions. The preacher who set out by proclaiming salvation for mankind invites us to contribute to the fund for the new organ." See Ellis, "Another Prophet: H. G. Wells," in *Views and Reviews: A Selection of Uncollected Articles 1884–1932*, First Series: 1884–1919 (London: Desmond Harmsworth, n.d.), pp. 204–12.

20. Wells offers a lengthy summary of his later views on eugenics in *The Work, Wealth and Happiness of Mankind*, 2, pp. 745–49. He does not object to the sterilization of "criminals convicted of brutish violence," nor to "the temporary or permanent sterilization of those who have contracted hereditable diseases." But he dismisses Francis Galton's theory that there are "large, indisputably superior people in the world, moving about amidst the small inferior multitudes, and that it would be possible to pick out, mate, and breed these superiors." This notion of "positive eugenics" overlooks the fact that "human relationships are complex and subtle," Wells argues; that "the characteristics of an individual are not the expression of all his hereditable possibilities."

21. See Jonathan Rose, *The Edwardian Temperament, 1895–1919* (Athens: Ohio University Press, 1986), p. 137. In chapter 4, "The Efficiency Men," Rose provides a good summary of the popular eugenical belief in turn-of-the-century Britain, noting—for example—that "A Liberal government, under considerable pressure, passed the Mental Deficiency Act of 1913, which authorized the forcible segregation and institutionalization of the feeble-minded." Churchill drafted the legislation. For more on Shaw's often overlooked totalitarian impulses, see Arnold Silver, *Bernard Shaw: The Darker Side* (Stanford: Stanford University Press, 1982). Shaw's own "destructive passion," writes Silver, "encompassing both sadistic and homicidal urges, was more gratified by dictatorships than by parliamentary systems, whose laws and habits of debate impeded the use of terror. In his comments on dictatorships Shaw clearly identified himself, not with the citizenry, but with the rulers who broke people, poured castor oil into them, exterminated them. He felt that Hitler should have given him credit for introducing the idea of gas chambers, and he congratulated himself for instilling in the Russian leaders the idea of liquidation. He thoroughly sympathized with Stalin's extermination of five million peasants by starvation, and he looked forward to introducing extermination procedures into England. According to his secretary, Blanche Patch, he startled a group of simple Lancashire chapel-goers with his remedy for idlers: 'I would like to take everyone before a tribunal, and, if it were found that they were not doing as much for the community as the community was doing for them, I would give them a few days to make their peace and put them in a lethal chamber.' Miss Patch insists on her employer's perfect sincerity in advancing this proposal, and it is of course an extension of his frequently propounded belief that all incorrigible criminals should be killed" (pp. 40–41).

22. Margaret Sanger, "Is Race Suicide Probable?" *Collier's* (August 15, 1925), p. 25.

23. Max Beerbohm, "Perkins and Mankind," in his *A Christmas Garland* (London: Heinemann, 1950), pp. 33–46.

24. For an insightful and entertaining discussion of Wells' relationship with James and Conrad during his time at Sandgate, see Nicholas Delbanco, *Group Portrait* (New York: William Morrow, 1982).

25. For an especially perceptive discussion of the responses of several British writers—including Wells—to the phenomenon of America, see Peter Conrad, *Imagining America* (New York: Oxford University Press, 1980).

26. In Dan H. Laurence, ed., *Bernard Shaw: Collected Letters, 1898–1910* (New York: Dodd, Mead & Company, 1972), p. 650.

27. Quoted in Parrinder, *H. G. Wells: The Critical Heritage*, p. 15.

28. John St. Loe Strachey, review of *Ann Veronica*, the *Spectator* (November 20, 1909), in Parrinder, *H. G. Wells: The Critical Heritage*, pp. 169–70.

29. Wilfred Whitten, review of *Ann Veronica*, *T. P.'s Weekly* (October 22, 1909), in Parrinder, *H. G. Wells: The Critical Heritage*, pp. 161, 164.

30. In Walter Hooper, ed., *They Stand Together: The Letters of C. S. Lewis to Arthur Greeves (1914–1963)* (London: Collins, 1979), p. 264. For a good discussion of Lewis's objections to writers who share a Wellsian worldview, see Michael D. Aeschliman, *The Restitution of Man: C. S. Lewis and the Case against Scientism* (Grand Rapids, Michigan: Eerdmans, 1983).

31. Rebecca West, review of *Marriage*, in Parrinder, *H. G. Wells: The Critical Heritage*, pp. 203–8.

32. Gordon N. Ray, *H. G. Wells & Rebecca West* (New Haven: Yale University Press, 1974), p. 7.

33. Anthony West, *H. G. Wells: Aspects of a Life* (New York: Random House, 1984), pp. 56–57.

34. Something of Wells's tendency to contradict himself can be found in his comments on this novel. In his preface to volume 25 of the "Atlantic" edition of his collected works (1927), Wells calls *The Secret Places of the Heart* "quite a good piece of work." Writing a decade or so later, in *Exasperations*, Wells dismisses the novel as "the worst bale of writing I ever committed, that I am glad to clear off my chest. I deplore it, but than Heaven! it is out of print and it can be kept so."

35. Victoria Glendinning, *Rebecca West: A Life* (London: Weidenfeld and Nicolson, 1987), p. 84.

36. Ibid., p. 50.

37. "The Younger Generation" is reprinted in full in Leon Edel and Gordon N. Ray, eds., *Henry James and H. G. Wells: A Record of their Friendship, their De-*

bate on the Art of Fiction, and their Quarrel (Urbana: University of Illinois Press, 1958), pp. 178–215. This volume contains the pertinent portions of Boon, as well as the letters between Wells and James that were exchanged in the wake of that book's publication.

38. Kenner, A Sinking Island, p. 73.

39. Rebecca West would offer a similar criticism of James's later style in her Henry James (New York: Henry Holt, 1916), pp. 107–8. "With sentences vast as the granite blocks of the pyramids, and a scene that would have made a site for a capital," James—writes West—" set about constructing a story the size of a hen-house. The type of these unhappier efforts of Mr. James' genius is The Sacred Fount (1901), where . . . he records how a weekend visitor spends more intellectual force than Kant can have used on The Critique of Pure Reason in an unsuccessful attempt to discover whether there exists between certain of his fellow-guests a relationship not more interesting among these vacuous people than it is among sparrows. The finely wrought descriptions of the leisured life make one feel as though one sat in a beautiful old castle, granting its beauty but not pleased, because one is a prisoner, while the small, mean story worries one like a rat nibbling at the wainscot." For more on the Wells / West attack on James and his defenders, see Delbanco, pp. 137–79.

40. See William James, "The Moral Equivalent of War," in Bruce W. Wilshire, ed., William James: The Essential Writings (Albany: State University of New York Press, 1984), pp. 349–61. James quotes from First and Last Things in this essay, noting that "H. G. Wells, as usual, sees the centre of the situation" regarding the need to move "contemporary man" to "a higher plane, into an atmosphere of service and cooperation and of infinitely more honorable emulations." In God the Invisible King, Wells calls James "my friend and master."

41. For more background on Wells's religious attitudes, see William Archer, God and Mr. Wells: A Critical Examination of "God the Invisible King" (London: Watts, 1917) and Willis B. Glover, "Religious Orientation of H. G. Wells: A Case Study in Scientific Humanism," Harvard Theological Review 65 (1972): pp. 117–35. Though Wells's religious views sparked discussion and debate, they were not entirely unique; indeed, by 1915, attempts by artists and intellectuals to synthesize a demystified form of Christianity with a spirit of social reform were commonplace. See, for example, Jonathan Rose's discussion of T. H. Green's philosophy in The Edwardian Temperament, pp. 17–20. As Glover notes, remnants of Wells's "new religion" persist in Julian Huxley's Religion Without Revelation (1957). Huxley, a grandson of T. H. Huxley, co-authored, with Wells, The Science of Life.

42. For an extensive discussion of Wells's prolonged debate with the highly persistent Jones, see Vincent Brome, Six Studies in Quarrelling (London: Cresset Press, 1958). Brome also discusses Wells's debates with Shaw, James, and Belloc.

43. A. W. Gomme, Mr. Wells as Historian: An Inquiry into those parts of Mr. H. G. Wells' "Outline of History" which Deal with Greece and Rome (Glasgow: Maclehose, Jackson & Company, 1921), p. 4. For a more recent evaluation of Wells's intentions and skills as a historian, see John Barker, The Superhistorians (New York: Scribner's, 1982).

44. See especially Hilaire Belloc, *A Companion to Mr. Wells's "Outline of History"* (London: Sheed and Ward, 1929) and Richard Downey, *Some Errors of H. G. Wells: A Catholic's Criticism of "The Outline of History"* (London: Burns Oates, 1921). "We know of no history," observes Downey, "in which the personal equation is so pronounced as in this work of Mr. Wells. We have here not so much a record of human affairs as the vision of an artist enraptured with the pageant of the ages; the passion of a democrat railing at kings and princes; the wail of a pacifist over the strifes of men; and in it all and through it all, the spirit of emancipation chafing at all restraint. This spirit is in some measure responsible for his attitude to the Catholic Church, but his marked antagonism has deeper roots. A church which is *semper eadem* cannot well be made to harmonize with a philosophy of change, and Mr. Wells is the Heraclitus of history proclaiming universal flux" (pp. 56–57).

45. E. M. Forster, review of *The Outline of History,* the *Athenaeum,* (July 2 and 9, 1920), in Parrinder, *H. G. Wells: The Critical Heritage,* p. 248.

46. H. L. Mencken, "H. G. Wells *Redivivus,"* in William H. Nolte, ed., *H. L. Mencken's "Smart Set" Criticism* (Washington, D.C.: Gateway Editions, 1987), p. 218.

47. Later, arguments also arose concerning the originality of Wells's design for the *Outline of History.* In 1928, Florence Deeks, a Canadian, filed suit against Wells, claiming that the *Outline* drew heavily upon her *The Web of History,* which had floated through various editorial offices in manuscript form. The suit—which was eventually dismissed in court—attracted much publicity and cost Wells and his publishers several thousand pounds.

48. In Wells, *The Story of a Great Schoolmaster* (New York: Macmillan, 1924), p. 167.

49. D. H. Lawrence, *"The World of William Clissold,"* in Edward D. McDonald, ed., *Phoenix: The Posthumous Papers of D. H. Lawrence* (Middlesex: Penguin, 1978), pp. 346, 350.

50. A. A. M. Thomson, *The World of Billiam Wissold* (London: Hurst and Blackett, 1928), p. 12.

51. H. L. Mencken, "The Late Mr. Wells," in *Prejudices: First Series* (New York: Knopf, 1919), pp. 24–26.

52. See H. L. Mencken, review of *The World of William Clissold, American Mercury* (December 1926), in Parrinder, *H. G. Wells: The Critical Heritage,* pp. 282–85.

53. Henry Hazlitt, "The Wellsian Bible," the *Nation* 133 (December 30, 1931), p. 727–28.

54. See, for example, Robert Bloom, *Anatomies of Egotism: A Reading of the Last Novels of H. G. Wells* (Lincoln: University of Nebraska Press, 1977), chapter 2, and John Batchelor, *H. G. Wells* (Cambridge: Cambridge University Press, 1985), pp. 145–53.

55. Joseph Wood Krutch, "Prophet into Historian," the *Nation* 136 (January 25, 1933), p. 97.

56. Malcolm Cowley, "Outline of Wells's History," *The New Republic* (November 14, 1934), p. 22.

57. Mackenzie, *The Life of H. G. Wells*, p. 384.

58. George Zebrowski, Introduction to *Things to Come* (Boston: Gregg Press, 1975), p. xxxiii.

59. Hadley Cantril, *The Invasion from Mars* (Princeton: Princeton University Press, 1947), p. vii.

60. Phillip Klass, "Wells, Welles and the Martians," *New York Times Book Review* (October 30, 1988), p. 1. For a more extensive discussion of the origins and consequences of Orson Welles's broadcast of *The War of the Worlds*, see Frank Brady, *Citizen Welles* (New York: Charles Scribner's Sons, 1989), pp. 162–80. As Brady notes, "some critics believed [wrongly] that H. G. Wells was actually instrumental in having his *War of the Worlds* modernized purposely to create a scandal for publicity. October 27, the day before the broadcast, was the publication date of his latest novel, *Apropos of Dolores*, and bookstores all over the country were displaying it for the first time."

61. Mackenzie, *The Life of H. G. Wells*, p. 411.

62. See C. P. Snow, "H. G. Wells," in *Variety of Men* (New York: Scribner's, 1967), pp. 63–85. As Snow notes, Wells in his later years was also increasingly frustrated because of his failure to gain membership into the Royal Society. "He wanted to be an F. R. S.," writes Snow. "And this desire, instead of becoming weaker as he got older, became more obsessive. He felt, in increasing despondency, that it would justify his career. I am fairly sure, though it is guesswork, that this was the reason that he did laborious scholarship at seventy for his D. Sc. It was to prove that he could do reputable scientific work." Despite help from his friend Richard Gregory, Wells was never granted an F. R. S., presumably because—as Snow explains—membership was then restricted, at least officially, to "people who have done scientific research and made original contributions to knowledge." Wells, comments Snow, "had been the prophet of twentieth century science, more effectively than any man alive. It was shocking that the Royal Society should be so wooden."

63. "The Rights of Man" is reprinted in full in David C. Smith's *H. G. Wells, Desperately Mortal* (New Haven: Yale University Press, 1986), pp. 490–92.

64. Wells's "My Auto-Obituary" and his "Complete Exposé of this Notorious Literary Humbug" are reprinted in J. R. Hammond, ed., *H. G. Wells: Interviews and Recollections* (London: Macmillan, 1980), pp. 108–17. Lionel Trilling, discussing "developments in the organized intellectual life of our day," writes thoughtfully on Wells's late, bleak worldview in *Mind in the Modern World* (New York: The Viking Press, 1973).

Chapter 2: The Scientific Romances

1. John J. Pierce, *Foundations of Science Fiction* (New York: Greenwood Press, 1987), p. 34.

2. See Wells's "Preface to *The Scientific Romances*," in Patrick Parrinder and Robert Philmus, eds., *H. G. Wells's Literary Criticism* (Towata, New Jersey: Barnes & Noble Books, 1980), pp. 240–45.

3. See Ingvald Raknem, *H. G. Wells and his Critics* (Oslo: Universitetsforlaset, 1962), chapter 22, "The Originality of Wells's Short Stories."

4. See Catherine Rainwater, "Encounters with the White Sphinx: Poe's Influence on Some Early Works of H. G. Wells," *English Literature in Transition* 26 (1983), pp. 35–51.

5. Many later writers of science fiction have shown themselves to be influenced not only by Wells's plots and techniques, but—in varying ways—by his values and ideas. See, for example, Arthur C. Clarke's *Childhood's End* (1953), Robert Heinlein's *Stranger in a Strange Land* (1961), and particularly, Stapledon's *Last and First Men* (1931). Stapledon is perhaps the clearest example of a s.f. writer shaped by a Wellsian view of the world. Brian Aldiss writes on Wells's contribution to the genre in *Billion Year Spree: The True History of Science Fiction* (Garden City, N.Y.: Doubleday, 1973). See especially chapter 5, "The Man Who Could Work Miracles: H. G. Wells," pp. 113–33. Aldiss calls Wells "the Shakespeare of science fiction."

6. "The Chronic Argonauts" is reprinted in Bernard Bergonzi's *The Early H. G. Wells* (Manchester: Manchester University Press, 1961), pp. 187–214, and in *The Definitive Time Machine*, Harry M. Geduld, ed. (Bloomington: Indiana University Press, 1987), pp. 135–52.

7. Sir Richard Gregory, "H. G. Wells: A Survey and a Tribute," *Nature* (September 21, 1946), pp. 400–401.

8. Chalmers Mitchell, review of *The Island of Doctor Moreau*, *Saturday Review* (April 11, 1896), in Parrinder, *H. G. Wells: The Critical Heritage*, p. 44.

9. Unsigned review of *The Island of Doctor Moreau*, the *Guardian* (June 3, 1896), in Parrinder, *H. G. Wells: The Critical Heritage*, p. 53.

10. W. T. Stead, review of *The Invisible Man*, *Review of Reviews* (April 1898), in Parrinder, *H. G. Wells: The Critical Heritage*, p. 62.

11. John St. Loe Strachey, review of *The War of the Worlds*, *Spectator* (January 29, 1898), in Parrinder, *H. G. Wells: The Critical Heritage*, p. 64.

12. T. S. Eliot, "Wells as Journalist," in Parrinder, *H. G. Wells: The Critical Heritage*, p. 320.

13. MacKenzie, *The Life of H. G. Wells*, p. 188.

14. V. S. Pritchett, "The Scientific Romances," in Bernard Bergonzi, ed., *H. G. Wells: A Collection of Critical Essays* (Englewood Cliffs, NJ: Prentice-Hall, 1976), pp. 34–35.

15. Gail Cunningham, *The New Woman and the Victorian Novel* (London: Macmillan, 1978), pp. 16–17.

16. Jefferson Hunter, *Edwardian Fiction* (Cambridge: Harvard University Press, 1982), pp. 13–14.

17. J. R. Hammond, *An H. G. Wells Companion* (London: Macmillan, 1979), pp. 109–10.

Chapter 3: The Edwardian Novels

1. See, for example, Fredric Warburg, "Wells as seen by his Publishers," in J. R. Hammond, ed., *H. G. Wells: Interviews & Recollections* (London: Macmillan, 1980), pp. 97–104.

2. "The Contemporary Novel" is reprinted in *H. G. Wells's Literary Criticism*, Patrick Parrinder and Robert Philmus, eds. (Towata, NJ: Barnes & Noble Books, 1980), pp. 192–202.

3. William Dean Howells, review of *Kipps*, the *North American Review* (October 31, 1906), in Parrinder, *H. G. Wells: The Critical Heritage*, pp. 128–31.

4. There are strong echoes of *Tono-Bungay* in *The Crying of Lot 49*. Set in Southern California, Pynchon's novel centers on a housewife, Oedipa Maas, who finds herself moving closer to the forces of American economic power, their maneuverings utterly unknown to the blundering masses. Oedipa's world is shrouded with smog and flooded with junk: it's a mind-numbing world of Muzak and Tupperware and flying aerosal cans—a world in which alienated men and women look fruitlessly for meaning, where paranoia reigns supreme. Like Wells, Pynchon was trained as a scientist, and seems similarly obsessed with the principle of entropy—with the knowledge that everything, including worlds, wear down. Certainly, the word waste echoes throughout the whole of *The Crying of Lot 49*—which like *Tono Bungay*, combines comedy with a deep sense of melancholy. One thinks, for example, of the scene near the end of the book in which Mucho Maas, a car salesman, recalls a recurring dream about a car lot, in which "I'd be going about a normal day's business and suddenly, with no warning, there'd be the sign. We were a member of the National Automobile Dealer's Association, N. A. D. A. Just this creaking metal sign that said nada, nada, against the blue sky. I used to wake up hollering" (p. 107).

5. Mark Schorer, "Technique as Discovery," *Hudson Review* 1 (Spring, 1948), p. 75.

6. J. R. Hammond, *H. G. Wells and the Modern Novel* (New York: St. Martin's Press, 1988), p. 103.

7. Vincent Brome, *H. G. Wells: A Biography* (London: Longmans, 1951), p. 110.

8. See H. L. Mencken, review of *The History of Mr. Polly*, *Smart Set* (July 1910), in Parrinder, *H. G. Wells: The Critical Heritage*, pp. 178–80.

9. Graham Greene, "Some Notes on Somerset Maugham," in *Collected Essays* (Middlesex: Penguin, 1985), p. 154.

Chapter 4: Wells and Women

1. Nancy Steffen-Fluhr, "Paper Tiger: Women and H. G. Wells," *Science Fiction Studies* 12 (1985), p. 314.

2. Victoria Glendinning, *Rebecca West: A Life* (London: Weidenfeld and Nicolson, 1987), p. 48.

3. Steffen-Fluhr, "Paper Tiger," p. 317.

4. Wells's "longed-for mate," suggest Norman and Jeanne Mackenzie, "would fuse the regal spendour of Britannia with the combative valour of Mrs Pankhurst." See their epilogue to *The Life of H. G. Wells*, pp. 449–60.

5. Thomas Huxley, "Emancipation—Black and White," in *Lay Sermons, Addresses, and Reviews* (New York: Appelton & Co., 1871), p. 24. For an extended—and highly provocative—discussion of the often-biased ways in which male Victorian scientists approached "the woman question," see Cynthia Eagle Russett, *Sexual Science: The Victorian Construction of Womanhood* (Cambridge: Harvard University Press, 1989).

6. Gail Cunningham, *The New Woman and the Victorian Novel* (London: Macmillan, 1978), pp. 59–61.

7. Vladimir Nabokov, in "Reputations revisited," in *Times Literary Supplement* (January 21, 1977): 66.

8. Walter Lippmann, review of *The Wife of Sir Isaac Harman*, *New Republic* (November 7, 1914), in Parrinder, *H. G. Wells: The Critical Heritage*, p. 220.

Chapter 5: The Later Novels

1. Unsigned review of *Mr. Britling Sees It Through*, *Times Literary Supplement* (September 21, 1916), in Parrinder, *H. G. Wells: The Critical Heritage*, p. 236.

2. Parrinder, introduction to *H. G. Wells: The Critical Heritage*, p. 24.

3. Robert Bloom, *Anatomies of Egotism: A Reading of the Last Novels of H. G. Wells* (Lincoln: University of Nebraska Press, 1977), pp. 4, 3.

4. Quoted in Mackenzie, *The Life of H. G. Wells*, pp. 338–39.

5. Krishan Kumar, *Utopia and Anti-Utopia in Modern Times* (Oxford: Basil Blackwell, 1987), p. 243.

6. See Alfred Mond, *Industry and Politics* (London: Macmillan, 1928), especially pp. 1–12.

7. See Somerset Maugham, "Some Novelists I Have Known," in *Mr. Maugham Himself* (Garden City, N.Y.: Doubleday, 1954), pp. 454–60.

Chapter 6: The Reputation

1. Odette Keun, "H. G. Wells—the Player," *Time and Tide* (October 13, 1934), p. 1251.

2. Sinclair Lewis, foreword to *The History of Mr. Polly* (New York: The Press of the Readers Club, 1941), p. v.

3. See Aldous Huxley, *Brave New World and Brave New World Revisited* (London: Chatto & Windus / The Hogarth Press, 1984), pp. 257–69.

4. Keun's comments are found in "H. G. Wells—the Player," published serially in *Time and Tide* between October 13 and October 27, 1934.

5. See Christopher Caudwell, "H. G. Wells: A Study in Utopianism," in *Studies and Further Studies in a Dying Culture* (New York: Monthly Review Press, 1971) pp. 73–95.

6. George Orwell, "Inside the Whale," in his *Collected Essays* (London: Secker & Warburg, 1961), p. 141.

7. See Orwell, "Wells, Hitler, and the World State," *Collected Essays*, pp. 160–66.

8. Virginia Woolf, *Mr. Bennett and Mrs. Brown* (London: The Hogarth Press, 1928). See especially pp. 11–13.

9. See Mark Schorer, "Technique as Discovery," *Hudson Review* 1 (Spring, 1948), pp. 67–88.

10. Jorge Luis Borges, "El Primer Wells," in Parrinder, *H. G. Wells: The Critical Heritage*, pp. 330–32.

11. Bernard Bergonzi, *The Early H. G. Wells* (Manchester: University of Manchester Press, 1961), p. 173. See especially chapter 1, "H. G. Wells and the 'Fin de Siècle.' "

12. David Lodge, *The Language of Fiction* (London: Routledge & Kegan Paul, 1966), pp. 214–42.

13. John Batchelor, *H. G. Wells* (Cambridge: Cambridge University Press, 1985), p. ix.

14. Kemp's comments are found in *H. G. Wells and the Culminating Ape* (New York: St. Martin's Press, 1982).

Select Bibliography

Books

Text Book of Biology, 2 volumes. London: Clive, 1893; volume 1 revised, 1894.

Select Conversations With An Uncle, Now Extinct, and Two Reminiscences. London: John Lane/New York: Merriam, 1895.

The Time Machine: An Invention. London: Heinemann, 1895; New York: Holt, 1895.

The Wonderful Visit. London: Dent/New York: Macmillan, 1895.

The Stolen Bacillus, And Other Incidents. London: Methuen, 1895.

The Island of Doctor Moreau. London: Heinemann, 1896; New York: Stone & Kimball, 1896.

The Wheels of Chance. London: Dent/New York: Macmillan, 1896.

The Plattner Story And Others. London: Methuen, 1897.

The Invisible Man, A Grotesque Romance. London: Pearson, 1897; enlarged edition, New York: Arnold, 1897; London: Pearson, 1900.

The War of the Worlds. London: Heinemann, 1898; New York & London: Harper, 1898.

When the Sleeper Wakes. London & New York: Harper, 1899; revised as *The Sleeper Awakes,* London: Nelson, 1910.

Love and Mr. Lewisham. London & New York: Harper, 1900.

The First Men in the Moon. London: Newnes, 1901; Indianapolis: Bowen-Merril, 1901.

Anticipations of the Reaction Of Mechanical and Scientific Progress upon Human Life and Thought. London: Chapman & Hall, 1901; New York & London: Harper, 1902.

The Discovery of the Future. London: Unwin, 1902; New York: Heubsch, 1913.

The Sea Lady. London: Methuen, 1902; New York: Appleton, 1902.

Mankind in the Making. London: Chapman & Hall, 1903; New York: Scribners, 1904.

The Food of the Gods, and How It Came to Earth. London: Macmillan, 1904; New York: Scribners, 1904.

A Modern Utopia. London: Chapman & Hall, 1905; New York: Scribners, 1905.

Kipps: The Story of a Simple Soul. London: Macmillan, 1905; New York: Scribners, 1905.

In the Days of the Comet. London: Macmillan, 1906; New York: Century, 1906.

The Future in America: A Search after Realities. London: Chapman & Hall, 1906; New York & London: Harper, 1906.

Faults of the Fabian. London: Fabian Society, 1906.

This Misery of Boots. London: Fabian Society, 1907; Boston: Ball, 1908. 1907.

New Worlds for Old. London: Constable, 1908; New York: Macmillan, 1908.

The War in the Air, and Particularly How Mr Bert Smallways Fare While It Lasted. London: Bell, 1908; New York: Macmillan, 1908.

First & Last Things: A Confession of Faith and Rule of Life. London: Constable, 1908; New York & London: Putnam's 1908; revised and enlarged edition, London, New York, Melbourne & Toronto: Cassell, 1917.

Tono-Bungay. New York: Duffield, 1908; London: Macmillan, 1909.

Ann Veronica: A Modern Love Story. London: Unwin, 1909; New York & Harper, 1909.

The History of Mr. Polly. London, Edinburgh, Dublin, New York, Leipzig & Paris: Nelson, 1910; New York: Duffield, 1910.

The New Machiavelli. New York: Duffield, 1910; London: John Lane/Bodley Head, 1911.

The Country of the Blind And other Stories. London: Edinburgh, Dublin, Leeds, New York, Leipzig & Paris: Nelson, 1911.

Marriage. London: Macmillan, 1912; New York: Duffield, 1912.

Little Wars: A Game for Boys from Twelve Years of Age to One Hundred and Fifty and for that More Intelligent Sort of Girls Who Like Boys' Games. London: Palmer, 1913; Boston: Small, Maynard, 1913; revised edition, London & Toronto: Dent, 1931.

The Passionate Friends. London: Macmillan, 1913; New York & London: Harper, 1913.

An Englishman Looks at the World. London, New York, Toronto & Melbourne: Cassell, 1914; republished as *Social Forces in England and America,* New York & London: Harper, 1914.

The World Set Free: A Story of Mankind. London: Macmillan, 1914; New York: Dutton, 1914.

The Wife of Sir Isaac Harman. London: Macmillan, 1914; New York: Macmillan, 1914.

The War that Will End War. London: Palmer, 1914; New York: Duffield, 1914.

Boon, The Mind of the Race, The Wild Asses of the Devil, and the Last Trump, Being a First Selection from the Literary Remains of George Boon, Appropriate to the Times, Prepared for Publication by Reginald

Bliss . . . With An Ambiguous Introduction by H. G. Wells. London: Unwin, 1915; New York: Doran, 1915.

Bealby: A Holiday. London: Methuen, 1915; New York: Macmillan, 1915.

The Research Magnificent. London: Macmillan, 1915; New York: Macmillan, 1915.

Mr. Britling Sees It Through. London, New York, Toronto & Melbourne: Cassell, 1916; New York: Macmillan, 1916.

God The Invisible King. London, New York, Toronto & Melbourne: Cassell, 1917; New York: Macmillan, 1917.

The Soul of a Bishop: A Novel (with Just a Little Love in It) about Conscience and Religion and The Real Troubles of Life. London, New York, Toronto & Melbourne: Cassell, 1917; New York: Macmillan, 1917.

Joan And Peter: The Story of an Education. London, New York, Toronto & Melbourne: Cassell, 1918; New York: Macmillan, 1918.

The Undying Fire. London, New York, Toronto & Melbourne: Cassell, 1919; New York: Macmillan, 1919.

The Idea of a League of Nations, with Viscount Grey, Gilbert Murray, J. A. Spender, A. E. Zimmern, H. Wickham Steed, Lionel Curtis, William Archer, and Viscount Bryce. London: Oxford University Press, 1919; Boston: Atlantic Monthly Press, 1919.

The Way to the League of Nations, with Grey, Murray, Spender, Zimmern, Steed, Curtis, Archer, Ernest Barker, G. Lowes Dickinson, John Hilton, and L. S. Woolf. London: Oxford University Press, 1919.

The Outline of History, Being a Plain History of Life and Mankind. 24 parts, London: Newnes, 1919–1920; 1 volume, London: Newnes, 1920; 2 volumes, New York: Macmillan, 1921.

Russia in the Shadows. London: Hodder & Stoughton, 1920; New York: Doran, 1921.

The Salvaging of Civilisation. London, New York, Toronto & Melbourne: Cassell, 1921; New York: Macmillan, 1921.

The Secret Places of the Heart. London, New York, Toronto & Melbourne: Cassell, 1922; New York: Macmillan, 1922.

A Short History of the World. London, New York, Toronto & Melbourne: Cassell, 1922; New York: Macmillan, 1922.

Men Like Gods. London, New York, Toronto & Melbourne: Cassell, 1923; New York: Macmillan, 1923.

The Story of a Great Schoolmaster, Being a Plain Account of the Life and Ideas of Sanderson of Oundle. London: Chatto & Windus, 1924; New York: Macmillan, 1924.

The Dream: A Novel. London: Cape, 1924; New York: Macmillan, 1924.

A Year of Prophesying. London: Unwin, 1924; New York: Macmillan, 1925.

The Atlantic Edition of the Works of H. G. Wells, 28 volumes, revised by
   Wells, London: Unwin, 1924; New York: Macmillan, 1924.
Christina Albert's Father. London: Cape, 1925; New York: Macmillan,
   1925.
The World of William Clissold: A Novel at a New Angle. 3 volumes,
   London: Benn, 1926; 2 volumes, New York: Doran, 1926.
Mr. Belloc Objects to the Outline of History. London: Watts, 1926; New
   York: Doran, 1926.
Meanwhile. London: Benn, 1927; New York: Doran, 1927.
Experiments on Animals: View For and Against, with George Bernard
   Shaw, London: British Union for the Abolition of Vivisection, 1927.
The Short Stories of H. G. Wells. London: Benn, 1927; Garden City:
   Doubleday, Doran, 1929.
The Way the World Is Going: Guesses and Forecasts of the Years Ahead.
   London: Benn, 1928; Garden City: Doubleday, Doran, 1929.
The Open Conspiracy: Blue Prints for a World Revolution. London:
   Gollancz, 1928; Garden City: Doubleday, Doran, 1928; revised edi-
   tion, London: Leonard & Virginia Woolf, 1930; revised again as *What
   Are We To Do With Our Lives?,* London: Heinemann, 1931; Garden
   City: Doubleday, Doran, 1931.
Mr. Blettsworthy on Rampole Island. London: Benn, 1928; Garden City:
   Doubleday, Doran, 1928.
The King Who Was a King: The Book of a Film. London: Benn, 1929;
   republished as *The King Who Was a King: An Unconventional Novel,*
   Garden City: Doubleday, Doran, 1929.
The Adventures of Tommy. London: Harrap, 1929; New York: Stokes,
   1929.
The Science of Life, with Julian Huxley, and G. P. Wells, 31 parts, Lon-
   don: Amalgamated Press, 1929–1930; 3 volumes, London: Amalgam-
   ated Press, 1930; 4 volumes, Garden City: Doubleday, Doran, 1931.
The Autocracy of Mr. Parham. London: Heinemann, 1930; Garden City:
   Doubleday, Doran, 1930.
The Work, Wealth and Happiness of Mankind. 2 volumes, Garden City:
   Doubleday, Doran, 1931; 1 volume, London: Heinemann, 1932.
The Bulpington of Blup. London: Hutchinson, 1932; New York: Mac-
   millan, 1933.
The Shape of Things to Come: The Ultimate Revolution. London:
   Hutchinson, 1933; New York: Macmillan, 1933.
*Experiment in Autobiography: Discoveries and Conclusions of a Very
   Ordinary Brain (Since 1866).* 2 volumes, London: Gollancz & Cresset,
   1934; New York: Macmillan, 1934.
*Things to Come: A Film Story Based on the Material Contained in His
   History of the Future 'The Shape of Things to Come'.* London:
   Cresset, 1935; New York: Macmillan, 1935.
The Anatomy of Frustration: A Modern Synthesis. London: Cresset,
   1936; London: Macmillan, 1936.

The Croquet Player: A Story. London: Chatto & Windus, 1936; New York: Viking, 1937.

The Idea of a World Encyclopaedia: A Lecture Delivered at the Royal Institution, November 20th, 1936. London: Leonard & Virginia Woolf, 1936.

Star Begotten: A Biological Fantasia. London: Chatto & Windus, 1937; New York: Viking, 1937.

Brynhild. London: Methuen, 1937; New York: Scribners, 1937.

The Camford Visitation. London: Methuen, 1937.

The Brothers: A Story. London: Chatto & Windus, 1938; New York: Viking, 1938.

World Brain. London: Methuen, 1938; Garden City: Doubleday, Doran, 1938.

Apropos of Delores. London: Cape, 1938; New York: Scribners, 1938.

The Holy Terror. London: Joseph, 1939; New York: Simon & Schuster, 1939.

Travels of a Republican in Search of Hot Water. Harmondsworth: Penguin, 1939.

The Fate of Homo Sapiens. London: Secker & Warburg, 1939; republished as *The Fate of Man,* New York: Alliance/Longmans, Green, 1939.

The Rights of Man, Or What Are We Fighting For? Harmondsworth & New York: Penguin, 1940.

Babes in the Darkling Wood. London: Secker & Warburg, 1940; New York: Alliance, 1940.

All Aboard for Ararat. London: Secker & Warburg, 1940; New York: Alliance, 1941.

You Can't Be Too Careful. A Sample of Life 1901–1951. London: Secker & Warburg, 1941; New York: Putnam's, 1942.

The Outlook for Homo Sapiens, "amalgamation and modernization" of *The Fate of Homo Sapiens* and *The New World Order.* London: Secker & Warburg, 1942.

Science and the World-Mind. London: New Europe Publishing, 1942.

Phoenix: A Summary of the Inescapable Conditions of World Organization. London: Secker & Warburg, 1942; Girard, Kans.: Haldeman-Julius, 1942.

A Thesis on the Quality of Illusion in the Continuity of Individual Life of the Higher Metazoa, with Particular Reference to the Species Homo Sapiens. London: Privately printed, 1942.

The Conquest of Time, by H. G. Wells: Written to Replace His First and Last Things. London: Watts, 1942.

Crux Ansata. An Indictment of the Roman Catholic Church. Harmondsworth & New York: Penguin, 1943; New York: Agora, 1944.

'42 to '44: A Contemporary Memoir upon Human Behaviour during the Crisis of the World Revolution. London: Secker & Warburg, 1944.

The Happy Turning: A Dream of Life. London & Toronto: Heinemann, 1945.

Mind at the End of Its Tether. London: Heinemann, 1945.

The Desert Daisy, ed. Gordon N. Ray, Urbana, Ill.: Beta Phi Mu, 1957.

Hoopdriver's Holiday, ed. Michael Timko, West Lafayette, Ind.: Purdue University Press, 1964.

The Wealth of Mr. Waddy: A Novel, ed. Harris Wilson, Carbondale: Southern Illinois University Press/London: Feffer & Simons, 1969.

H. G. Wells: Early Writings in Science and Science Fiction, ed. Robert M. Philmus and David Y. Hughes, Berkeley & London: University of California Press, 1975.

H. G. Wells's Literary Criticism. ed. Patrick Parrinder and Philmus, Brighton, U.K.: Harvester, 1980; Totowa, N.J.: Barnes & Noble, 1980.

H. G. Wells in Love, ed. G. P. Wells, London & Boston: Faber & Faber, 1984.

The Man with a Nose and Other Uncollected Short Stories. ed. J. R. Hammond, London: Athlone, 1984.

Secondary Sources

Aldiss, Brian. *Billion Year Spree*. Garden City, NY: Doubleday, 1973.

Amis, Kingsley. *New Maps of Hell: A Survey of Science Fiction*. New York: Arno Press, 1975.

Archer, William. *God and Mr. Wells: A Critical Examination of "God the Invisible King*. London: Watts, 1917.

Arnold, Mathew. *Culture and Anarchy*. Ann Arbor: The University of Michigan Press, 1965.

Ash, Brian. *Who's Who in H. G. Wells*. London: Elm Tree Books, 1979.

Batchelor, John. *H. G. Wells*. Cambridge: Cambridge University Press, 1985.

———. *The Edwardian Novelists*. London: Duckworth, 1982.

Barker, John. *The Superhistorians: Makers of Our Past*. New York: Scribner's, 1982.

Barrie, James M. *When A Man's Single*. New York: William L. Allison, no date.

Beerbohm, Max. *A Christmas Garland*. London: Heinemann, 1950.

Belloc, Hilaire. *A Companion to Mr. Wells's "Outline of History*." London: Sheed and Ward, 1929.

Bergonzi, Bernard. *The Early H. G. Wells*. Manchester: Manchester University Press, 1961.

———, ed. *H. G. Wells: A Collection of Critical Essays*. Englewood Cliffs, N.J.: Prentice-Hall, 1976.

Bloom, Robert. *Anatomies of Egotism: A Reading of the Last Novels of H. G. Wells*. Lincoln: University of Nebraska Press, 1977.

Brady, Frank. *Citizen Welles*. New York: Charles Scribner's, 1989.

Brome, Vincent. *H. G. Wells*. London: Longman's Green and Co., 1951.

———. *Six Studies in Quarrelling*. London: Cresset Press, 1958.

Burgess, Anthony. "Inexhaustible Wells," *But Do Blondes Prefer Gentlemen?* New York: McGraw-Hill, 1986.

Cantril, Hadley. *The Invasion From Mars.* Princeton: Princeton University Press, 1947.

Chadwick, Owen. *The Secularization of the European Mind in the Nineteenth Century.* Cambridge: Cambridge University Press, 1975.

Conrad, Peter. *Imagining America.* New York: Oxford University Press, 1980.

Costa, Richard Hauer. *H. G. Wells,* rev. ed. Boston, Twayne, 1985.

Cowley, Malcolm. "Outline of Wells's History," *The New Republic* LXXXI (November 14, 1934): 504–5.

Cunningham, Gail. *The New Woman and the Victorian Novel.* London: Macmillan, 1978.

Darwin, Charles. *The Origin of Species* and *The Descent of Man.* New York: The Modern Library, no date.

Delbanco, Nicholas. *Group Portrait.* New York: Morrow, 1982.

Dickson, Lovat. *H. G. Wells: His Turbulent Life and Times.* New York: Atheneum, 1969.

Downey, Richard. *Some Errors of H. G. Wells: A Catholic's Criticism of "The Outline of History".* London: Burns Oates, 1921.

Edel, Leon & Gordon N. Ray, eds. *Henry James and H. G. Wells: A Record of their Friendship, their Debate on the Art of Fiction, and their Quarrel.* Urbana: University of Illinois Press, 1958.

Eliot, George. *The Poetical Works of George Eliot.* New York: Thomas Y. Crowell, no date.

Ellis, Havelock. "Another Prophet: H. G. Wells," *Views and Reviews: A Selection of Uncollected Articles 1884–1932.* First Series, 1884–1919. London: Desmond Harmsworth, 1933, pp. 204–12.

Glendinning, Victoria. *Rebecca West: A Life.* London: Weidenfeld and Nicolson, 1987.

Glover, Willis B. "Religious Orientations of H. G. Wells: A Case Study in Scientific Humanism," *Harvard Theological Review* 65 (1972): 117–135.

Gomme, A. W. *Mr. Wells as Historian: An Inquiry into those Parts of Mr. Wells' "Outline of History" which Deal with Greece and Rome.* Glasgow: Maclehose, Jackson & Company, 1921.

Greene, Graham. "Some Notes on Somerset Maugham," *Collected Essays.* New York: Penguin, 1970, pp. 148–54.

Gregory, Sir Richard. "H. G. Wells: A Survey and Tribute," *Nature* 158 (September 21, 1946): 399–402.

Hammond, J. R. *H. G. Wells and the Modern Novel.* New York: St. Martin's, 1988.

———, ed. *H. G. Wells: Interviews & Recollections.* London: Macmillan, 1980.

Haynes, Roslynn D. *H. G. Wells: Discoverer of the Future*. New York: New York University Press, 1980.

Hazliltt, Henry. "The Wellsian Bible," the *Nation* 133 (December?????

Hillegas, Mark R. *The Future as Nightmare: H. G. Wells and the Anti-Utopians*. New York: Oxford University Press, 1967.

Hooper, Walter, ed. *They Stand Together: The Letters of C. S. Lewis to Arthur Greeves (1914–1963)*. London: Collins, 1979.

Hunter, Jefferson. *Edwardian Fiction*. Cambridge: Harvard University Press, 1982.

Huxley, Thomas. *Selections from the Essays of Thomas Huxley*. Ed. Alburey Castell. New York: Appelton-Century-Crofts, 1948.

———. *Lay Sermons, Addresses, and Reviews*. New York: D. Appleton & Company, 1871.

Kemp, Peter. *H. G. Wells and the Culminating Ape*. London: Macmillan, 1982.

Kenner, Hugh. *A Sinking Island: The Modern English Writers*. New York: Knopf, 1988.

Keun, Odette. "H. G. Wells. The Player." *Time and Tide* 13, 20 and 27 October 1934, pp. 1249–51, pp. 1307–9. pp. 1346–1348.

Klass, Philip. "Wells, Welles and the Martians," *The New York Times Book Review,* October 30, 1988, pp. 1, 48.

Krutch, Joseph Wood. "Prophet into Historian," *The Nation* 136 (January 25, 1933): 97–8.

Kumar, Krishan. *Utopia & Anti-Utopia in Modern Times*. Oxford: Basil Blackwell, 1987.

Laurence, Dan H., ed. *Bernard Shaw: Collected Letters, 1898–1910*. New York: Dodd, Mead & Company, 1972.

Lawrence, D. H. *Phoenix: The Posthumous Papers of D. H. Lawrence*. Ed. Edward D. McDonald. Middlesex: Penguin, 1978.

Lewis, Sinclair. Foreward to *The History of Mr. Polly*. New York: The Press of the Readers Club, 1941.

Lodge, David. *The Language of Fiction*. New York: Columbia University Press, 1966.

MacKenzie, Norman and Jeanne. *The Life of H. G. Wells: The Time Traveller,* rev ed. London: The Hogarth Press, 1987.

Maugham, Somerset. "Some Novelists I Have Known," *Mr. Maugham Himself.* Garden City: Doubleday, 1954, pp. 454–60.

McConnell, Frank. *The Science Fiction of H. G. Wells*. New York: Oxford University Press, 1981.

Mencken, H. L. "The Late Mr. Wells," *Prejudices: First Series*. New York: Alfred Knopf, 1919, pp. 22–35.

Mond, Alfred, *Industry and Politics*. London: Macmillan, 1928.

Orwell, George. "Wells, Hitler and the World State," *Collected Essays*. London: Secker & Warburg, 1961, pp. 160–66.

———. *The Collected Essays, Journalism and Letters of George Orwell,* volume IV, eds. Sonia Orwell and Ian Angus. London: Secker & Warburg, 1968.

Parrinder, Patrick, ed. *H. G. Wells: The Critical Heritage.* London: Routledge & Kegan Paul, 1972.

Phelps, William Lyon. *The Advance of the English Novel.* New York: Dodd, Mead and Company, 1916.

Pierce, John J. *Foundations of Science Fiction.* New York: Greenwood Press, 1987.

Poupard, Dennis, ed. *Twentieth Century Literary Criticism,* vol. 12. Detroit: Gale, 1984.

Pynchon, Thomas. *The Crying of Lot 49.* New York: Bantam Books, 1966.

Rainwater, Catherine. "Encounters with the White Sphinx: Poe's Influence on Some Early Works of H. G. Wells," *English Literature in Transition* 26 (1983): 35–51.

Raknem, Ingvald. *H. G. Wells and his Critics.* Oslo: Universitesforlaget, 1962.

Ray, Gordon. *H. G. Wells & Rebecca West.* New Haven: Yale University Press, 1974.

Reade, Winwood. *The Martyrdom of Man.* New York: The Truth Seeker Company, no date.

Reed, John R. *The Natural History of H. G. Wells.* Athens: Ohio University Press, 1982.

"Reputations revisited," *The Times Literary Supplement,* Jan. 21, 1977.

Rose, Jonathan. *The Edwardian Temperament.* Athens: Ohio University Press, 1986.

Russett, Cynthia Eagle. *Sexual Science. The Victorian Constitution of Womanhood.* Cambridge: Harvard University Press, 1989.

Sanger, Margaret. "Is Race Suicide Probable?" *Colliers* (August 15, 1925).

Schorer, Mark. "Technique as Discovery," *The Hudson Review* 1 (Spring 1948), pp. 67–87.

Shaw, George Bernard. "The Man I Knew." *The New Statesman and Nation,* (August 17, 1946): 115.

Smith, David C. *H. G. Wells, Desperately Mortal.* New Haven: Yale University Press, 1986.

Snow, C. P. *Variety of Men.* New York: Charles Scribner's Sons, 1967.

Steffen-Fluhr, Nancy. "Paper Tiger: Women and H. G. Wells," *Science Fiction Studies* 12 (1985): 311–29.

Suvin, Darko and Robert M. Philmus, eds. *H. G. Wells and Modern Science Fiction.* Lewisburg: Bucknell University Press, 1977.

Thomson, A. A. M. *The World of Billiam Wissold.* London: Hurst and Blackett, 1928.

Trilling, Lionel. *Mind in the Modern World.* New York: The Viking Press, 1972.

Watkins, A. H. ed., *The Catalogue of H. G. Wells Collection in the Bromley Public Libraries.* Bromley: London Borough of Bromley Public Libraries, 1974.

Weldon, Fay. *Rebecca West.* New York: Viking, 1985.

West, Anthony. *H. G. Wells: Aspects of a Life.* New York: Random House, 1984.

West, Geoffrey. *H. G. Wells.* New York: W. W. Norton, 1930.

West, Rebecca. *The New Meaning of Treason.* New York: The Viking Press, 1967.

———. *Henry James.* New York: Henry Holt, 1916.

Woolf, Virginia. *Mr. Bennet and Mrs. Brown.* London: The Hogarth Press, 1928.

Zebrowski, George. Introduction to *Things to Come.* Boston, Gregg Press, 1985.

Index